Applied Chemistry

Applied Chemistry

Dr. R.K. Singh

AMIGA PRESS. INC
Delhi -110051

AMIGA
PRESS INC.
AMIGA PRESS INC.
Registered Office:
19 DBS Building, Ansari Road, Darya Ganj, Delhi. 110002, India
Phone: +91-11-23283333 Email: amigapress@gmail.com

This edition is published by Amiga Press.Inc

ISBN : 978-93-84533-17-5

First Published 2018

Reprint 2026

Printed and bound in India by Replika Press Pvt. Ltd.

Preface

Applied chemistry, is often the bridge between chemistry and chemical engineering (large scale-process industries). Not only is it a study on the basic chemistry principles (organic chemistry, inorganic chemistry), it is also the study of analytical instruments and apparatus used in industrial work.

Chemistry is the science concerned with the composition, structure, and properties of matter, as well as the changes it undergoes during chemical reactions. It is a physical science for studies of various atoms, molecules, crystals and other aggregates of matter whether in isolation or combination, which incorporates the concepts of energy and entropy in relation to the spontaneity of chemical processes. Modern chemistry evolved out of alchemy following the chemical revolution (1773).

Disciplines within chemistry are traditionally grouped by the type of matter being studied or the kind of study. These include inorganic chemistry, the study of inorganic matter; organic chemistry, the study of organic matter; biochemistry, the study of substances found in biological organisms; physical chemistry, the energy related studies of chemical systems at macro, molecular and submolecular scales; analytical chemistry, the analysis of material samples to gain an understanding of their chemical composition and structure. Many more specialized disciplines have emerged in recent years, e.g. neurochemistry the chemical study of the nervous system.

A chemical reaction is a transformation of some substances into one or more other substances. It can be symbolically depicted through a chemical equation. The number of atoms on the left and the right in the equation for a chemical transformation is most often equal. The nature of chemical reactions a substance may undergo and the energy changes that may accompany it are constrained by certain basic rules, known as chemical laws.

The concept of chemical element is related to that of chemical substance. A chemical element is characterized by a particular number of protons in the nuclei of its atoms. This number is known as the atomic number of the element. For example, all atoms with 6 protons in their nuclei are atoms of the chemical element carbon, and all atoms with 92 protons in their nuclei are atoms of the element uranium.

However, several isotopes of an element, that differ from one another in the number of neutrons present in the nucleus, may exist.

The most convenient presentation of the chemical elements is in the periodic table of the chemical elements, which groups elements by atomic number. Due to its ingenious arrangement, groups, or columns, and periods, or rows, of elements in the table either share several chemical properties, or follow a certain trend in characteristics such as atomic radius, electronegativity, etc. Lists of the elements by name, by symbol, and by atomic number are also available.

This book is comprehensive package for knowledge sharing on applied chemistry. The language of the book is simple and self explanatory, this will help the students to grasp the fundamentals of the subject easily.

—Editor

Contents

1

Introduction

OVERVIEW

Chemistry is the scientific study of interaction of chemical substances that are constituted of atoms or the subatomic particles: protons, electrons and neutrons. Atoms combine to produce molecules or crystals. Chemistry is often called "the central science" because it connects the other natural sciences, such as astronomy, physics, material science, biology, and geology. The genesis of chemistry can be traced to certain practices, known as alchemy, which had been practiced for several millennia in various parts of the world, particularly the Middle East.

The structure of objects we commonly use and the properties of the matter we commonly interact with, are a consequence of the properties of chemical substances and their interactions. For example, steel is harder than iron because its atoms are bound together in a more rigid crystalline lattice; wood burns or undergoes rapid oxidation because it can react spontaneously with oxygen in a chemical reaction above a certain temperature; sugar and salt dissolve in water because their molecular/ionic properties are such that dissolution is preferred under the ambient conditions.

The transformations that are studied in chemistry are a result of interaction either between different chemical substances or between matter and energy. Traditional chemistry involves study of interactions between substances in a chemistry laboratory using various forms of laboratory glassware.

A chemical reaction is a transformation of some substances into one or more other substances. It can be symbolically depicted through a chemical equation. The number of atoms on the left and the right in the equation for a chemical transformation is most often equal. The nature of chemical reactions a substance may undergo and the energy changes that may accompany it are constrained by certain basic rules, known as chemical laws. Energy and entropy considerations are invariably important in almost all chemical studies.

Chemical substances are classified in terms of their structure, phase as well as their chemical compositions. They can be analysed using the tools of chemical analysis, e.g. spectroscopy and chromatography.

Chemistry is an integral part of the science curriculum both at the high school as well as the early college level. At these levels, it is often called 'general chemistry' which is an introduction to a wide variety of fundamental concepts that enable the student to acquire tools and skills useful at the advanced levels, whereby chemistry is invariably studied in any of its various sub-disciplines. Scientists, engaged in chemical research are known as chemists. Most chemists specialize in one or more sub-disciplines.

HISTORY

Ancient Egyptians pioneered the art of synthetic "wet" chemistry up to 4,000 years ago. By 1000 BC ancient civilizations were using technologies that formed the basis of the various branches of chemistry, such as; extracting metal from their ores, making pottery and glazes, fermenting beer and wine, making pigments for cosmetics and painting, extracting chemicals from plants for medicine and perfume, making cheese, dying cloth, tanning leather, rendering fat into soap, making glass, and making alloys like bronze.

The genesis of chemistry can be traced to the widely observed phenomenon of burning that led to metallurgy- the art and science of processing ores to get metals (e.g. metallurgy in ancient India). The greed for gold led to the discovery of the process for its purification, even though, the underlying principles were not well understood — it was thought to be a transformation rather than purification. Many scholars in those days thought it reasonable to believe that there exist means for transforming cheaper (base) metals into gold. This gave way to alchemy, and the search for the Philosopher's Stone, which was believed to bring about such a transformation by mere touch.

Greek atomism dates back to 440 BC, as what might be indicated by the book *De Rerum Natura* (The Nature of Things) written by the Roman Lucretius in 50 BC. Much of the early development of purification methods is described by Pliny the Elder in his *Naturalis Historia*.

Some consider medieval Arabs and Persians to be the earliest chemists, who introduced precise observation and controlled experimentation into the field, and discovered numerous chemical substances.

The most influential Muslim chemists were Geber (d. 815), al-Kindi (d. 873), al-Razi (d. 925), and al-Biruni (d. 1048). The works of Geber became more widely known in Europe through Latin translations by a pseudo-Geber in 14th century Spain, who also wrote some of his own books under the pen name "Geber". The contribution of Indian alchemists and metallurgists in the development of chemistry was also quite significant.

The emergence of chemistry in Europe was primarily due to the recurrent incidence of the plague and blights there during the so called Dark Ages. This gave rise to a need for medicines. It was thought that there exists a universal medicine called the Elixir of Life that can cure all diseases, but like the Philosopher's Stone, it was never found.

For some practitioners, alchemy was an intellectual pursuit, over time, they got better at it. Paracelsus (1493-1541), for example, rejected the 4-elemental theory and with only a vague understanding of his chemicals and medicines, formed a hybrid of alchemy and science in what was to be called *iatrochemistry*. Similarly, the influences of philosophers such as Sir Francis Bacon (1561-1626) and Rene Descartes (1596-1650), who demanded more rigor in mathematics and in removing bias from scientific observations, led to a scientific revolution. In chemistry, this began with Robert Boyle (1627-1691), who came up with an equations known as the Boyle's Law about the characteristics of gaseous state. Chemistry indeed came of age when Antoine Lavoisier (1743-1794), developed the theory of Conservation of mass in 1783; and the development of the Atomic Theory by John Dalton around 1800. The Law of Conservation of Mass resulted in the reformulation of chemistry based on this law and the oxygen theory of combustion, which was largely based on the work of Lavoisier.

Lavoisier's fundamental contributions to chemistry were a result of a conscious effort to fit all experiments into the framework of a single theory. He established the consistent use of the chemical balance, used oxygen to overthrow the phlogiston theory, and developed a new system of chemical nomenclature and made contribution to the modern metric system. Lavoisier also worked to translate the archaic and technical language of chemistry into something that could be easily understood by the largely uneducated masses, leading to an increased public interest in chemistry. All these advances in chemistry led to what is usually called the chemical revolution. The contributions of Lavoisier led to what is now called modern chemistry - the chemistry that is studied in educational institutions all over the world. It is because of these and other contributions that Antoine Lavoisier is often celebrated as the "Father of Modern Chemistry". The later discovery of Friedrich Wohler that many natural substances, organic compounds, can indeed be synthesized in a chemistry laboratory also helped the modern chemistry to mature from its infancy.

The discoveries of the chemical elements has a long history from the days of alchemy and culminating in the creation of the periodic table of the chemical elements by Dmitri Mendeleev (1834-1907) and later discoveries of some synthetic elements.

ETYMOLOGY

The word *chemistry* comes from the earlier study of alchemy, which is a pseudoscientific practice which encompasses elements of chemistry, metallurgy, philosophy, astrology, astronomy, mysticism and medicine. Alchemy is commonly thought of as the quest to turn lead or another common starting material into gold. As to the origin of the word "alchemy" the question is a debatable one; it certainly can be traced back to the Greeks, and some, following E. Wallis Budge, have also asserted Egyptian origins.

Many believe that the word "alchemy" is derived from the word Chemi or Kimi, which is the name of Egypt in Egyptian. The word was subsequently borrwed by the Greeks, and from the Greeks by the Arabs when they occupied Alexandria (Egypt) in the 7th century. The Arabs added the Arabic definite article "al" to the word, resulting in the word "al-kimiya", from which is derived the old French *alkemie*. A tentative outline is as follows:

1. Egyptian alchemy [3,000 BCE – 400 BCE], formulate early "element" theories such as the Ogdoad.
2. Greek alchemy [332 BCE – 642 CE], the Greek king Alexander the Great conquers Egypt and founds Alexandria, having the world's largest library, where scholars and wise men gather to study.
3. Arab alchemy [642 CE – 1200], the Arabs invade Alexandria; Jabir is the main chemist
4. European alchemy [1300 – present], Pseudo-Geber builds on Arabic chemistry
5. Chemistry [1661], Boyle writes his classic chemistry text *The Sceptical Chymist*
6. Chemistry [1787], Lavoisier writes his classic *Elements of Chemistry*
7. Chemistry [1803], Dalton publishes his *Atomic Theory*.

Thus, an alchemist was called a 'chemist' in popular speech, and later the suffix "-ry" was added to this to describe the art of the chemist as "chemistry".

DEFINITIONS

In retrospect, the definition of chemistry seems to invariably change per decade, as new discoveries and theories add to the functionality of the science. Shown below are some of the standard definitions used by various noted chemists:

- Alchemy (330) – the study of the composition of waters, movement, growth, embodying, disembodying, drawing the spirits from bodies and bonding the spirits within bodies (Zosimos).

- Chymistry (1661) – the subject of the material principles of mixt bodies (Boyle).
- Chymistry (1663) – a scientific art, by which one learns to dissolve bodies, and draw from them the different substances on their composition, and how to unite them again, and exalt them to an higher perfection (Glaser).
- Chemistry (1730) – the art of resolving mixt, compound, or aggregate bodies into their principles; and of composing such bodies from those principles (Stahl).
- Chemistry (1837) – the science concerned with the laws and effects of molecular forces (Dumas).
- Chemistry (1947) – the science of substances: their structure, their properties, and the reactions that change them into other substances (Pauling).
- Chemistry (1998) – the study of matter and the changes it undergoes (Chang).

BASIC CONCEPTS

Several concepts are essential for the study of chemistry, some of them are:

Atom

An atom is the basic unit of an element. It is a collection of matter consisting of a positively charged core (the atomic nucleus) which contains protons and neutrons, and which maintains a number of electrons to balance the positive charge in the nucleus. The atom is also the smallest entity that can be envisaged to retain some of the chemical properties of the element, such as electronegativity, ionization potential, preferred oxidation state(s), coordination number, and preferred types of bonds to form (e.g., metallic, ionic, covalent).

Element

The concept of chemical element is related to that of chemical substance. A chemical element is characterized by a particular number of protons in the nuclei of its atoms. This number is known as the atomic number of the element. For example, all atoms with 6 protons in their nuclei are atoms of the chemical element carbon, and all atoms with 92 protons in their nuclei are atoms of the element uranium.

However, several isotopes of an element, that differ from one another in the number of neutrons present in the nucleus, may exist.

The most convenient presentation of the chemical elements is in the periodic table of the chemical elements, which groups elements by atomic number. Due to its ingenious arrangement, groups, or columns, and periods, or rows, of elements in the table either share several chemical properties, or follow a certain trend in characteristics such as atomic radius, electronegativity, etc. Lists of the elements by name, by symbol, and by atomic number are also available.

Compound

A compound is a substance with a particular ratio of atoms of particular chemical elements which determines its composition, and a particular organization which determines chemical properties. For example, water is a compound containing hydrogen and oxygen in the ratio of two to one, with the oxygen between the hydrogens, and an angle of 104.5° between them. Compounds are formed and interconverted by chemical reactions.

Substance

A chemical substance is a kind of matter with a definite composition and set of properties. Strictly speaking, a mixture of compounds, elements or compounds and elements is not a chemical substance, but it may be called a chemical. Most of the substances we encounter in our daily life are some kind of mixture, e.g. air, alloys, biomass etc.

Nomenclature of substances is a critical part of the language of chemistry. Generally it refers to a system for naming chemical compounds. Earlier in the history of chemistry substances were given name by their discoverer, which often led to some confusion and difficulty.

However, today the IUPAC system of chemical nomenclature allows chemists to specify by name specific compounds amongst the infinite variety of possible chemicals. The standard nomenclature of chemical substances is set by the International Union of Pure and Applied Chemistry (IUPAC). There are well-defined systems in place for naming chemical species. Organic compounds are named according to the organic nomenclature system. Inorganic compounds are named according to the inorganic nomenclature system. In addition the Chemical Abstracts Service has devised a method to index chemical substance. In this scheme each chemical substance is identifiable by a numeric number known as CAS registry number.

Molecule

A molecule is the smallest indivisible portion, beside an atom, of a pure chemical substance that has its unique set of chemical properties, that is, its potential to undergo a certain set of chemical reactions with other substances.

Molecules can exist as electrically neutral units unlike ions. Molecules are typically a set of atoms bound together by covalent bonds, such that the structure is electrically neutral and all valence electrons are paired with other electrons either in bonds or in lone pairs.

One of the main characteristic of a molecule is its geometry often called its structure. While the structure of diatomic, triatomic or tetra atomic molecules may be trivial, (linear, angular pyramidal etc.) the structure of polyatomic molecules, that are constituted of more than six atoms (of several elements) can be crucial for its chemical nature.

Mole

A mole is the amount of a substance that contains as many elementary entities (atoms, molecules or ions) as there are atoms in 0.012 kilogram (or 12 grams) of carbon-12, where the carbon-12 atoms are unbound, at rest and in their ground state. This number is known as the Avogadro constant, and is determined empirically. The currently accepted value is 6.02214179(30)×1023 mol-1 (2007 CODATA). It is much like the term "a dozen" in that it is an absolute number (having no units) and can describe any type of elementary object, although the mole's use is usually limited to measurement of subatomic, atomic, and molecular structures.

The number of moles of a substance in one litre of a solution is known as its molarity. Molarity is the common unit used to express the concentration of a solution in physical chemistry.

Ions and Salts

An ion is a charged species, an atom or a molecule, that has lost or gained one or more electrons. Positively charged cations (e.g. sodium cation Na+) and negatively charged anions (e.g. chloride Cl–) can form a crystalline lattice of neutral salts (e.g. sodium chloride NaCl). Examples of polyatomic ions that do not split up during acid-base reactions are hydroxide (OH–) and phosphate (PO43–). Ions in the gaseous phase is often known as plasma.

Acidity and Basicity

A substance can often be classified as an acid or a base. This is often done on the basis of a particular kind of reaction, namely the exchange of protons between chemical compounds. However, an extension to this mode of classification was brewed up by the American chemist, Gilbert Newton Lewis; in this mode of classification the reaction is not limited to those occurring in an aqueous solution, thus is no longer limited to solutions in water. According to concept as per Lewis, the crucial things being exchanged are charges. There are several other ways in which a substance may be classified as an acid or a base, as is evident in the history of this concept.

Phase

In addition to the specific chemical properties that distinguish different chemical classifications chemicals can exist in several phases. For the most part, the chemical classifications are independent of these bulk phase classifications; however, some more exotic phases are incompatible with certain chemical properties. A phase is a set of states of a chemical system that have similar bulk structural properties, over a range of conditions, such as pressure or temperature. Physical properties, such as density and refractive index tend to fall within values characteristic of the phase. The phase of matter is defined by the phase transition, which is when energy put into or taken out of the system goes into rearranging the structure of the system, instead of changing the bulk conditions.

Sometimes the distinction between phases can be continuous instead of having a discrete boundary, in this case the matter is considered to be in a supercritical state. When three states meet based on the conditions, it is known as a triple point and since this is invariant, it is a convenient way to define a set of conditions.

The most familiar examples of phases are solids, liquids, and gases. Many substances exhibit multiple solid phases. For example, there are three phases of solid iron (alpha, gamma, and delta) that vary based on temperature and pressure. A principal difference between solid phases is the crystal structure, or arrangement, of the atoms. Less familiar phases include plasmas, Bose-Einstein condensates and fermionic condensates and the paramagnetic and ferromagnetic phases of magnetic materials. While most familiar phases deal with three-dimensional systems, it is also possible to define analogs in two-dimensional systems, which has received attention for its relevance to systems in biology.

Redox

It is a concept related to the ability of atoms of various substances to lose or gain electrons. Substances that have the ability to oxidize other substances are said to be oxidative and are known as oxidizing agents, oxidants or oxidizers. An oxidant removes electrons from another substance. Similarly, substances that have the ability to reduce other substances are said to be reductive and are known as reducing agents, reductants, or reducers. A reductant transfers electrons to another substance, and is thus oxidized itself. And because it "donates" electrons it is also called an electron donor. Oxidation and reduction properly refer to a change in oxidation number—the actual transfer of electrons may never occur. Thus, oxidation is better defined as an increase in oxidation number, and reduction as a decrease in oxidation number.

Chemical Bond

A chemical bond is a concept for understanding how atoms stick together in molecules. It may be visualized as the multipole balance between the positive charges in the nuclei and the negative charges oscillating about them. More than simple attraction and repulsion, the energies and distributions characterize the availability of an electron to bond to another atom. These potentials create the interactions which holds together atoms in molecules or crystals. In many simple compounds, Valence Bond Theory, the Valence Shell Electron Pair Repulsion model (VSEPR), and the concept of oxidation number can be used to predict molecular structure and composition. Similarly, theories from classical physics can be used to predict many ionic structures. With more complicated compounds, such as metal complexes, valence bond theory fails and alternative approaches, primarily based on principles of quantum chemistry such as the molecular orbital theory, are necessary.

Chemical Reaction

Chemical reaction is a concept related to the transformation of a chemical substance through its interaction with another, or as a result of its interaction with some form of energy. A chemical reaction may occur naturally or carried out in a laboratory by chemists in specially designed vessels which are often laboratory glassware. It can result in the formation or dissociation of molecules, that is, molecules breaking apart to form two or more smaller molecules, or rearrangement of atoms within or across molecules. Chemical reactions usually involve the making or breaking of chemical bonds. Oxidation, reduction, dissociation, acid-base neutralization and molecular rearrangement are some of the commonly used kinds of chemical reactions.

A chemical reaction can be symbolically depicted through a chemical equation. While in a non-nuclear chemical reaction the number and kind of atoms on both sides of the equation are equal, for a nuclear reaction this holds true only for the nuclear particles viz. protons and neutrons.

The sequence of steps in which the reorganization of chemical bonds may be taking place in the course of a chemical reaction is called its mechanism. A chemical reaction can be envisioned to take place in a number of steps, each of which may have a different speed. Many reaction intermediates with variable stability can thus be envisaged during the course of a reaction. Reaction mechanisms are proposed to explain the kinetics and the relative product mix of a reaction. Many physical chemists specialize in exploring and proposing the mechanisms of various chemical reactions. Several empirical rules, like the Woodward-Hoffmann rules often come handy while proposing a mechanism for a chemical reaction.

A stricter definition is that "a chemical reaction is a process that results in the interconversion of chemical species". Under this definition, a chemical reaction may be an elementary reaction or a stepwise reaction. An additional caveat is made, in that this definition includes cases where the interconversion of conformers is experimentally observable. Such detectable chemical reactions normally involve sets of molecular entities as indicated by this definition, but it is often conceptually convenient to use the term also for changes involving single molecular entities (i.e. 'microscopic chemical events').

Energy

In the context of chemistry, energy is an attribute of a substance as a consequence of its atomic, molecular or aggregate structure. Since a chemical transformation is accompanied by a change in one or more of these kinds of structure, it is invariably accompanied by an increase or decrease of energy of the substances involved. Some energy is transferred between the surroundings and the reactants of the reaction in the form of heat or light, thus the products of a reaction may have more or less energy than the reactants.

A reaction is said to be exothermic if the final state is lower on the energy scale than the initial state; in case of endothermic reactions the situation is otherwise.

Chemical reactions are invariably not possible unless the reactants surmount an energy barrier known as the activation energy. The speed of a chemical reaction (at given temperature T) is related to the activation energy E, by the Boltzmann's population factor e–E/kT-that is the probability of molecule to have energy greater than or equal to E at the given temperature T. This exponential dependence of a reaction rate on temperature is known as the Arrhenius equation. The activation energy necessary for a chemical reaction can be in the form of heat, light, electricity or mechanical force in the form of ultrasound.

A related concept free energy, which incorporates entropy considerations too, is a very useful means for predicting the feasibility of a reaction and determining the state of equilibrium of a chemical reaction, in chemical thermodynamics. A reaction is feasible only if the total change in the Gibbs free energy is negative, $\Delta G \leq 0$; if it is equal to zero the chemical reaction is said to be at equilibrium.

There are only a limited possible states of energy for electrons, atoms and molecules. These are determined by the rules of quantum mechanics, which require quantization of energy of a bound system. The atoms/molecules in a higher energy state are said to be excited. The molecules/atoms of substance in an excited energy state are often much more reactive, that is amenable to chemical reactions.

The phase of a substance is invariably determined by its energy and those of its surroundings. When the intermolecular forces of a substance are such that energy of the surroundings is not sufficient to overcome them, it occurs in a more ordered phase like liquid or solid as is the case with water (H2O), a liquid at room temperature because its molecules are bound by hydrogen bonds. Whereas hydrogen sulfide (H2S) is a gas at room temperature and standard pressure, as its molecules are bound by weaker dipole-dipole interactions.The transfer of energy from one chemical substance to other depend on the size of energy quanta emitted from one substance. However, heat energy is easily transferred from almost any substance to another mainly because the vibrational and rotational energy levels in a substance are very closely placed. Because, the electronic energy levels are not so closely spaced, ultraviolet electromagnetic radiation is not transferred with equal felicity, as is also the case with electrical energy.

The existence of characteristic energy levels for different chemical substances is useful for their identification by the analysis of spectral lines of different kinds of spectra often used in chemical spectroscopy e.g. IR, microwave, NMR, ESR etc. This is used to identify the composition of remote objects - like stars and far galaxies - by analyzing their radiation.

The term chemical energy is often used to indicate the potential of a chemical substance to undergo a transformation through a chemical reaction or transform other chemical substances.

CHEMICAL LAWS

Chemical reactions are governed by certain laws, which have become fundamental concepts in chemistry. Some of them are:

- Law of conservation of mass, according to the modern physics it is actually energy that is conserved, and that energy and mass are related; a concept which becomes important in nuclear chemistry.
- Law of conservation of Energy leads to the important concepts of equilibrium, thermodynamics, and kinetics.
- Law of definite composition, although in many systems (notably biomacromolecules and minerals) the ratios tend to require large numbers, and are frequently represented as a fraction.
- Law of multiple proportions
- Hess's Law

- Beer-Lambert law
- Fick's law of diffusion
- Raoult's Law
- Henry's law
- Boyle's law (1662, relating pressure and volume)
- Charles's law (1787, relating volume and temperature)
- Gay-Lussac's law (1809, relating pressure and temperature)
- Avogadro's law

SUBDISCIPLINES

Chemistry is typically divided into several major sub-disciplines. There are also several main cross-disciplinary and more specialized fields of chemistry.

- Analytical chemistry is the analysis of material samples to gain an understanding of their chemical composition and structure. Analytical chemistry incorporates standardized experimental methods in chemistry. These methods may be used in all subdisciplines of chemistry, excluding purely theoretical chemistry.
- Biochemistry is the study of the chemicals, chemical reactions and chemical interactions that take place in living organisms. Biochemistry and organic chemistry are closely related, as in medicinal chemistry or neurochemistry. Biochemistry is also associated with molecular biology and genetics.
- Inorganic chemistry is the study of the properties and reactions of inorganic compounds. The distinction between organic and inorganic disciplines is not absolute and there is much overlap, most importantly in the sub-discipline of organometallic chemistry.
- Materials chemistry is the preparation, characterization, and understanding of substances with a useful function. The field is a new breadth of study in graduate programs, and it integrates elements from all classical areas of chemistry with a focus on fundamental issues that are unique to materials. Primary systems of study include the chemistry of condensed phases (solids, liquids, polymers) and interfaces between different phases.
- Nuclear chemistry is the study of how subatomic particles come together and make nuclei. Modern Transmutation is a large component of nuclear chemistry, and the table of nuclides is an important result and tool for this field.
- Organic chemistry is the study of the structure, properties, composition, mechanisms, and reactions of organic compounds. An organic compound is defined as any compound based on a carbon skeleton.

- Physical chemistry is the study of the physical and fundamental basis of chemical systems and processes. In particular, the energetics and dynamics of such systems and processes are of interest to physical chemists. Important areas of study include chemical thermodynamics, chemical kinetics, electrochemistry, statistical mechanics, and spectroscopy. Physical chemistry has large overlap with molecular physics. Physical chemistry involves the use of infinitesimal calculus in deriving equations. It is usually associated with quantum chemistry and theoretical chemistry. Physical chemistry is a distinct discipline from chemical physics.
- Theoretical chemistry is the study of chemistry via fundamental theoretical reasoning (usually within mathematics or physics). In particular the application of quantum mechanics to chemistry is called quantum chemistry. Since the end of the Second World War, the development of computers has allowed a systematic development of computational chemistry, which is the art of developing and applying computer programs for solving chemical problems. Theoretical chemistry has large overlap with (theoretical and experimental) condensed matter physics and molecular physics.

CHEMICAL INDUSTRY

The chemical industry represents an important economic activity. The global top 50 chemical producers in 2004 had sales of 587 billion US dollars with a profit margin of 8.1% and research and development spending of 2.1% of total chemical sales.

2

Analytical Chemistry

Analytical chemistry is the study of the chemical composition of natural and artificial materials. Unlike other major sub disciplines of chemistry such as inorganic chemistry and organic chemistry, analytical chemistry is not restricted to any particular type of chemical compound or reaction.

Properties studied in analytical chemistry include geometric features such as molecular morphologies and distributions of species, as well as features such as composition and species identity. The contributions made by analytical chemists have played critical roles in the sciences ranging from the development of concepts and theories (pure science) to a variety of practical applications, such as biomedical applications, environmental monitoring, quality control of industrial manufacturing and forensic science (applied science).

OVERVIEW

Analytical chemistry is a sub discipline of chemistry that has the broad mission of understanding the chemical composition of all matter and developing the tools and experiments to make either qualitative or quantitative measurements.

In a nutshell, analytical chemistry applies measurement science principles along with an understanding of chemical systems to provide useful information; and it has significant overlap with other branches of chemistry through the measurement methods that it provides. For example, the field of bioanalytical chemistry is a growing area of analytical chemistry that addresses analytical questions in biochemistry, (the chemistry of life). Experimental physical chemistry and analytical chemistry show similarity in that both have a measurement science focus.

While there is occasional overlap between these two disciplines, the goal of physical chemistry experiments is to determine the dynamics of how energy affects the chemical system by making kinetic, thermodynamic, and spectroscopic measurements, while analytical chemistry sometimes uses such energy-based measurements to determine matter-related properties such as chemical identity and quantity. Analytical chemistry is also focused on improvements in experimental design and the creation of new measurement tools to provide better chemical information.

Traditionally, analytical chemistry was particularly concerned with the questions of "what chemicals are present, what are their characteristics and in what quantities are they present?"

These questions are often involved in questions that are more dynamic such as what chemical reaction an enzyme catalyzes or how fast it does it, or even more dynamic such as what is the transition state of the reaction.

The next logical steps of understanding what it means, how it fits into a larger system, how can this result be generalized into theory, or how it can be used all result from information provided by analytical chemistry methods.

Analytical chemists work to improve the reliability of existing techniques to meet the demands for better chemical measurements which arise constantly in our society. They adapt proven methodologies to new kinds of materials or to answer new questions about their composition. They carry out research to discover completely new principles of measurement and are at the forefront of the utilization of major discoveries such as lasers and microchip devices for practical purposes. They make important contributions to many other fields as diverse as forensic chemistry, archaeology, and space science.

TRADITIONAL ANALYTICAL TECHNIQUES

Although modern analytical chemistry is dominated by sophisticated instrumentation, the roots of analytical chemistry and some of the principles used in modern instruments are from traditional techniques many of which are still used today.

These techniques also tend to form the backbone of most undergraduate analytical chemistry educational labs. Examples include:

Titration

Titration involves the addition of a reactant to a solution being analyzed until some equivalence point is reached. Often the amount of material in the solution being analyzed may be determined. Most familiar to those who have taken college chemistry is the acid-base titration involving a color changing indicator.

There are many other types of titrations, for example potentiometric titrations. These titrations may use different types of indicators to reach some equivalence point.

Gravimetry

Gravimetric analysis involves determining the amount of material present by weighing the sample before and/or after some transformation.

A common example used in undergraduate education is the determination of the amount of water in a hydrate by heating the sample to remove the water such that the difference in weight is due to the water lost.

Inorganic Qualitative Analysis

Inorganic qualitative analysis generally refers to a systematic scheme to confirm the presence of certain, usually aqueous, ions or elements by performing a series of reactions that eliminate ranges of possibilities and then confirms suspected ions with a confirming test.

Sometimes small carbon containing ions are included in such schemes. With modern instrumentation these tests are rarely used but can be useful for educational purposes and in field work or other situations where access to state-of-the-art instruments are not available or expedient.

Instrumental Analysis

Mass Spectrometry: Mass spectrometry measures mass-to-charge ratio of molecules using electric and magnetic fields. There are several ionization methods: electron impact, chemical ionization, electrospray, fast atom bombardment, matrix assisted laser desorption ionization, and others.

Also, mass spectrometry is categorized by approaches of mass analyzers: magnetic-sector,quadrupole mass analyzer, quadrupole ion trap, Time-of-flight, Fourier transform ion cyclotron resonance, and so on.

Crystallography: Crystallography is a technique that characterizes the chemical structure of materials at the atomic level by analyzing the diffraction patterns of usually x-rays that have been deflected by atoms in the material. From the raw data the relative placement of atoms in space may be determined.

Electrochemical Analysis

Electroanalytical methods measure the potential (volts) and/or current (amps) in an electrochemical cell containing the analyte. These methods can be categorized according to which aspects of the cell are controlled and which are measured.

The three main categories are potentiometry (the difference in electrode potentials is measured), coulometry (the cell's current is measured over time), and voltammetry (the cell's current is measured while actively altering the cell's potential). Thermal Analysis: Calorimetry and thermogravimetric analysis measure the interaction of a material and heat.

Separation

Separation processes are used to decrease the complexity of material mixtures. Chromatography and electrophoresis are representative of this field.

Hybrid Techniques

Combinations of the above techniques produce "hybrid" or "hyphenated" techniques.

Several examples are in popular use today and new hybrid techniques are under development. For example, Gas chromatography-mass spectrometry, LC-MS, GC-IR, LC-NMR, LC-IR, CE-MS, and so on.

Hyphenated separation techniques refers to a combination of two (or more) techniques to detect and separate chemicals from solutions. Most often the other technique is some form of chromatography.

Hyphenated techniques are widely used in chemistry and biochemistry. A slash is sometimes used instead of hyphen, especially if the name of one of the methods contains a hyphen itself.

Examples of hyphenated techniques:

1. LC-MS (or HPLC-MS)
2. HPLC/ESI-MS
3. LC-DAD
4. CE-MS
5. CE-UV
6. GC-MS
7. LC-IR.

Microscopy

The visualization of single molecules, single cells, biological tissues and nano- micro materials is very important and attractive approach in analytical science.

Also, hybridization with other traditional analytical tools is revolutionizing analytical science. Microscopy can be categorized into three different fields: optical microscopy, electron microscopy, and scanning probe microscopy. Recently, this field is rapidly progressing because of the rapid development of computer and camera industries.

Lab-on-a-chip

Devices that integrate (multiple) laboratory functions on a single chip of only millimeters to a few square centimeters in size and that are capable of handling extremely small fluid volumes down to less than pico liters.

Methods and Data Analysis

Standard Curve

A standard method for analysis of concentration involves the creation of a calibration curve. This allows for determination of the amount of a chemical in a material by comparing the results of unknown sample to those of a series known standards.If the concentration of element or compound in a sample is too high for the detection range of the technique, it can simply be diluted in a pure solvent.

If the amount in the sample is below an instrument's range of measurement, the method of addition can be used. In this method a known quantity of the element or compound under study is added, and the difference between the concentration added, and the concentration observed is the amount actually in the sample.

Internal Standards

Sometimes an internal standard is added at a known concentration directly to an analytical sample to aid in quantitation. The amount of analyte present is then determined relative to the internal standard as a calibrant.

Trends

Analytical chemistry research is largely driven by performance (sensitivity, selectivity, robustness, linear range, accuracy, precision, and speed), and cost (purchase, operation, training, time, and space).

Among the main branches of contemporary analytical atomic spectrometry, the most widespread and universal are optical and mass spectrometry.

In the direct elemental analysis of solid samples, the new leaders are laser-induced breakdown and laser ablation mass spectrometry, and the related techniques with transfer of the laser ablation products into inductively coupled plasma.

Advances in design of diode lasers and optical parametric oscillators promote developments in fluorescence and ionization spectrometry and also in absorption techniques where uses of optical cavities for increased effective absorption pathlength are expected to expand.

Steady progress and growth in applications of plasma- and laser-based methods are noticeable. An interest towards the absolute (standardless) analysis has revived, particularly in the emission spectrometry.

A lot of effort is put in shrinking the analysis techniques to chip size. Although there are few examples of such systems competitive with traditional analysis techniques, potential advantages include size/portability, speed, and cost. (micro Total Analysis System (μTAS) or Lab-on-a-chip). Microscale chemistry reduces the amounts of chemicals used. Much effort is also put into analyzing biological systems. Examples of rapidly expanding fields in this area are:

- Genomics - DNA sequencing and its related research. Genetic fingerprinting and DNA microarray are very popular tools and research fields.
- Proteomics - the analysis of protein concentrations and modifications, especially in response to various stressors, at various developmental stages, or in various parts of the body.
- Metabolomics - similar to proteomics, but dealing with metabolites.
- Transcriptomics- mRNA and its associated field
- Lipidomics - lipids and its associated field
- Peptidomics - peptides and its associated field
- Metalomics - similar to proteomics and metabolomics, but dealing with metal concentrations and especially with their binding to proteins and other molecules.

Analytical chemistry has played critical roles in the understanding of basic science to a variety of practical applications, such as biomedical applications, environmental monitoring, quality control of industrial manufacturing, forensic science and so on.

The recent developments of computer automation and information technologies have innervated analytical chemistry to initiate a number of new biological fields. For example, automated DNA sequencing machines were the basis to complete human genome projects leading to the birth of genomics. Protein identification and peptide sequencing by mass spectrometry opened a new field of proteomics. Furthermore, a number of ~omics based on analytical chemistry have become important areas in modern biology.

Also, analytical chemistry has been an indispensable area in the development of nanotechnology. Surface characterization instruments, electron microscopes and scanning probe microscopes enables scientists to visualize atomic structures with chemical characterizations.

Analytical chemistry is pursuing the development of practical applications and commercial instruments rather than elucidating scientific fundamentals. This may be an arguable difference from overlapping science areas such as physical chemistry and biophysics, although there isn't any distinct boundaries among disciplines in contemporary science and technology. However, this aspect may attract many engineers' interest; thus, it is not difficult to see papers from engineering departments in analytical chemistry journals.

Among active contemporary analytical chemistry research fields, micro total analysis system is considered as a great promise of revolutionary technology. In this approach, integrated and miniaturized analytical systems are being developed to control and analyze single cells and single molecules. This cutting-edge technology has a promising potential of leading a new revolution in science as integrated circuits did in computer developments.

MODERN ANALYTICAL CHEMISTRY

Modern analytical chemistry is dominated by instrumental analysis. Many analytical chemists focus on a single type of instrument. Academics tend to either focus on new applications and discoveries or on new methods of analysis. The discovery of a chemical present in blood that increases the risk of cancer would be a discovery that an analytical chemist might be involved in. An effort to develop a new method might involve the use of a tunable laser to increase the specificity and sensitivity of a spectrometric method. Many methods, once developed, are kept purposely static so that data can be compared over long periods of time. This is particularly true in industrial quality assurance (QA), forensic and environmental applications. Analytical chemistry plays an increasingly important role in the pharmaceutical industry where, aside from QA, it is used in discovery of new drug candidates and in clinical applications where understanding the interactions between the drug and the patient are critical.

History

Much of early chemistry (1661-~1900AD) was analytical chemistry since the questions of what elements and chemicals were present in the world around us and what are their fundamental natures is very much in the realm of analytical chemistry. There was also significant early progress in synthesis and theory which of course are not analytical chemistry. During this period significant analytical contributions to chemistry include the development of systematic elemental analysis by Justus von Liebig and systematized organic analysis based on the specific reactions of functional groups.

The first instrumental analysis was flame emissive spectrometry developed by Robert Bunsen and Gustav Kirchhoff who discovered rubidium (Rb) and caesium (Cs) in 1860. Most of the major developments in analytical chemistry take place after 1900. During this period instrumental analysis becomes progressively dominant in the field. In particular many of the basic spectroscopic and spectrometric techniques were discovered in the early 20th century and refined in the late 20th century. The separation sciences follow a similar time line of development and also become increasingly transformed into high performance instruments.

In the 1970s many of these techniques began to be used together to achieve a complete characterization of samples. Starting in approximately the

1970s into the present day analytical chemistry has progressively become more inclusive of biological questions (bioanalytical chemistry), whereas it had previously been largely focused on inorganic or small organic molecules.

Lasers have been increasingly used in chemistry as probes and even to start and influence a wide variety of reactions. The late 20th century also saw an expansion of the application of analytical chemistry from somewhat academic chemical questions to forensic, environmental, industrial and medical questions, such as in histology.

TYPES

Traditionally, analytical chemistry has been split into two main types, qualitative and quantitative:

Qualitative

- Qualitative inorganic analysis seeks to establish the presence of a given element or inorganic compound in a sample.

Quantitative

- Quantitative analysis seeks to establish the amount of a given element or compound in a sample.

Approaches

Most modern analytical chemistry is categorized by two different approaches such as analytical targets or analytical methods. Analytical Chemistry (journal) reviews two different approaches alternatively in the issue 12 of each year.

By Analytical Targets

- Bioanalytical chemistry
- Environmental analysis
- Forensics

By Analytical Methods

- Spectroscopy
- Chromatography and Electrophoresis
- Crystallography
- Microscopy
- Electrochemistry.

3

Surface and Colloids Chemistry

INTRODUCTION

Because of the range of dimensions involved in colloidal structures, the surface-to-volume ratio is high and a significant proportion of the molecules in such systems lie within or close to the region of inhomogeneity associated with particle/medium interfaces. These molecules will have properties (energy, molecular conformation) different from those in the bulk phases more distant from the interface. It is then no longer possible (as we do in bulk thermodynamics) to describe the whole system simply in terms of the sum of the contributions from the molecules in the bulk phases, calculated as though both phases had the same properties as they have in the bulk state.

A significant and often dominating contribution comes from the molecules in the interfacial region. This is why surface chemistry plays such an important part in colloid science and why colloidal properties begin to become evident when the particle size falls below 1 μm.

We can see this in the following way: The surface area associated with a given mass of material subdivided into equal-size particles increases in inverse proportion to the linear dimensions of the particles. Thus the area exposed by unit mass (the specific surface area, as) is given by 6/d, (Where d is the density of the material and d is the edge length in the case of cubic particles or the diametre in the case of spheres). If the material is made up of molecules of linear dimension h and molecular volume ~h^3, then the fraction of molecules in the surface layer is given approximately by 6(h/d). Thus for a substance of molar volume 30 cm^3 mol -1 or of molecular volume 0.05 nm^3 (silver bromide) h = 0.37 nm. For a 1-cm cube only two or three molecules in ten million are surface molecules, and these have a negligible influence on its properties. However, when divided into 10^{12} particles of 1 μm, one molecule in four hundred and fifty is a surface molecule, and the properties of the system begin to be affected.

At 10 nm the ratio rises to nearly one in four and surface effects became dominant. Beyond this it is hardly possible to decide what we mean by a surface molecule and, as indicated above, special considerations apply to the size range 1-10 nm. To illustrate this point, variation of the percentage of surface molecules with particle size for the typical case of silver bromide.

Variation of the percentage of molecules in the surface as a function of particle size for a substance with a molar volume of 30 cm^3 mol^{-1}. This approach to colloids, emphasizing the importance of surface or interfacial properties, suggests a more meaningful description of colloids as microheterogeneous systems, the microheterogeneity being characterized by lengths in the range 1-1000 nm.

It should be noted, however, that some typically colloidal phenomena, such as light scattering, are exhibited (though very weakly) by systems in which the microheterogeneity arises from random kinetic fluctuations in density in an otherwise uniform system of small molecules such as a gas or a liquid, while in some cases (suspensions of relatively coarse solid particles) certain colloid-like properties may persist to particle sizes much larger than the above maximum.

Nomenclature

Before proceeding further, it will be helpful to introduce a number of additional terms, which are widely used in the description of colloidal behaviour. Disperse systems in which all the particles are of (approximately) the same size are said to be monodisperse (or isodisperse); conversely, if a range of particle sizes is present, they are polydisperse.

In certain circumstances, to be discussed in greater detail later, the particles of a dispersion may adhere to one another and form aggregates of successively increasing size which may, despite the tendency of thermal motion to keep them in suspension, separate out under the influence of gravity. The nature of the aggregated material may depend on the conditions of its formation, or it may change with time. An initially formed, rather open aggregate is called a floc and the process of its formation flocculation. The floc may or may not separate out.

If the aggregate changes to, or is produced in, a much denser form, it is said to undergo coagulation with the formation of a coagulum. An aggregate usually separates out either by sedimentation (if it is more dense than the medium) or by creaming (if it is less dense than the medium). Since in many cases it is not readily apparent which type of aggregate is formed, the terms flocculation and coagulation have often been used interchangeably, but the more specific meanings introduced above are gaining more general acceptance.

One characteristic that is sometimes used to infer a distinction between the two is whether aggregation is reversible. It is usually supposed that coagulation is irreversible whereas flocculation can be reversed in the process of deflocculation. However, conditions can sometimes be found under which even coagulated systems can be redispersed. The meaning of the term stability as applied to colloid systems is to be considered both for the conditions of initial dispersion, floc or coagulum and redispersion.

Historical Perspective

Although the true nature of colloids was not appreciated until relatively recently, Man has observed and made use of colloidal systems and their properties since the earliest days of civilization. Moreover, colloids have played in geological time, and play today, an important role in many natural phenomena.

Perhaps the oldest record of a colloidal phenomenon is that of the deposition of silt at river mouths mentioned in the Babylonian Creation myth which, incidentally, was inscribed on tablets of clay, themselves an example of a colloidal material. The Book of Genesis refers to clouds and the fall of rain. But early Man must also have been familiar with many other colloidal phenomena, such as the effect of walking on wet sand and the treachery of quicksand. He soon exploited them in the preparation of butter, cheese, and yogurt and in the making of bread.

His early technology, too, often depended on colloids and their properties:

- The making of bricks
- The extraction of glue from bones
- The preparation of inks and pigments.

Indeed, there can have been few aspects of his domestic life that were independent of the behaviour of colloids, either of natural occurrences or prepared by him. *The same is even truer today*: the list of colloids and colloidal processes of vital importance to modern living and industrial technology is almost unlimited.

Their diversity can be appreciated by quoting just a few examples, which include the following:

- The products of modern food technology
- Pharmaceutical and cosmetic preparations of many kinds
- Agricultural and horticultural chemicals
- Paints

- Dyestuffs
- Paper
- The processes involved in mineral extraction
- Oil recovery
- Water treatment
- Photography
- Biotechnology
- SynLube™ lubricants

The difference today is that colloid technology is rapidly becoming more rational and scientifically based and is leaving behind many of the empiricisms that characterized those earlier crafts which depended on controlling and using colloidal materials. Despite this long history, the scientific study of colloids is a relatively recent development.

It is true that the alchemists prepared and used two important forms of colloidal gold, namely potable gold (supposedly the Elixir of Life) and Purple of Cassius, used to make ruby glass. But the first experimental studies date from the early years of the nineteenth century, when Selmi prepared what were then called demulsions of sulfur and silver halides.

It was not until 1856 that Michael Faraday made the first systematic study of colloidal gold, which will be outlined in the following section, and put forward ideas which can still be seen in modern theories concerning the factors responsible for the stability of these dispersions. The word 'colloid' was coined later by Thomas Graham in 1861 to describe systems, which exhibited slow rates of diffusion through a porous membrane, of which glue solutions were a typical example.

The usefulness of this definition depends on the significant decrease in the diffusion rate when the size of the diffusing particle exceeds a few nanometres. However, such solutions are but one example of the wide class of disperse systems described above, although this was not appreciated immediately. The slow progress in the understanding of colloidal behaviour compared with that in other branches of chemistry and physics was in large part due to the extreme difficulty of preparing well-characterized materials with reproducible properties. As exemplified by the quotation heading this section, and in part to the absence of adequate theoretical knowledge to provide a basis for understanding the factors controlling these properties.

Recent progress has followed the reduction and, in some cases, the elimination of these barriers. Thus methods of preparing well-characterized colloids have made it possible to perform quantitative and reproducible experiments, while the development of theories of intermolecular forces, electrolyte solutions, and polymers was essential before the concepts they introduced could be brought together and applied in colloid science. Coupled with these factors, and playing an increasingly important role, has been the application to colloids of sophisticated modern instrumental techniques, including:

- High-resolution microscopy
- Scanning electron microscopy
- Laser light scattering in its various forms
- Neutron scattering
- Nuclear magnetic resonance
- Optical spectroscopy (infrared and Raman in particular)
- Greatly improved rheological techniques

The guidance provided by basic research into the fundamental factors controlling colloidal behaviour has proved, and is increasingly proving, of immense value in enhancing industrial processes that involve colloids and in developing new processes and products.

Among the many examples, which have taken place in the last, twenty to thirty years are:

- The dramatic improvements in paint technology
- New drug delivery systems

These are based in large measure on an increased understanding of the principles of colloid and surface chemistry.

Antonino Tabascio first initiated the marriage of colloid chemistry and Tribology in 1944 and SynLube™ Lube-4-Life™ lubricants are direct result of his Syn-Sol experiments.

Colloidal Gold

It so happens that one of the first colloidal dispersions to have been examined systematically will suit our purpose admirably. During 1856-7 Michael Faraday first prepared colloidal gold by reducing an aqueous solution of gold chloride with phosphorus to yield a ruby-coloured liquid. He showed by chemical tests that the gold was no longer present in an ionic form but that reagents that dissolve metallic gold were able to remove the colour. He concluded that the gold was dispersed in the liquid in a very finely divided form, the presence of which could be detected by the bluefish opalescence observed when a narrow, intense beam of light is passed through the liquid.

This phenomenon was subsequently investigated by Tyndall and is known as the Tyndall effect. Faraday observed that the addition of a small amount of various salts changed the colour from ruby towards blue and that the blue liquid tended to deposit solid. Neither the blue liquid nor these deposits could be changed back to ruby. Faraday found that the gold sol could also be produced in the presence of a warm gelatine solution, which on cooling set to a jelly. Moreover, when prepared in this way addition of salt to the warm solution did not change the colour to blue.

Faraday concluded that the change from ruby to blue resulted from an increase in particle size. *Of the particles in the ruby liquid he said*:"Whether the particles be considered as mutually repulsive, or else as molecules** of gold with associated envelopes of water, they differ from those particles which by the application of salt or other substances are rendered mutually adhesive, and so fall and clot together.'"

His observations on the jellied samples implied, he believed:"a like association (of the gold particles) with that animal substance", which explained their stability in the ruby form.

In this series of experiments Faraday thus demonstrated some of the more important properties of colloidal dispersions: light scattering, sedimentation, coagulation by salts, and their `protection' from the effects of salt by gelatine. His interpretation of these observations was remarkably perceptive, in contrast to the speculations of some of his contemporaries. He correctly surmised that the change induced by changing conditions"is not a change of the gold as gold, but rather a change in the relations of the surface of the particle to the surrounding medium".

It is perhaps surprising that Faraday did not examine the effect of an electric current on his gold sols. Had he done so, he would have discovered the one additional factor which in due course provided the clue to many of their properties, namely that colloidal particles in an aqueous medium (except under special circumstances) move under the influence of an electric field. The phenomenon of electrophoresis shows that colloidal particles usually carry an electric charge, which in the case of gold sols is negative. The discussion the origin of these charges and the factors that determine their sign is beyond the scope of this brief introduction. For the moment it is sufficient to know that they exist. This brief account of the properties of one typical colloidal dispersion we are now in a position to examine in the next section the factors that are responsible for the stability of dispersions.

CLASSIFICATION OF COLLOIDAL

Colloidal systems may be grouped into three general classifications:

1. Colloidal dispersions are thermodynamically unstable owing to their high surface free energy and are irreversible systems in the sense that they are not easily reconstituted after phase separation.

2. True solutions of macromolecular material (natural or synthetic) are thermodynamically stable and reversible in the sense that they are easily reconstituted after separation of solute from solvent.
3. Association colloids which are thermodynamically stable.

The particles in a colloidal dispersion are sufficiently large for definite surfaces of separation to exist between the particles and the medium in which they are dispersed. Simple colloidal dispersions are, therefore, two-phase systems.

The phases are distinguished by the terms dispersed phase (for the phase forming the particles) anddispersion medium (for the medium in which the particles are distributed) — The physical nature of a dispersion depends, of course, on the respective roles of the constituent phases; for example, an oil-in-water (O/W) emulsion and a water-in-oil (W/O) emulsion could have almost the same overall composition, but their physical properties would be notably different.

Dispersions

Sols and emulsions are by far the most important types of colloidal dispersion. The term sol is used to distinguish colloidal suspensions from macroscopic suspensions; there is, of course, no sharp line of demarcation. When the dispersion medium is aqueous, the term hydrosol is usually used. If the dispersed phase is polymeric in nature, the dispersion is called a latex (pl. latices or latexes). Foams are somewhat different in that it is the dispersion medium which has colloidal dimensions.

The Importance of the Unterface

A characteristic feature of colloidal dispersions is the large area-to-volume ratio for the particles involved. At the interfaces between the dispersed phase and the dispersion medium characteristic surface properties, such as adsorption and electric double layer effects, are evident and play a very important part in determining the physical properties of the system as a whole. It is the material within a molecular layer or so of the interface which exerts by far the greatest influence on particle-particle and particle-dispersion medium interactions.

Despite this large area-to-volume ratio, the amount of material required to give a significant molecular coverage and modification of the interfaces in a typical colloidal dispersion can be quite small, and substantial modification of the overall bulk properties of a colloidal dispersion can often be effected by small quantities of suitable additives. For example, pronounced changes in the consistency of certain clay suspensions (such as those used in oil-well drilling) can be effected by the addition of small amounts of calcium ions (thickening) or phosphate ions (thinning).

Surface science is, therefore, closely linked with colloid science; indeed, colloid science is inevitably a part of surface science, although the reverse does not necessarily hold.

The surface or interfacial phenomena associated with colloidal systems such as emulsions and foams are often studied by means of experiments on artificially prepared flat surfaces rather than on the colloidal systems themselves. Such methods provide a most useful indirect approach to the various problems involved.

Lyophilic and Lyophobic Systems

The terms lyophilic (liquid-loving) and lyophobic (liquid-hating) are frequently used to describe the tendency of a surface or functional group to become wetted or solvated. If the liquid medium is aqueous, the terms hydrophilic and hydrophobic are used.

Lyophilic surfaces can be made lyophobic, and vice versa. For example, clean glass surfaces, which are hydrophilic, can be made hydrophobic by a coating of wax; conversely, the droplets in a hydrocarbon oil-in-water emulsion, which are hydrophobic, can be made hydrophilic by the addition of protein to the emulsion, the protein molecules adsorbing on to the droplet surfaces.

This terminology is particularly useful when one considers the phenomenon of surface activity. The molecules of surface-active materials have a strong affinity for interfaces, because they contain both hydrophilic and lipophilic (oil-loving) regions.

The general usage of the terms 'lyophilic' and 'lyophobic' in describing colloidal systems is somewhat illogical. 'Lyophobic' traditionally describes liquid dispersions of solid or liquid particles produced by mechanical or chemical action; however, in these so-called 'lyophobic sols'. dispersions of powdered alumina or silica in water) there is often a high affinity between the particles and the dispersion medium - *i.e.* the particles are really lyophilic. Indeed, if the term 'lyophobic' is taken to imply no affinity between particles and dispersion medium (an unreal situation), then the particles would not be wetted and no dispersion could, in fact, be formed. 'Lyophilic' traditionally describes soluble macromolecular material; however, lyophobic regions are often present. For example, proteins are partly hydrophobic (hydrocarbon regions) and partly hydrophilic (peptide linkages, and amino and carboxyl groups).

DEFINITION OF COLLOIDS

Colloid science concerns systems in which one or more of the components has at least one dimension within the nanometre (10^{-9}m) to micrometre (10^{-6}m) range, *i.e.* it concerns, in the main, systems containing large molecules and/or small particles. The adjective 'microheterogeneous' provides an appropriate description of most colloidal systems. There is, however, no sharp distinction between colloidal and non-colloidal systems.

The range of colloidal systems of practical importance is vast, as is the range of processes where colloid/surface chemical phenomena are involved.

Examples of systems which are colloidal (at least in some respects) are:

Aerosols	Foodstuffs
Agrochemicals	Ink
Cement	Paint
Cosmetics	Paper
Dyestuffs	Pharmaceuticals
Emulsions	Plastics
Fabrics	Rubber
Foams	Soil

Examples of processes which rely heavily on the application of colloid/surface phenomena are:

Adhesion	Ore flotation
Chromatography	Precipitation
Detergency	Road surfacing
Electrophoretic deposition	Sewage disposal
Emulsion polymerization	Soil conditioning
Food processing	Sugar refining
Grinding	Water clarification
Heterogeneous catalysis	Water evaporation control
Ion exchange	Water repellency
Lubrication	Wetting
Oil-well drilling	

As can be seen from the second of these lists, the existence of matter in the colloidal state may be a desirable or an undesirable state of affairs, and so it is important to know both how to make and how to destroy colloidal systems.

Colloid science is very much an interdisciplinary subject, albeit with certain areas of physics and physical chemistry most prominent. Owing to the complexity of most colloidal systems, the subject often cannot be treated readily with the exactness that tends to be associated with much of these major subject areas. It is probably a combination of this lack of precision and its interdisciplinary nature, rather than lack of importance, that has been responsible in the past for an unjustifiable tendency to neglect colloid science during undergraduate academic training.

Until the last few decades colloid science stood more or less on its own as an almost entirely descriptive subject which did not appear to fit within the general framework of physics and chemistry. The use of materials of doubtful compositions which put considerable strain on the questions of reproducibility and interpretation, was partly responsible for this state of affairs. Nowadays, the tendency is to work whenever possible with well-defined systems. monodispersed dispersions, pure surface-active agents, well-defined polymeric material) which act as models, both in their own right and for real life systems under consideration.

Despite the large number of variables which are often involved, research of this nature coupled with advances in the understanding of the fundamental principles of physics and chemistry has made it possible to formulate coherent, if not always comprehensive, theories relating to many of the aspects of colloidal behaviour. Since it is important that colloid science be understood at both descriptive and theoretical levels, the study of this subject can range widely from relatively simple descriptive material to extremely complex theory.

The natural laws of physics and chemistry which describe the behaviour of matter in the massive and molecular states also, of course, apply to the colloidal state. The characteristic feature of colloid science lies in the relative importance which is attached to the various physicochemical properties of the systems being studied.

As we shall see, the factors which contribute most to the overall nature of a colloidal system are:

- Particle size
- Particle shape and flexibility
- Surface (including electrical) properties
- Particle-particle interactions
- Particle-solvent interactions

Colloidal Silver

The Herald of Provo Utah, February 2, 1992, ran an article on Pg. D1, in which a member of the administrative staff of Brigham Young University by the name of Daryl Tichy has been successfully experimenting with colloidal silver in the treatment of AIDS, along with warts and parvo virus in a dog."Tichy said he had the material [colloidal silver] tested at two different labs; results showed the solution killed a variety of pathogens, including the HIV virus." Tichy then states,"I don't have a doubt in my mind." He says he has not been able to obtain funds to continue his research.

This should not be a surprise, considering what other researchers have been telling us. There is much more evidence to support Tichy's conclusion. Extensive evidence points to the fact that colloidal silver destroys all types of virii including the AIDS virus and greatly enhances the immune system in general. Colloidal Silver supports the T-cells in their fight against foreign organisms in the blood. It virtually forms a second immune system, actually protecting and defending the T-cells, as well as doing their work for them. It is strongly suggested by research scientists such as Dr. Gary Smith and others that silver ions are essential to the immune system.

In"Use of Colloids in Health and Disease", author Dr. Henry Crooks says colloidal silver is highly anti-viral. In laboratory tests he found that"all fungus, virii, bacterium, streptococcus, staphylococcus, and other pathogenic organisms are killed in three or four minutes. In fact, there is no microbe known that is not killed by colloidal silver in six minutes or less in a dilution as little as five parts per million." Dr. Crooks tells us there are no serious side effects whatsoever from high concentrations. Research scientist Dr. Gary Smith reports that he has noticed a correlation between low silver levels, sickness and immune deficiency. He found people who have low silver levels tend to be frequently sick and to have innumerable colds, flu's, fevers, and other illnesses. The research of Dr. Gary Smith would seem to support the belief that colloidal silver is an entirely natural healing agent.

HIV and AIDS are a two sided medical condition. First is the HIV virus, which attacks the immune system. Second are the main outward effects, the conditions resulting from the weakened immune system. Research evidence shows that Colloidal Silver is a two edged sword. It attacks the HIV virus directly and effectively, and then forms virtually its own immune system to ward off the various health problems the immune system has not been able to handle.

Parasites are being recognised more and more as a cause of failing health. Hulda Clark, Ph.D., N.D., author of"The Cure for All Cancers" and"The Cure for HIV and AIDS", tells us that neither cancer nor HIV can exist without parasites and that if we eliminate the parasites, the disease will be gone. Health Consciousness, Vol. 15, No. 4 says:"Parasites are also killed [by colloidal silver], as they have an egg-stage in their reproductive cycle, which is one celled and therefore killed in six minutes or less." In as much as there are many kinds of parasites, this may be inconclusive. However, tests have shown that mosquito larva are effectively killed by colloidal silver. It should be remembered that to rid oneself of parasites by killing the eggs or larvae means that one must continue the treatment until all of the adults die, probably of old age. More research is needed. But if the AIDS or Cancer and other conditions can be effectively treated with colloidal silver, then any effects on parasites is a free benefit.

In as much as AIDS is the result of a virtually destroyed immune system, it would be surprising to find that colloidal silver did not have a dramatic effect on AIDS. AIDS is a viral disease, and antibiotics seldom have any effect on any virus, but the colloidal silver ion is highly effective. The evidence strongly supports the theory that colloidal silver is highly effective against all strains of virus, curing even the common cold in one dose. Where many drugs on the market suppress certain symptoms of a cold, colloidal silver is said to kill off the virus that causes it to hang on. AIDS, like all other viral infections, is unaffected by antibiotics, which each kill off only a few strains of bacteria and none are effective against the virus, yeast's, or fungi. Yet, researchers are telling us that colloidal silver is highly effective against all of these.

One serious condition typical of AIDS is rapid ageing. Ageing is generally considered as due to a slowing down of the body's ability to replace worn out cells fast enough. This slowing down begins by the time of adulthood and continues into old age. In"Report: Colloidal Silver, Health Consciousness, Vol. 15, No. 4, it is stated that"Silver aids the developing foetus in growth, health, and eases the delivery and recovery."

If colloidal silver aids the growth of a foetus so noticeably, will it reduce the ageing process? From the research of Dr. Becker, it would seem colloidal silver will produce the dedifferentiated cells necessary to prevent this slowdown of cell replacement. It is probable that the weakened immune system is incapable of producing the undifferentiated cells necessary to rebuild worn out cells. Colloidal silver produced the needed cells to make this possible. All of this is being discovered and rediscovered at the same time that disease bacterium are developing immunity to modern antibiotics.

Furthermore, immunity to the antibiotics seems to be developing all over the world, even in isolated areas. The medical profession is alarmed. Can silver save us? Many authorities think so!

Colloidal Silver Versus Bacteria and Viruses

As single celled creatures called bacteria use a common type enzyme or'chemical lung" for their oxygen metabolism, the presence of colloidal silver cripples the enzyme, therefore causing the organism to suffocate. Any and all bacteria are therefore killed within the 6-minute time frame, without causing any adverse effect on the surrounding tissue cells. Dr Becker also states in his book:"Positive silver kills all types of bacteria". This is exiting, because no other single antibiotic works against all types of bacteria. Positive silver, however, offers several advantages over previous forms. There are no ions besides silver to burden tide tissues. It works against all types of bacteria and viruses, even killing antibiotic resistant strains as well as all fungal infections."

To carry the fight to fungal infection, one must firstly understand fungal growths. A fungus is a series of single cells that have small tubes of the material from which the cell is made, which stretches between the cell walls.

Whether more linear in its spread and expand mode or, alternatively, more like a fabric in its reproductive mode, a fungus will still exhibit that characteristic of any one celled bacterium, that particular type of chemical lung, which is almost completely and permanently disabled by the presence of colloidal silver in the body, as the silver suffocates the organism.

How it Works Against Viruses

A single virus will invade a living cell within the body tissue. Then the insidious pathogen will take over the nucleus of the cell and alter it's production and reproduction mechanism to replicate the virus instead of the enzyme, hormone, or other chemical that the body would normally have produced for itself within that cell.

Later, the newly produced virus will be released from that cell and into the blood stream. However, another very interesting thing takes place. As the virus affects the cell for its own purposes, part of the response of that living cell is that it reverts back to a more primitive form of cell structure and chemistry. The oxygen metabolising enzyme, or chemical lung in the cell wall, reverts as well.

This more primitive form of enzyme is vulnerable to the effects of colloidal silver. The catalyst effect of the colloidal silver simply being in close proximity to the enzyme of this cell results in the enzyme becoming permanently disabled. It cannot function to bring oxygen into the cell, and the virus producing cell dies by suffocation.

Colloidal Sllver and Hiv

HIV is caused by a particular type of virus. This virus attacks and invades a single tissue cell and takes over the operation of the cell's reproductive mechanism. Part of the cells response to this viral attack is for the cell to revert back to a different primitive one celled type of enzyme or chemical lung, the kind that is crippled by the presence of colloidal silver, The cell then suffocates and dies and, as it is no longer useful to the body, it is flushed out. The colloidal silver has killed the mutated cell, virus and all. Silver kills all viruses, precluding future mutations as it also kills the HIV virus-invaded cell within minutes. As a catalyst, colloidal silver is not affected in the reaction, and it continues to kill any other single celled pathogen that is in its presence.

Colloidal Silver as a Preventative Substance

As a preventative, colloidal silver is unsurpassed. Sufficient colloidal silver taken daily precludes infection, viruses, disease, contagion outbreak and serious burn toxicity. The daily ingestion of colloidal silver is like having a second immune system. It lessens the load on the body's natural immune system, and effectively kills the many thousands of viruses and bacteria that are present throughout the body.

In addition, it lessens the toxicity due to the average amount of virus and bacterial activity that occurs naturally in the body. However, tests have shown that, due to the high absorption of silver into the small intestine, the "friendly bacteria in the large intestine are unaffected".

This "second immune system" acts parallel to, and independent of, the body's own first line of defence, which is a major advantage in warding off outbreaks of influenza or other germ, plaque or pestilence. By taking colloidal silver at the correct dose rate is to have protection that is unsurpassed against serious burn toxicity. Severe burn cases, such as from a house fire or motor accident, will have a much greater survival rate than those who do not take colloidal silver before such a catastrophe. Often, people who survive such horrific injuries later die of complications that occur some days, even weeks after the injury is sustained.

This is because several of the body's systems become overloaded and cannot cope. Colloidal silver has proven to be extremely effective in helping the body's immune system and sustained in the fire or accident.

With reference to the healing powers of colloidal silver, an American surgeon, Dr William Stewart Halstedwrote in 1913, after referring to the age old practice of placing pure silver wire in and around wounds. "I know of nothing that could take its place, nor have I known anyone to abandon it who has thoroughly familiarised him or herself with the technique of its employment. We may have only scratched the surface of tale medical brilliance of silver. Already it is an amazing tool, as it stimulates bone-forming cells, cures the most stubborn infections, and stimulates healing of skin tissue. "Some established uses for colloidal silver Below is a list of diseases colloidal silver will successfully treat. This is a partial list, as there are over 650 in all.

- Acne
- Aids
- Allergies
- Appendicitis
- Arthritis
- Athletes foot
- Bladder infection
- Blood parasites
- Blood poisoning
- Boils
- Burns
- Cancer
- Candida
- Chronic fatigue
- Colitis
- Conjunctivitis
- Cystitis
- Dandruff
- Dermatitis
- Diabetes
- Diphtheria
- Eczema
- Gastro-enteritis
- Gonorrhoea
- Hayfever
- Hepatitis
- Herpes
- Impetigo
- Indigestion
- Keratitus
- Leprosy
- Leukaemia
- Malaria
- Meningitis
- Neurasthenia
- Parasitic infection
- Pneumonia
- Prostate infection
- Pruritis ani
- Psoriasis
- Rheumatics
- Rhinitis
- Ring worm
- Scarlet fever
- Septic conditions
- Seborreah septicaemia
- Shingles
- Staph and streptococcal
- Ulcers
- Viruses
- Warts
- Chest infections etc..

The above may be an impressive array of nasty viruses and diseases, but they are but a few that form a much larger group. Colloidal silver can also be applied directly to open wounds and sores to eliminate infection. It does not sting, burn or smart in any way.

Other antiseptics sting when applied to a wound because they are killing the surrounding wall tissue cells, as well as attempting to kill the germs. Colloidal silver will not harm the surrounding cells or tissue. After washing the face thoroughly, colloidal silver may be used as the only medication or, in amount each day, the affliction will disappear. On open wounds, colloidal silver may be used as the only medication or, in conjunction with other medication. Just sprinkle the colloidal silver over the effected area and bandage. This application is also good for the removal of warts.

4

Nuclear Chemistry

Nuclear chemistry is a subfield of chemistry dealing with radioactivity, nuclear processes and nuclear properties. * It is the chemistry of radioactive elements such as the actinides, radium and radon together with the chemistry associated with equipment (such as nuclear reactors) which are designed to perform nuclear processes.

This includes the corrosion of surfaces and the behaviour under conditions of both normal and abnormal operation (such as during an accident). An important area is the behaviour of objects and materials after being placed into a waste store or otherwise disposed of.

- the study of the chemical effects resulting from the absorption of radiation within living animals, plants, and other materials. The radiation chemistry controls much of radiation biology as radiation has an effect on living things at the molecular scale, to explain it another way the radiation alters the biochemicals within an organism, the alteration of the biomolecules then changes the chemistry which occurs within the organism, this change in biochemistry then can lead to a biological outcome. As a result nuclear chemistry greatly assists the understanding of medical treatments (such as cancer radiotherapy) and has enabled these treatments to improve.
- the study of the production and use of radioactive sources for a range of processes. These include radiotherapy in medical applications; the use of radioactive tracers within industry, science and the environment; and the use of radiation to modify materials such as polymers.
- the study and use of nuclear processes in *non-radioactive* areas of human activity. For instance, nuclear magnetic resonance (NMR) spectroscopy is commonly used in synthetic organic chemistry and physical chemistry and for structural analysis in macromolecular chemistry.

Early History

After the discovery of X-rays by Wilhelm Rontgen, many scientists began to work on ionizing radiation. One of these was Henri Becquerel, who investigated the relationship between phosphorescence and the blackening of photographic plates. When Becquerel (working in France) discovered that, with no external source of energy, the uranium generated rays which could blacken (or *fog*) the photographic plate, radioactivity was discovered. Marie Curie (working in Paris) and her husband Pierre Curie isolated two new radioactive elements from uranium ore.

They used radiometric methods to identify which stream the radioactivity was in after each chemical separation; they separated the uranium ore into each of the different chemical elements that were known at the time, and measured the radioactivity of each fraction. They then attempted to separate these radioactive fractions further, to isolate a smaller fraction with a higher specific activity (radioactivity divided by mass). In this way, they isolated polonium and radium. It was noticed in about 1901 that high doses of radiation could cause an injury in humans, Becquerel had carried a sample of radium in his pocket and as a result he suffered a high localised dose which resulted in a radiation burn this injury resulted in the biological properties of radiation being investigated, which in time resulted in the development of medical treatments.

Marie Curie's daughter (Irène Joliot-Curie) and her husband were the first to 'create' radioactivity: they bombarded boron with alpha particles to make a proton-rich isotope of nitrogen; this isotope emitted positrons. In addition, they bombarded aluminium and magnesium with neutrons to make new radioisotopes. Ernest Rutherford, working in Canada and England, showed that radioactivity decay can be described by a simple equation (a linear first degree derivative equation, now called first order kinetics), implying that a given radioactive substance has a characteristic "half life" (the time taken for the amount of radioactivity present in a source to diminish by half). He also coined the terms alpha, beta and gamma rays, he converted nitrogen into oxygen, and most importantly he supervised the students who did the Geiger-Marsden experiment (gold leaf experiment) which showed that the 'plum pudding model' of the atom was wrong. In the plum pudding model, proposed by J. J. Thomson in 1904, the atom is composed of electrons surrounded by a 'cloud' of positive charge to balance the electrons' negative charge. To Rutherford, the gold foil experiment implied that the positive charge was confined to a very small nucleus leading first to the Rutherford model, and eventually to the Bohr model of the atom, where the positive nucleus is surrounded by the negative electrons.

Main Areas

Radiochemistry is the chemistry of radioactive materials, where radioactive isotopes of elements are used to study the properties and chemical reactions of non-radioactive isotopes (often within radiochemistry the absence of radioactivity leads to a substance being described as being *inactive* as the isotopes are *stable*).

Radiation Chemistry

Radiation chemistry is the study of the chemical effects of radiation on matter; this is very different to radiochemistry as no radioactivity needs to be present in the material which is being chemically changed by the radiation. An example is the conversion of water into hydrogen gas and hydrogen peroxide.

Study of Nuclear Reactions

A combination of radiochemistry and radiation chemistry is used to study nuclear reactions such as fission and fusion. Some early evidence for nuclear fission was the formation of a shortlived radioisotope of barium which was isolated from neutron irradiated uranium (^{139}Ba, with a half-life of 83 minutes and ^{140}Ba, with a half-life of 12.8 days, are major fission products of uranium). At the time, it was thought that this was a new radium isotope, as it was then standard radiochemical practice to use a barium sulphate carrier precipitate to assist in the isolation of radium.. More recently, a combination of radiochemical methods and nuclear physics has been used to try to make new 'superheavy' elements; it is thought that islands of relative stability exist where the nuclides have half-lives of years, thus enabling weighable amounts of the new elements to be isolated. For more details of the original discovery of nuclear fission see the work of Otto Hahn.

The Nuclear Fuel Cycle

The chemistry associated with any part of the nuclear fuel cycle, including nuclear reprocessing. The fuel cycle includes all the operations involved in producing fuel, from mining, ore processing and enrichment to fuel production (*Front end of the cycle*). It also includes the 'in-pile' behaviour (use of the fuel in a reactor) before the *back end* of the cycle. The *back end* includes the management of the used nuclear fuel in either a cooling pond or dry storage, before it is disposed of into an underground waste store or reprocessed.

Normal and Abnormal Conditions

The nuclear chemistry associated with the nuclear fuel cycle can be divided into two main areas, one area is concerned with operation under the intended conditions while the other area is concerned with maloperation conditions where some alteration from the normal operating conditions has occurred or (*more rarely*) an accident is occurring.

Reprocessing

Law

PUREX Chemistry: The current method of choice is to use the PUREX liquid-liquid extraction process which uses a tributyl phosphate/hydrocarbon mixture to extract both uranium and plutonium from nitric acid. This extraction is of the nitrate salts and is classed as being of a solvation mechanism. For example the extraction of plutonium by an extraction agent (S) in a nitrate medium occurs by the following reaction.

$$Pu^{4+}_{aq} + 4NO^{-}_{3\,aq} + 2S_{organic} \longrightarrow [Pu(NO_3)_4S_2]_{organic}$$

A complex is formed between the metal cation, the nitrates and the tributyl phosphate, and a model compound of a dioxouranium(VI) complex with two nitrates and two triethyl phosphates has been characterised by X-ray crystallography.

When the nitric acid concentration is high the extraction into the organic phase is favoured, and when the nitric acid concentration is low the extraction is reversed (the organic phase is *stripped* of the metal). It is normal to dissolve the used fuel in nitric acid, after the removal of the insoluble matter the uranium and plutonium are extracted from the highly active liquor. It is normal to then back extract the loaded organic phase to create a *medium active* liquor which contains mostly uranium and plutonium with only small traces of fission products.

This medium active aqueous mixture is then extracted again by tributyl phosphate/hydrocarbon to form a new organic phase, the metal bearing organic phase is then stripped of the metals to form an aqueous mixture of only uranium and plutonium. The two stages of extraction are used to improve the purity of the actinide product, the organic phase used for the first extraction will suffer a far greater dose of radiation.

The radiation can degrade the tributyl phosphate into dibutyl hydrogen phosphate. The dibutyl hydrogen phosphate can act as an extraction agent for both the actinides and other metals such as ruthenium. The dibutyl hydrogen phosphate can make the system behave in a more complex manner as it tends to extract metals by an ion exchange mechanism (extraction favoured by low acid concentration), to reduce the effect of the dibutyl hydrogen phosphate it is common for the used organic phase to be washed with sodium carbonate solution to remove the acidic degradation products of the tributyl phosphate.

NUCLEAR SCIENCE

Nuclear Science is a subfield of chemistry dealing with radioactivity, nuclear processes and nuclear properties. It is the chemistry of radioactive elements such as the actinides, radium and radon together with the chemistry associated with equipment (such as nuclear reactors) which are designed to perform nuclear processes. This includes the corrosion of surfaces and the behaviour under conditions of both normal and abnormal operation (such as during an accident). An important area is the behaviour of objects and materials after being placed into a waste store or otherwise disposed of.

- The study of the chemical effects resulting from the absorption of radiation within living animals, plants, and other materials. The radiation chemistry controls much of radiation biology as radiation has an effect on living things at the molecular scale, to explain it another way the radiation alters the biochemicals within an organism, the alteration of the biomolecules then changes the chemistry which occurs within the organism, this change in biochemistry then can lead to a biological outcome. As a result nuclear chemistry greatly assists the understanding of medical treatments (such as cancer radiotherapy) and has enabled these treatments to improve.
- The study of the production and use of radioactive sources for a range of processes. These include radiotherapy in medical applications; the use of radioactive tracers within industry, science and the environment; and the use of radiation to modify materials such as polymers.
- The study and use of nuclear processes in *non-radioactive* areas of human activity. For instance, nuclear magnetic resonance (NMR) spectroscopy is commonly used in synthetic organic chemistry and physical chemistry and for structural analysis in macromolecular chemistry.

Early history

After the discovery of X-rays by Wilhelm Röntgen, many scientists began to work on ionizing radiation. One of these was Henri Becquerel, who investigated the relationship between phosphorescence and the blackening of photographic plates. When Becquerel (working in France) discovered that, with no external source of energy, the uranium generated rays which could blacken (or *fog*) the photographic plate, radioactivity was discovered.

Marie Curie (working in Paris) and her husband Pierre Curie isolated two new radioactive elements from uranium ore. They used radiometric methods to identify which stream the radioactivity was in after each chemical separation; they separated the uranium ore into each of the different chemical elements that were known at the time, and measured the radioactivity of each fraction. They then attempted to separate these radioactive fractions further, to isolate a smaller fraction with a higher specific activity (radioactivity divided by mass). In this way, they isolated polonium and radium.

It was noticed in about 1901 that high doses of radiation could cause an injury in humans, Becquerel had carried a sample of radium in his pocket and as a result he suffered a high localised dose which resulted in a radiation burn this injury resulted in the biological properties of radiation being investigated, which in time resulted in the development of medical treatments.

Marie Curie's daughter and her husband were the first to 'create' radioactivity: they bombarded boron with alpha particles to make a proton-rich isotope of nitrogen; this isotope emitted positrons. In addition, they bombarded aluminium and magnesium with neutrons to make new radioisotopes. Ernest Rutherford, working in Canada and England, showed that radioactivity decay can be described by a simple equation (a linear first degree derivative equation, now called first order kinetics), implying that a given radioactive substance has a characteristic "half life" (the time taken for the amount of radioactivity present in a source to diminish by half).

He also coined the terms alpha, beta and gamma rays, he converted nitrogen into oxygen, and most importantly he supervised the students who did the Geiger-Marsden experiment (gold leaf experiment) which showed that the 'plum pudding model' of the atom was wrong. In the plum pudding model, proposed by J. J. Thomson in 1904, the atom is composed of electrons surrounded by a 'cloud' of positive charge to balance the electrons' negative charge. To Rutherford, the gold foil experiment implied that the positive charge was confined to a very small nucleus leading first to the Rutherford model, and eventually to the Bohr model of the atom, where the positive nucleus is surrounded by the negative electrons.

Main areas

Radiochemistry is the chemistry of radioactive materials, where radioactive isotopes of elements are used to study the properties and chemical reactions of non-radioactive isotopes (often within radiochemistry the absence of radioactivity leads to a substance being described as being *inactive* as the isotopes are *stable*).

Radiation Chemistry

Radiation chemistry is the study of the chemical effects of radiation on matter; this is very different to radiochemistry as no radioactivity needs to be present in the material which is being chemically changed by the radiation. An example is the conversion of water into hydrogen gas and hydrogen peroxide.

Study of Nuclear Reactions

A combination of radiochemistry and radiation chemistry is used to study nuclear reactions such as fission and fusion. Some early evidence for nuclear fission was the formation of a shortlived radioisotope of barium which was isolated from neutron irradiated uranium (^{139}Ba, with a half-life of 83 minutes and ^{140}Ba, with a half-life of 12.8 days, are major fission products of uranium).

At the time, it was thought that this was a new radium isotope, as it was then standard radiochemical practice to use a barium sulphate carrier precipitate to assist in the isolation of radium. More recently, a combination of radiochemical methods and nuclear physics has been used to try to make new 'superheavy' elements; it is thought that islands of relative stability exist where the nuclides have half-lives of years, thus enabling weighable amounts of the new elements to be isolated.

The nuclear fuel cycle

The chemistry associated with any part of the nuclear fuel cycle, including nuclear reprocessing. The fuel cycle includes all the operations involved in producing fuel, from mining, ore processing and enrichment to fuel production (*Front end of the cycle*).

It also includes the 'in-pile' behaviour (use of the fuel in a reactor) before the *back end* of the cycle. The *back end* includes the management of the used nuclear fuel in either a cooling pond or dry storage, before it is disposed of into an underground waste store or reprocessed.

Normal and Abnormal Conditions

The nuclear chemistry associated with the nuclear fuel cycle can be divided into two main areas, one area is concerned with operation under the intended conditions while the other area is concerned with maloperation conditions where some alteration from the normal operating conditions has occurred or (*more rarely*) an accident is occurring.

Reprocessing

Law: In the USA it is normal to use fuel once in a power reactor before placing it in a waste store. The long term plan is currently to place the civil used power reactor fuel in a deep store. This policy of not reprocessing was started in March 1977 for nuclear weapons proliferation reasons. The President Jimmy Carter issued a Presidential directive which indefinitely suspended the commercial reprocessing and recycling of plutonium in the USA.

This Presidential directive is likely to have been an attempt by the USA to lead other countries by example, but many other nations continue to reprocess spent nuclear fuels. It is noteworthy that the government under Putin (President of Russia) repealed a law which had banned the import of used nuclear fuel into Russia, this change in Russian law now permits the Russians to offer a reprocessing service for clients outside Russia (In a similar way to that offered by BNFL).

PUREX Chemistry

The current method of choice is to use the PUREX liquid-liquid extraction process which uses a tributyl phosphate/hydrocarbon mixture to extract both uranium and plutonium from nitric acid. This extraction is of the nitrate salts and is classed as being of a solvation mechanism. For example the extraction of plutonium by an extraction agent (S) in a nitrate medium occurs by the following reaction.

$$Pu^{4+}{}_{aq} + 4NO_3^-{}_{aq} + 2S_{organic} \rightarrow [Pu(NO_3)_4S_2]_{organic}$$

A complex is formed between the metal cation, the nitrates and the tributyl phosphate, and a model compound of a dioxouranium(VI) complex with two nitrates and two triethyl phosphates has been characterised by X-ray crystallography.

When the nitric acid concentration is high the extraction into the organic phase is favoured, and when the nitric acid concentration is low the extraction is reversed (the organic phase is *stripped* of the metal). It is normal to dissolve the used fuel in nitric acid, after the removal of the insoluble matter the uranium and plutonium are extracted from the highly active liquor.

It is normal to then back extract the loaded organic phase to create a *medium active* liquor which contains mostly uranium and plutonium with only small traces of fission products. This medium active aqueous mixture is then extracted again by tributyl phosphate/hydrocarbon to form a new organic phase, the metal bearing organic phase is then stripped of the metals to form an aqueous mixture of only uranium and plutonium. The two stages of extraction are used to improve the purity of the actinide product, the organic phase used for the first extraction will suffer a far greater dose of radiation. The radiation can degrade the tributyl phosphate into dibutyl hydrogen phosphate. The dibutyl hydrogen phosphate can act as an extraction agent for both the actinides and other metals such as ruthenium.

The dibutyl hydrogen phosphate can make the system behave in a more complex manner as it tends to extract metals by an ion exchange mechanism (extraction favoured by low acid concentration), to reduce the effect of the dibutyl hydrogen phosphate it is common for the used organic phase to be washed with sodium carbonate solution to remove the acidic degradation products of the tributyl phosphate.

New Methods being Considered for Future use

The PUREX process can be modified to make a UREX (URanium EXtraction) process which could be used to save space inside high level nuclear waste disposal sites, such as Yucca Mountain, by removing the uranium which makes up the vast majority of the mass and volume of used fuel and recycling it as reprocessed uranium.

The UREX process is a PUREX process which has been modified to prevent the plutonium being extracted. This can be done by adding a plutonium reductant before the first metal extraction step. In the UREX process, ~99.9% of the Uranium and >95% of Technetium are separated from each other and the other fission products and actinides.

The key is the addition of acetohydroxamic acid (AHA) to the extraction and scrub sections of the process. The addition of AHA greatly diminishes the extractability of Plutonium and Neptunium, providing greater proliferation resistance than with the plutonium extraction stage of the PUREX process.

Adding a second extraction agent, octyl(phenyl)-N, N-dibutyl carbamoylmethyl phosphine oxide(CMPO) in combination with tributylphosphate, (TBP), the PUREX process can be turned into the TRUEX (TRansUranic EXtraction) process this is a process which was invented in the USA by Argonne National Laboratory, and is designed to remove the transuranic metals (Am/Cm) from waste. The idea is that by lowering the alpha activity of the waste, the majority of the waste can then be disposed of with greater ease. In common with PUREX this process operates by a solvation mechanism.

As an alternative to TRUEX, an extraction process using a malondiamide has been devised. The DIAMEX (DIAMideEXtraction) process has the advantage of avoiding the formation of organic waste which contains elements other than Carbon, Hydrogen, Nitrogen, and Oxygen. Such an organic waste can be burned without the formation of acidic gases which could contribute to acid rain.

The DIAMEX process is being worked on in Europe by the French CEA. The process is sufficiently mature that an industrial plant could be constructed with the existing knowledge of the process. In common with PUREX this process operates by a solvation mechanism.

Selective ActiNide EXtraction. As part of the management of minor actinides it has been proposed that the lanthanides and trivalent minor actinides should be removed from the PUREX raffinate by a process such as DIAMEX or TRUEX. In order to allow the actinides such as americium to be either reused in industrial sources or used as fuel the lanthanides must be removed.

The lanthanides has large neutron cross sections and hence they would poison a neutron driven nuclear reaction. To date the extraction system for the SANEX process has not been defined, but currently several different research groups are working towards a process. For instance the French CEA is working on a bis-triaiznyl pyridine (BTP) based process.

Other systems such as the dithiophosphinic acids are being worked on by some other workers.

This is the *UNiversal* EXtraction process which was developed in Russia and the Czech Republic, it is a process designed to remove all of the most troublesome (Sr, Cs and minor actinides) radioisotopes from the raffinates left after the extraction of uranium and plutonium from used nuclear fuel.

The chemistry is based upon the interaction of caesium and strontium with poly ethylene oxide (poly ethylene glycol) and a cobalt carborane anion (known as chlorinated cobalt dicarbollide).

The actinides are extracted by CMPO, and the diluent is a polar aromatic such as nitrobenzene. Other dilents such as *meta*-nitrobenzotrifluoride and phenyl trifluoromethyl sulfone have been suggested as well.

Absorption of Fission Products on Surfaces

Another important area of nuclear chemistry is the study of how fission products interact with surfaces; this is thought to control the rate of release and migration of fission products both from waste containers under normal conditions and from power reactors under accident conditions.

It is interesting to note that, like chromate and molybdate, the $^{99}TcO_4$ anion can react with steel surfaces to form a corrosion resistant layer. In this way, these metaloxo anions act as anodic corrosion inhibitors. The formation of $^{99}TcO_2$ on steel surfaces is one effect which will retard the release of ^{99}Tc from nuclear waste drums and nuclear equipment which has been lost before decontamination (eg submarine reactors lost at sea). This $^{99}TcO_2$ layer renders the steel surface passive, inhibiting the anodic corrosion reaction.

The radioactive nature of technetium makes this corrosion protection impractical in almost all situations. It has also been shown that $^{99}TcO_4$ anions react to form a layer on the surface of activated carbon (charcoal) or aluminium. A short review of the biochemical properties of a series of key long lived radioisotopes can be read on line.

It is important to note that ^{99}Tc in nuclear waste may exist in chemical forms other than the $^{99}TcO_4$ anion, these other forms have different chemical properties. Similarly, the release of iodine-131 in a serious power reactor accident could be retarded by absorption on metal surfaces within the nuclear plant.

Spinout areas

Some methods first developed within nuclear chemistry and physics have become so widely used within chemistry and other physical sciences that they may be best thought of as separate from *normal* nuclear chemistry.

For example, the isotope effect is used so extensively to investigate chemical mechanisms and the use of cosmogenic isotopes and long-lived unstable isotopes in geology that it is best to consider much of isotopic chemistry as separate from nuclear chemistry.

Kinetics (Use within Mechanistic Chemistry)

The mechanisms of chemical reactions can be investigated by observing how the kinetics of a reaction are changed by making an isotopic modification of a substrate. This is now a standard method in organic chemistry.

Briefly, replacing normal hydrogens (protons) by deuterium within a chemical compound causes the rate of molecular vibration (C-H, N-H and O-H bonds show this) to decrease. This then can lead to a decrease in the reaction rate if the rate-determining step involves breaking a bond between hydrogen and another atom.

Thus, if the reaction changes in rate when protons are replaced by deuteriums, it is reasonable to assume that the breaking of the bond to hydrogen is part of the step which determines the rate.

Uses within Geology, Biology and Forensic Science

Cosmogenic isotopes are formed by the interaction of cosmic rays with the nucleus of an atom. These can be used for dating purposes and for use as natural tracers. In addition, by careful measurement of some ratios of stable isotopes it is possible to obtain new insights into the origin of bullets, ages of ice samples, ages of rocks, and the diet of a person can be identified from a hair or other tissue sample.

Biology

Within living things, isotopic labels (both radioactive and nonradioactive) can be used to probe how the complex web of reactions which makes up the metabolism of an organism converts one substance to another. For instance a green plant uses light energy to convert water and carbon dioxide into glucose by photosynthesis.

If the oxygen in the water is labeled, then the label appears in the oxygen gas formed by the plant and not in the glucose formed in the chloroplasts within the plant cells.

For biochemical and physiological experiments and medical methods, a number of specific isotopes have important applications.

- Stable isotopes have the advantage of not delivering a radiation dose to the system being studied; however, a significant excess of them in the organ or organism might still interfere with its functionality, and the availability of sufficient amounts for whole-animal studies is limited for many isotopes. Measurement is also difficult, and usually requires mass spectroscopy to determine how much of the isotope is present in particular compounds, and there is no means of localizing measurements within the cell.
- H-2 (deuterium), the stable isotope of hydrogen, is a stable tracer, the concentration of which can be measured by mass spectroscopy or NMR. It is incorporated into all cellular structures. Specific deuterated compound can also be produced.
- N-15, the stable isotope of nitrogen, has also been used. It is incorporated mainly into proteins.
- Radioactive isotopes have the advantages of being detectable in very low quantities, in being easily measured by scintillation counting or other radiochemical methods, and in being localizable to particular regions of a cell, and quantifiable by autoradiography. Many compounds with the radioactive atoms in specific positions can be prepared, and are widely available commercially. In high quantities they require precautions to guard the workers from the effects of radiation—and they can easily contaminate laboratory glassware and other equipment. For some isotopes the half-life is so short that preparation and measurement is difficult.

By organic synthesis it is possible to create a complex molecule with a radioactive label that can be confined to a small area of the molecule. For short-lived isotopes such as ^{11}C, very rapid synthetic methods have been developed to permit the rapid addition of the radioactive isotope to the molecule. For instance a palladium catalysed carbonylation reaction in a microfluidic device has been used to rapidly form amides and it might be possible to use this method to form radioactive imaging agents for PET imaging.

- ^{3}H, Tritium, the radioisotope of hydrogen, it available at very high specific activities, and compounds with this isotope in particular positions are easily prepared by standard chemical reactions such as hydrogenation of unsaturated precursors. The isotope emits very soft beta radiation, and can be detected by scintillation counting.

- ^{11}C, Carbon-11 can be made using a cyclotron, boron in the form of boric oxide is reacted with protons in a (p,n) reaction. An alternative route is to react ^{10}B with deuterons. By rapid organic synthesis, the ^{11}C compound formed in the cyclotron is converted into the imaging agent which is then used for PET.
- ^{14}C, Carbon-14 can be made (as above), and it is possible to convert the target material into simple inorganic and organic compounds. In most organic synthesis work it is normal to try to create a product out of two approximately equal sized fragments and to use a convergent route, but when a radioactive label is added, it is normal to try to add the label late in the synthesis in the form of a very small fragment to the molecule to enable the radioactivity to be localised in a single group. Late addition of the label also reduces the number of synthetic stages where radioactive material is used.
- ^{18}F, fluorine-18 can be made by the reaction of neon with deuterons, ^{20}Ne reacts in a (d,^{4}He) reaction. It is normal to use neon gas with a trace of stable fluorine ($^{19}F_2$). The $^{19}F_2$ acts as a carrier which increases the yield of radioactivity from the cyclotron target by reducing the amount of radioactivity lost by absorption on surfaces. However, this reduction in loss is at the cost of the specific activity of the final product.

Nuclear Magnetic Resonance (NMR)

NMR spectroscopy uses the net spin of nuclei in a substances upon energy absorption to identify molecules. This has now become a standard spectroscopic tool within synthetic chemistry. One major use of NMR is to determine the bond connectivity within an organic molecule.

NMR imaging also uses the net spin of nuclei (commonly protons) for imaging. This is widely used for diagnostic purposes in medicine, and can provide detailed images of the inside of a person without inflicting any radiation upon them. In a medical setting, NMR is often known simply as "magnetic resonance" imaging, as the word 'nuclear' has negative connotations for many people.

Nuclear Chemistry

Nuclear Chemistry deals with the nuclei of atoms breaking apart. Atoms are continually undergoing decay. When studying nuclear chemistry, there is a typical format used to represent specific isotopes.

$$\underset{\text{Charge or Atomic Number}}{\overset{\text{Mass Number}}{{}^{238}_{92}\text{U}}} \leftarrow \text{Element}$$

Nuclear equations are typically written in the format shown below. There are 5 different types of radioactive decay.

1. *Alpha decay follows the form:*

$$^{X}_{Z}A \rightarrow \underset{\text{Alpha Particle}}{{}^{4}_{2}He} + {}^{X-4}_{Z-2}B$$

Where A is the parent isotope (the atom being broken apart) B is the daughter isotope or the isotope formed. When an element is broken down in alpha decay it looses two neutrons and two (2) protons. This means hat the name of the element will change as well, moving back two (2) places on the periodic table. Alpha decay is is not very penetrating because the He atoms capture electrons before traveling very far. However it is very damaging because the alpha particles can knock atoms off of molecules.Alpha decay is the most common in elements with an atomic number greater than 83.

2. *Beta negative decay follows the form:*

$$^{X}_{Z}A \rightarrow \underset{\text{Beta Particle}}{{}^{0}_{-1}e^{-1}} + {}^{X}_{Z-1}B$$

The beta emission increases the atomic number by one (1) by adding one (1) proton. At the same time, one (1) neutron is lost so the mass of the daughter isotope is the same as the parent isotope. Beta negative decay is more penetrating than alpha decay because the particles are smaller, but less penetrating than gamma decay. Beta electrons can penetrate through about one (1) cm of flesh before they are brought to a halt because of electrostatic forces. Beta decay is most common in elements with a high neutron to proton ratio.

3. *Gamma decay follows the form:*

$$^{X}_{Z}A \rightarrow \underset{\text{Gamma Particle}}{{}^{0}_{0}\gamma} + {}^{X}_{Z}B$$

In gamma emission, neither the atomic number or the mass number is changed. A high energy gamma ray is given off when the parent isotope falls into a lower energy state. Gamma radiation is the most penetrating of all.

These photons can pass through the body and cause damage by ionizing all the molecules in their way.

4. *Positron emission (also called Beta positive decay) follows the form:*

$$ {}^{X}_{Z}A \rightarrow \underset{\substack{\downarrow \\ \text{Positron Particle}}}{{}^{0}_{1}e} + {}^{X}_{Z-1}B $$

In this reaction a positron is emitted. A positron is exactly like an electron in mass and charge force except with a positive charge. It is formed when a proton breaks into a neutron with mass and no charge and this positron with no mass and the positive charge. Positron emission is most common in lighter elements with a low neutron to proton ratio.

5. *Electron capture follows the form:*

$$ {}^{X}_{Z}A + \underset{\substack{\downarrow \\ \text{Electron Particle}}}{{}^{0}_{-1}e} + {}^{X}_{Z-1}B $$

In this reaction a nucleus captures one (1) of its own atom's inner shell electrons which reduces the atomic number by one. This captured electron joins with a proton in the nucleus to form a neutron. Electron capture is common in larger elements with a low neutron to proton ratio.

All elements with an atomic number over 83 are considered radioactive. Radioactivity can be measured using a geiger counter, a cylinder containing a low-pressure gas and two (2) electrodes. Radiation ionizes the atoms in the cylinder and allows current to flow between the electrodes. The half life of a radioactive substance is the time required for half of the initial number of nuclei to disintegrate.

The decay rate expresses the speed at which a substance disintegrates. The following equation represents the relationship between the number of nuclei remaining, N, the number of nuclei initially present, N_O, the rate of decay, k, and the amount of time, t.

$$ \text{In}\frac{N}{N_0} = -kt $$

The relationship between the half-life of a radioactive substance and k, the rate at which it decays can also be found.

$$ t_{1/2}\frac{.693}{k} $$

By using these equations, it is possible to calculate how much of a nuclear substance will be left after a certain time and how much of a substance originally existed. A common example is isotopic dating in which the ages of archeological artifacts are determined by measuring the activity of the isotopes.

RADIOACTIVITY: HISTORICAL FIGURES

Access Excellence Classic Collection

This article will focus on the efforts of four scientists: Wilhelm Conrad Roentgen, Antoine Henri Becquerel, Marie Sklodowska Curie, and Ernest Rutherford.

It emphasizes their contributions to the elucidation of radioactivity and the "key" experiments they performed pertaining to their discoveries. The biographies and photographs are adapted from The Health Physics Society Centennial Calendar by permission of the Health Physics Society.

Wilhelm Conrad Roentgen

On November 8, 1895, at the University of Wurzburg, Wilhelm Roentgen's attention was drawn to a glowing fluorescent screen on a nearby table.

Roentgen immediately determined that the fluorescence was caused by invisible rays originating from the partially evacuated glass Hittorf-Crookes tube he was using to study cathode rays (i.e., electrons). Surprisingly, these mysterious rays penetrated the opaque black paper wrapped around the tube. Roentgen had discovered X rays, a momentous event that instantly revolutionized the field of physics and medicine.

However, prior to his first formal correspondence to the University Physical-Medical Society, Roentgen spent two months thoroughly investigating the properties of X rays. Silvanus Thompson complained that Roentgen left "little for others to do beyond elaborating his work." For his discovery, Roentgen received the first Nobel Prize in physics in 1901. When later asked what his thoughts were at the moment of his discovery, he replied "I didn't think, I investigated. "It was the crowning achievement in a career beset by more than its share of difficulties.

As a student in Holland, Roentgen was expelled from the Utrecht Technical School for a prank committed by another student. Even after receiving a doctorate, his lack of a diploma initially prevented him from obtaining a position at the University of Wurzburg. He even was accused of having stolen the discovery of X rays by those who failed to observe them.

Nevertheless, Roentgen was a brilliant experimentalist who never sought honors or financial profit for his research. He rejected a title (i.e., von Roentgen) that would have provided entry into the German nobility, and donated the money he received from the Nobel Prize to his University.

Roentgen did accept the honorary degree of Doctor of Medicine offered to him by the medical faculty of his own University of Wurzburg. However, he refused to take out any patents in order that the world could freely benefit from his work. At the time of his death, Roentgen was nearly bankrupt from the inflation that followed World War I.

Antoine Henri Becquerel

Henri Becquerel was born into a family of scientists. His grandfather had made important contributions in the field of electrochemistry while his father had investigated the phenomena of fluorescence and phosphorescence. Becquerel not only inherited their interest in science, he also inherited the minerals and compounds studied by his father.

And so, upon learning how Wilhelm Roentgen discovered X rays from the fluorescence they produced, Becquerel had a ready source of fluorescent materials with which to pursue his own investigations of these mysterious rays.

The material Becquerel chose to work with was potassium uranyl sulfate, $K_2UO_2(SO_4)_2$, which he exposed to sunlight and placed on photographic plates wrapped in black paper. When developed, the plates revealed an image of the uranium crystals. Becquerel concluded "that the phosphorescent substance in question emits radiation which penetrates paper opaque to light." Initially he believed that the sun's energy was being absorbed by the uranium which then emitted X rays.

Further investigation, on the 26th and 27th of February, was delayed because the skies over Paris were overcast and the uranium-covered plates Becquerel intended to expose to the sun were returned to a drawer. On the first of March, he developed the photographic plates expecting only faint images to appear. To his surprise, the images were clear and strong. This meant that the uranium emitted radiation without an external source of energy such as the sun. Becquerel had discovered radioactivity, the spontaneous emission of radiation by a material.

Later, Becquerel demonstrated that the radiation emitted by uranium shared certain characteristics with X rays but, unlike X rays, could be deflected by a magnetic field and therefore must consist of charged particles. For his discovery of radioactivity, Becquerel was awarded the 1903 Nobel Prize for physics.

Marie Curie

By the time he met Marie Sklodowska, Pierre Curie had already established an impressive reputation. In 1880, he and his brother Jacques had discovered piezoelectricity whereby physical pressure applied to a crystal resulted in the creation of an electric potential.

He also had made important investigations into the phenomenon of magnetism including the identification of a temperature, the curie point, above which a material's magnetic properties disappear. However, shortly after his marriage to Marie in 1895, Pierre subjugated his research to her interests.

Together, they began investigating the phenomenon of radioactivity recently discovered in uranium ore. Although the phenomenon was discovered by Henri Becquerel, the term radioactivity was coined by Marie. After chemical extraction of uranium from the ore, Marie noted the residual material to be more "active" than the pure uranium.

She concluded that the ore contained, in addition to uranium, new elements that were also radioactive. This led to their discoveries of the elements of polonium and radium, but it took four more years of processing tons of ore under oppressive conditions to isolate enough of each element to determine its chemical properties.

For their work on radioactivity, the Curies were awarded the 1903 Nobel Prize in physics. Tragically, Pierre was killed three years later in an accident while crossing a street in a rainstorm. Pierre's teaching position at the Sorbonne was given to Marie. Never before had a woman taught there in its 650 year history!

Her first lecture began with the very sentence her husband had used to finish his last. In his honour, the 1910 Radiology Congress chose the curie as the basic unit of radioactivity: the quantity of radon in equilibrium with one gram of radium (current definition: $1 \text{ Ci} = 3.7 \times 10^{10}$ dps). A year later, Marie was awarded the Nobel Prize in chemistry for her discoveries of radium and polonium, thus becoming the first person to receive two Nobel Prizes.

For the remainder of her life she tirelessly investigated and promoted the use if radium as a treatment for cancer. Marie Curie died July 4, 1934, overtaken by pernicious anemia no doubt caused by years of overwork and radiation exposure.

Ernest Rutherford

Ernest Rutherford is considered the father of nuclear physics. Indeed, it could be said that Rutherford invented the very language to describe the theoretical concepts of the atom and the phenomenon of radioactivity. Particles named and characterized by him include the alpha particle, beta particle and proton.

Even the neutron, discovered by James Chadwick, owes its name to Rutherford. The exponential equation used to calculate the decay of radioactive substances was first employed for that purpose by Rutherford and he was the first to elucidate the related concepts of the half-life and decay constant.

With Frederick Soddy at McGill University, Rutherford showed that elements such as uranium and thorium became different elements (i.e., transmuted) through the process of radioactive decay. At the time, such an incredible idea was not to be mentioned in polite company: it belonged to the realm of alchemy, not science.

For this work, Rutherford won the 1908 Nobel Prize in chemistry. In 1909, now at the University of Manchester, Rutherford was bombarding a thin gold foil with alpha particles when he noticed that although almost all of them went through the gold, one in eight thousand would "bounce" (i.e., scatter) back. The amazed Rutherford commented that it was "as if you fired a 15-inch naval shell at a piece of tissue paper and the shell came right back and hit you."

From this simple observation, Rutherford concluded that the atom's mass must be concentrated in a small positively-charged nucleus while the electrons inhabit the farthest reaches of the atom. Although this planetary model of the atom has been greatly refined over the years, it remains as valid today as when it was originally formulated by Rutherford.

In 1919, Rutherford returned to Cambridge to become director of the Cavendish laboratory where he had previously done his graduate work under J.J. Thomson. It was here that he made his final major achievement, the artificial alteration of nuclear and atomic structure. By bombarding nitrogen with alpha particles, Rutherford demonstrated the production of a different element, oxygen. "Playing with marbles" is what he called; the newspapers reported that Rutherford had "split the atom." After his death in 1937, Rutherford's remains were buried in Westminster Abbey near those of Sir Isaac Newton.

NEW METHODS BEING CONSIDERED FOR FUTURE USE

The PUREX process can be modified to make a UREX (URanium EXtraction) process which could be used to save space inside high level nuclear waste disposal sites, such as Yucca Mountain, by removing the uranium which makes up the vast majority of the mass and volume of used fuel and recycling it as reprocessed uranium.

The UREX process is a PUREX process which has been modified to prevent the plutonium being extracted. This can be done by adding a plutonium reductant before the first metal extraction step. In the UREX process, ~99.9% of the Uranium and >95% of Technetium are separated from each other and the other fission products and actinides. The key is the addition of acetohydroxamic acid (AHA) to the extraction and scrub sections of the process. The addition of AHA greatly diminishes the extractability of Plutonium and Neptunium, providing greater proliferation resistance than with the plutonium extraction stage of the PUREX process.

Adding a second extraction agent, octyl(phenyl)-N, N-dibutyl carbamoylmethyl phosphine oxide(CMPO) in combination with tributylphosphate, (TBP), the PUREX process can be turned into the TRUEX (TRansUranic EXtraction) process this is a process which was invented in the USA by Argonne National Laboratory, and is designed to remove the transuranic metals (Am/Cm) from waste. The idea is that by lowering the alpha activity of the waste, the majority of the waste can then be disposed of with greater ease. In common with PUREX this process operates by a solvation mechanism.

As an alternative to TRUEX, an extraction process using a malondiamide has been devised. The DIAMEX (DIAMideEXtraction) process has the advantage of avoiding the formation of organic waste which contains elements other than Carbon, Hydrogen, Nitrogen, and Oxygen. Such an organic waste can be burned without the formation of acidic gases which could contribute to acid rain. The DIAMEX process is being worked on in Europe by the French CEA. The process is sufficiently mature that an industrial plant could be constructed with the existing knowledge of the process. In common with PUREX this process operates by a solvation mechanism.

Selective ActiNide EXtraction. As part of the management of minor actinides it has been proposed that the lanthanides and trivalent minor actinides should be removed from the PUREX raffinate by a process such as DIAMEX or TRUEX. In order to allow the actinides such as americium to be either reused in industrial sources or used as fuel the lanthanides must be removed. The lanthanides has large neutron cross sections and hence they would poison a neutron driven nuclear reaction. To date the extraction system for the SANEX process has not been defined, but currently several different research groups are working towards a process. For instance the French CEA is working on a bis-triaiznyl pyridine (BTP) based process.

Other systems such as the dithiophosphinic acids are being worked on by some other workers.

This is the *UNiversal* EXtraction process which was developed in Russia and the Czech Republic, it is a process designed to remove all of the most troublesome (Sr, Cs and minor actinides) radioisotopes from the raffinates left after the extraction of uranium and plutonium from used nuclear fuel. The chemistry is based upon the interaction of caesium and strontium with poly ethylene oxide (poly ethylene glycol) and a cobalt carborane anion (known as chlorinated cobalt dicarbollide). The actinides are extracted by CMPO, and the diluent is a polar aromatic such as nitrobenzene. Other dilents such as *meta*-nitrobenzotrifluoride and phenyl trifluoromethyl sulfone have been suggested as well.

ABSORPTION OF FISSION PRODUCTS ON SURFACES

Another important area of nuclear chemistry is the study of how fission products interact with surfaces; this is thought to control the rate of release and migration of fission products both from waste containers under normal conditions and from power reactors under accident conditions. It is interesting to note that, like chromate and molybdate, the $^{99}TcO_4$ anion can react with steel surfaces to form a corrosion resistant layer. In this way, these metaloxo anions act as anodic corrosion inhibitors.

The formation of $^{99}TcO_2$ on steel surfaces is one effect which will retard the release of ^{99}Tc from nuclear waste drums and nuclear equipment which has been lost before decontamination (eg submarine reactors lost at sea). This $^{99}TcO_2$ layer renders the steel surface passive, inhibiting the anodic corrosion reaction. The radioactive nature of technetium makes this corrosion protection impractical in almost all situations. It has also been shown that $^{99}TcO_4$ anions react to form a layer on the surface of activated carbon (charcoal) or aluminium. A short review of the biochemical properties of a series of key long lived radioisotopes can be read on line.

It is important to note that ^{99}Tc in nuclear waste may exist in chemical forms other than the $^{99}TcO_4$ anion, these other forms have different chemical properties. Similarly, the release of iodine-131 in a serious power reactor accident could be retarded by absorption on metal surfaces within the nuclear plant.

Spinout Areas

Some methods first developed within nuclear chemistry and physics have become so widely used within chemistry and other physical sciences that they may be best thought of as separate from *normal* nuclear chemistry. For example, the isotope effect is used so extensively to investigate chemical mechanisms and the use of cosmogenic isotopes and long-lived unstable isotopes in geology that it is best to consider much of isotopic chemistry as separate from nuclear chemistry.

Kinetics (use within mechanistic chemistry)

The mechanisms of chemical reactions can be investigated by observing how the kinetics of a reaction are changed by making an isotopic modification of a substrate. This is now a standard method in organic chemistry. Briefly, replacing normal hydrogens (protons) by deuterium within a chemical compound causes the rate of molecular vibration (C-H, N-H and O-H bonds show this) to decrease. This then can lead to a decrease in the reaction rate if the rate-determining step involves breaking a bond between hydrogen and another atom. Thus, if the reaction changes in rate when protons are replaced by deuteriums, it is reasonable to assume that the breaking of the bond to hydrogen is part of the step which determines the rate.

Uses within Geology, Biology and Forensic Science

Cosmogenic isotopes are formed by the interaction of cosmic rays with the nucleus of an atom. These can be used for dating purposes and for use as natural tracers. In addition, by careful measurement of some ratios of stable isotopes it is possible to obtain new insights into the origin of bullets, ages of ice samples, ages of rocks, and the diet of a person can be identified from a hair or other tissue sample.

Biology

Within living things, isotopic labels (both radioactive and nonradioactive) can be used to probe how the complex web of reactions which makes up the metabolism of an organism converts one substance to another. For instance a green plant uses light energy to convert water and carbon dioxide into glucose by photosynthesis. If the oxygen in the water is labeled, then the label appears in the oxygen gas formed by the plant and not in the glucose formed in the chloroplasts within the plant cells.

For biochemical and physiological experiments and medical methods, a number of specific isotopes have important applications.

- Stable isotopes have the advantage of not delivering a radiation dose to the system being studied; however, a significant excess of them in the organ or organism might still interfere with its functionality, and the availability of sufficient amounts for whole-animal studies is limited for many isotopes. Measurement is also difficult, and usually requires mass spectroscopy to determine how much of the isotope is present in particular compounds, and there is no means of localizing measurements within the cell.
- H-2 (deuterium), the stable isotope of hydrogen, is a stable tracer, the concentration of which can be measured by mass spectroscopy or NMR. It is incorporated into all cellular structures. Specific deuterated compound can also be produced.
- N-15, the stable isotope of nitrogen, has also been used. It is incorporated mainly into proteins.

- Radioactive isotopes have the advantages of being detectable in very low quantities, in being easily measured by scintillation counting or other radiochemical methods, and in being localizable to particular regions of a cell, and quantifiable by autoradiography. Many compounds with the radioactive atoms in specific positions can be prepared, and are widely available commercially. In high quantities they require precautions to guard the workers from the effects of radiation—and they can easily contaminate laboratory glassware and other equipment. For some isotopes the half-life is so short that preparation and measurement is difficult.

By organic synthesis it is possible to create a complex molecule with a radioactive label that can be confined to a small area of the molecule. For short-lived isotopes such as ^{11}C, very rapid synthetic methods have been developed to permit the rapid addition of the radioactive isotope to the molecule. For instance a palladium catalysed carbonylation reaction in a microfluidic device has been used to rapidly form amides and it might be possible to use this method to form radioactive imaging agents for PET imaging.

- ^{3}H, Tritium, the radioisotope of hydrogen, it available at very high specific activities, and compounds with this isotope in particular positions are easily prepared by standard chemical reactions such as hydrogenation of unsaturated precursors. The isotope emits very soft beta radiation, and can be detected by scintillation counting.
- ^{11}C, Carbon-11 can be made using a cyclotron, boron in the form of boric oxide is reacted with protons in a (p,n) reaction. An alternative route is to react ^{10}B with deuterons. By rapid organic synthesis, the ^{11}C compound formed in the cyclotron is converted into the imaging agent which is then used for PET.
- ^{14}C, Carbon-14 can be made (as above), and it is possible to convert the target material into simple inorganic and organic compounds. In most organic synthesis work it is normal to try to create a product out of two approximately equal sized fragments and to use a convergent route, but when a radioactive label is added, it is normal to try to add the label late in the synthesis in the form of a very small fragment to the molecule to enable the radioactivity to be localised in a single group. Late addition of the label also reduces the number of synthetic stages where radioactive material is used.
- ^{18}F, fluorine-18 can be made by the reaction of neon with deuterons, ^{20}Ne reacts in a (d,^{4}He) reaction. It is normal to use neon gas with a trace of stable fluorine ($^{19}F_2$). The $^{19}F_2$ acts as a carrier which increases the yield of radioactivity from the cyclotron target by reducing the

amount of radioactivity lost by absorption on surfaces. However, this reduction in loss is at the cost of the specific activity of the final product.

NUCLEAR MAGNETIC RESONANCE (NMR)

NMR spectroscopy uses the net spin of nuclei in a substances upon energy absorption to identify molecules. This has now become a standard spectroscopic tool within synthetic chemistry. One major use of NMR is to determine the bond connectivity within an organic molecule. NMR imaging also uses the net spin of nuclei (commonly protons) for imaging. This is widely used for diagnostic purposes in medicine, and can provide detailed images of the inside of a person without inflicting any radiation upon them. In a medical setting, NMR is often known simply as "magnetic resonance" imaging, as the word 'nuclear' has negative connotations for many people.

ACTIVITY

Ideally, the first activity provides the necessary know-how for the pursuit of the second, but in practice, the help it can give is only partial, and the second activity has to fall back on trial and error techniques in order to achieve its ends. This means that a good chemist is one who not only has a mastery of chemical theory, but also a good knowledge of chemical facts. With such a knowledge he can direct a trial-and error approach to practical problems in the most promising directions.

Organic chemistry is usually defined as the chemistry of compounds of carbon, inorganic chemistry being then the chemistry of all the other elements. This distinction is not a completely satisfactory one, however, since there are many compounds of carbon that are quite different from those studied by organic chemists (*e.g.* tungsten carbide, used for tipping cutting tools) and there are many compounds of other elements that are very similar to those studied under organic chemistry (*e.g.* the silicon analogues of the hydrocarbons).

It is best, therefore, to think of inorganic chemistry as the chemistry of all the elements, with organic chemistry as being a more detailed study of certain important aspects of one of them - *viz.* the hydrocarbons and their derivatives.

Thinking of inorganic chemistry in this way brings together aspects of the chemistry of an element that would otherwise tend to become separated. For example, alcohols and ethers are usually dealt with under organic chemistry and are not thought of as being part of the chemistry of oxygen.

Once they are, however, they can be set alongside the other compounds of oxygen, and a relationship immediately becomes apparent that might otherwise be lost, *viz.* that expressed by the formulae:

H–O–H R–O–H R–O–R′

Foundation Inorganic Chemistry covers, as the name suggests, the basic concepts of inorganic chemistry. If you have studied A level chemistry then all of what follows should be familiar to you.

States of Matter

Matter comes in three basic types, solid, liquid and gas (three phases of matter). In many cases it is possible to covert matter from one phase to another, perhaps by heating (we can melt, or fuse, a solid) or by cooling (the cooling of water to form ice for example).

Elements, Compounds and Mixtures

Elements are the basic building blocks of matter. If you examine the periodic table, you will see that there are about 110 elements, each given its own unique symbol. Of these hundred or so elements, about 90 exists naturally, either in their elemental (uncombined) form or in compounds where they have combined with one or more other elements. The remaining "non naturally occurring" elements have been produced artificially.

Some of the elements will be familiar to you, oxygen, which is in the air around us, carbon which forms the "lead" in our pencils and diamonds and many of the metals which we see in common use such as iron and aluminium. Others may be less familiar, praseodymium, (Pr), promethium, (Pm) and protactinium, (Pa) for example.

Some of these, more exotic elements have fierce sounding names but really we need not be concerned about these elements in the first year. We will, by and large, be concerned with the first 36 elements of the periodic table and you should make an effort to learn the names and chemical symbols of these 36 elements.When elements combine by chemical bonding, they form compounds. Compounds consist of two or more elements joined together by a chemical bond.

Everyday examples include water (H_2O—two hydrogen atoms joined to an oxygen atom), table salt (NaCl—a sodium atom combining with a chlorine atom) and acetic acid (which is found in vinegar and involves carbon, oxygen and hydrogen bonding together to give CH_3COOH).When elements or compounds are mixed together and no chemical bonding occurs, we have a mixture, an example is the air we breathe which is a mixture (among other things) of nitrogen, oxygen, carbon dioxide and water vapour. The components of the mixture may be separated, so for example it is possible to liquefy air and obtain pure nitrogen and oxygen.

The Periodic Table

Reference has already been made to the periodic table in these notes. The periodic table is a classification of the 100 or so elements. Each element has its own place in the table, its position determined by its atomic number. Hydrogen, with atomic number 1 is the first element. At first the arrangement of the elements within the periodic table may seem a little strange. Hydrogen, for example is often placed on it own with no particular position, sometimes it appears above the first column. Hydrogen and helium are found at the top of the table in a row of two elements, the next row (starting with lithium) contains eight elements (ending in neon, Ne). Then we have another row of eight followed by a row of eighteen and so on. The elements are the building blocks of matter, and to a certain extent this is true.

However the elements themselves are built up from atoms. We could define an atom as the smallest particle of an element capable of displaying the properties of that element, although I am sure you will find alternative and probably better definitions elsewhere. This is not the end of the story however. Although atoms are very small (with diameters of about 10^{-10} m) they themselves are composed of sub-atomic particles.

The three sub-atomic particles that concern us are the proton, the neutron and the electron. Both protons and neutrons reside in the nucleus of the atom (they are the nucleons). The nucleus can be thought of in terms of the core of the atom. The nucleus is very small, having a diameter of about 10^{-15}m. It is also very dense, both the proton and neutron have a mass of about 10^{-24}g, which although seems very small is confined in an extremely small volume. Given that the atom has a diameter of about 10^{-10}m and the diameter of the nucleus is about 10^{-15}m we can see that the vast majority of the atomic volume is outside the nucleus.

It is in this extra-nuclear region that is occupied by the electrons. The electron has a mass of about 10^{-28}g (*i.e.* 10000 lighter than the proton). We must be careful about how we describe the electron however since (and I hope this doesn't confuse you) it has the properties of a particle and of a wave.

If you want to know more see my notes on atomic structure. These figures for mass are obviously not very convenient and so chemists have assigned different units to record atomic masses. The Atomic Mass Unit (amu) is used, 1 amu = 1.66×10^{-24}g. On this scale the mass of the proton and neutron is 1.0 amu and the electron is 1/1836 amu (or 5×10^{-4} amu). Whilst the chemical properties of the elements are largely dictated by the number and arrangement of the electrons, it is the nucleons which dictate the mass of the atom (and hence the element). For reasons we will come to shortly, atoms are arrange not in terms of their mass but in terms of the number of protons in the nucleus, this is the atomic number (usually given the symbol Z).

Charges of Sub-atomic Particles

The proton is a positively charged particle (+1) whilst the neutron is neutral and the electron is negatively charge (-1). In an uncharged atom, therefore, there will be an equal number of protons and electrons. Atoms may gain or lose electrons and in the process become ions. Atoms which lose electrons become cations (positively charged) and become anions when they gain electrons (negatively charged).

Isotopes

The chemical properties of the atom is by the number of electrons. Given that in a neutral atom, the number of electrons is equal to the number of protons, it follows that all atoms of a particular element will have the same number of protons. So all atoms of carbon, for instance, will have six protons. The same cannot be said for the number of neutrons. The number of neutrons in the nucleus of an element can vary. For example, the nucleus of a carbon atom can contain 6, 7 or 8 neutrons.

Each of these is still a carbon atom, since each still has only six protons but the mass of each will depend upon the number of neutrons present.

The mass number (A) of an element is given by the number of protons + the number of neutrons present. Hence we can have carbon-12 (with six protons + six neutrons), carbon-13 (six protons, seven neutrons) and carbon-14 (six protons and eight neutrons). These are isotopes of carbon. *Isotopes have the same value of Z but different values for A*. The mass of the element will then be determined by the relative proportions of the various isotopes present.

The atomic mass of chlorine is 35.45. Chlorine exists as a mixture of isotope Cl-35 and Cl-37. 75.53% of chlorine is Cl-35 and the remaining 24.47% as Cl-37. We can calculate the average mass of chlorine as (75.53% × 35) + (24.47% × 37) = 35.45

Electrons

We have seen that the protons and neutrons are found in the nucleus and that electrons are "somewhere" outside the nucleus. Actually the term "somewhere" isn't as odd as at first it might seem, but that's another story. You will see elsewhere that electrons occupy energy levels outside the nucleus.

We can classify them as "orbital". You should not, however, confuse this term with planetary orbits such as the earth around the sun. For the present, we will confine ourselves to recognising that certain energy levels exist within the atom. Lower energy levels are close to the nucleus, higher energy levels further away. Electrons will occupy these energy levels starting by filling the lowest energy level possible. The first energy level, or shell can accommodate 2 electrons, the next level 8.

This starts to give us some idea of why the periodic table looks like it does. Energy levels are assigned a value, n. So n = 1 indicates the first shell. Each shell can contain 2n2 electrons. So when n=1 we have 2 electrons, n=2 we have 8 and when n=3 we have 18. Of course if you look at the periodic table this seems a little odd, since row 3 has only eight elements when we might expect 18.

The explanation for this begins with something I said earlier about electrons entering energy levels at the lowest possible energy. And involves the make up of shells. Within each shell there are different types of orbitals. More detail on these are given in the atomic structure notes. Within the energy level n = 3, there are a group of orbitals labelled "3d", filling of these orbitals by electrons does not start until we get to the transition elements (starting atomic number 21 = Sc). Hence, the increase in the number of elements per row does not occur until we reach this point. When we reach scandium, the filling of the 3d orbitals begins and we have the series of 10 elements called the 3d transition metals.

Some Comments on the Periodic Table

The periodic table is divided into Groups and rows. The Groups are the columns, for example Group I which contains the alkali metals lithium, sodium, potassium, rubidium, caesium and francium. You may also see this labelled as Group 1A. The elements within each group will have similar properties, for example the Group I elements have a tendency to form compounds in which they are cations of +1 charge (NaCl being Na^+ Cl^-).

On a more general note, the elements to the left of the periodic table are electropositive which means they tend to lose electrons when they form compounds.

- The elements to the right are electronegative, they tend to gain electrons.
- The elements in the centre (excluding the transition metals) tend to form compounds by sharing electrons.
- When an electropositive element combines with an electronegative element we get ionic bonding.

- When electropositive elements combine with other electropositive elements we get metallic bonding.
- When an electronegative element combines with another electronegative element we get covalent bonding.
- Ionic bonding involves the transfer of electron(s), covalent bonding involves the sharing of electrons.
- To the left of the periodic table we have the metals and to the right the non-metals.

Elements and Compounds

All elements might be said to be equally important. The chemistry of each has to be understood in detail if the chemistry of matter as a whole is to be understood in detail. From the point of view of the world at large, however, the relative importance of different elements varies widely, and some elements are little more that chemical curiosities.

In a university course of inorganic chemistry a balance has to be struck between a uniform treatment of all of the elements, and a greater concentration on the socially more important ones. The question of which are the socially more important elements is to some extent a matter of opinion. A chemist working in the plastics industry would doubtless come up with a different list from one working in the metals industry, and someone working with agricultural chemicals would doubtless have different ideas from someone working on ceramics.

Most people would agree, however, that among the most important elements are:

- The more abundant elements,
- Elements that are consumed on a very large scale, and
- Elements that are actively sought for despite very poor resources.

The Relative Abundance of Different Elements

The tables below give the relative abundance of different elements in the atmosphere, the hydrosphere, the lithosphere, and the biosphere. The figures are necessarily approximate, and slightly different values may be found in other places. The percentages are percentages by mass— the percentage numbers of atoms would of course be different. All abundances over 0.1% have been included. The figures reveal that some 99% of the matter in the world around us is made up of as few as 14 elements. Note, however, that many of the remaining elements in the biosphere, despite their low concentration, are essential to its healthy continuance.

Atmosphere		Hydrosphere	
Nitrogen	75.5%	Oxygen	85.8%
Oxygen	23.0%	Hydrogen	10.7%
Argon	1.4%	Chlorine	2.1%
		Sodium	1.1%
Total	99.9%	Total	99.7%
Lithosphere		**Biosphere**	
Oxygen	46.6%	Oxygen	52.4%
Silicon	27.7%	Carbon	39.4%
Aluminium	8.1%	Hydrogen	6.6%
Iron	5.0%	Nitrogen	0.5%
Calcium	3.6%	Calcium	0.4%
Sodium	2.8%	Potassium	0.2%
Potassium	2.6%		
Magnesium	2.1%		
Titanium	0.4%		
Total	98.9%	Total	99.5%

The Relative Consumption of Different Elements

The table below give the annual world consumption of different elements, as elements and compounds, in millions of tons. The table vary from year to year and are necessarily approximate. Siliceous materials and limestone used for building purposes have been excluded, and a lower limit has been set at 0.1 million tons.

	Millions of tons per year
Carbon	1000–10000
Iron, sodium	100–1000
Calcium, nitrogen, oxygen, potassium, sulfur	10–100
Aluminium, barium, chlorine, chromium, copper, fluorine, hydrogen, lead, magnesium, manganese, phosphorus, zinc	1–10
Boron, nickel, tin, titanium, zirconium	0.1–1

Of the 25 elements in the table, 10 are very plentiful, Of the remainder, the majority occur in relatively concentrated deposits, from which they or their compounds can be extracted fairly easily (*e.g.* hydrocarbons from petroleum). For copper, lead, zinc, nickel, and tin, demand is such that less concentrated deposits have to be worked, down to 0.5% in the case of copper and 0.2% in the case of tin.

Elements Sought after from Very Low-grade Ores

The following table gives the minimum metal content that an ore must have before it can be mined and smelted economically with present-day technology. Values are given up to a limit of 0.5%, and may be compared with the value for iron of 25%.

Platinum	0.0003%
Gold	0.001%
Silver	0.01%
Uranium	0.2%
Mercury	0.2%
Tin	0.2%
Molybdenum	0.3%
Copper	0.5%

5

Photochemistry

INTRODUCTION

The study of chemical reactions, isomerizations and physical behaviour that may occur under the influence of visible and/or ultraviolet light is called Photochemistry. Two fundamental principles are the foundation for understanding photochemical transformations:

- The first law of photochemistry, the Grotthuss-Draper law, states that light must be absorbed by a compound in order for a photochemical reaction to take place.
- The second law of photochemistry, the Stark-Einstein law, states that for each photon of light absorbed by a chemical system, only one molecule is activated for subsequent reaction. This "photoequivalence law" was derived by Albert Einstein during his development of the quantum (photon) theory of light.

What is the Importance of Photochemistry?

Today photochemistry has become one of the most powerful research tool. Compounds of different molecules are occurred through various photochemical reactions like CO_2, NH_3 and methane. Other examples of photochemical reactions are formation of O_3, smog, Vitamin D and many more. A new field in photochemistry called photobiology helps us to understand the mechanism of photosynthesis (process by which plants make their own food by the absorption of sunlight).

Also photochemistry helps us to form some typical compounds like D_2, cubanes, and several cleaning agents which all are made by various chemical reactions of photochemistry. The formation of laser light is only possible through photochemistry. LASER stands for Light Amplification by Stimulated Emission of Radiations. LASER contain monochromatic rays with coherent radiations, these rays can be easily focused to a small point. Due to this property, LASER light is used for cutting hard material like metal, diamond etc, also there is some application of LASER light in medical field.

PROCESS OF PHOTOCHEMICAL

The efficiency with which a given photochemical process occurs is given by its Quantum Yield. Since many photochemical reactions are complex, and may compete with unproductive energy loss, the quantum yield is usually specified for a particular event. Thus, we may define quantum yield as "the number of moles of a stated reactant disappearing, or the number of moles of a stated product produced, per einstein of monochromatic light absorbed.", where an einstein is one mole of photons.

For example, irradiation of acetone with 313 nm light (3130 Å) gives a complex mixture of products. The quantum yield of these products is less than 0.2, indicating there are radiative (fluorescence & phosphorescene) and non-radiative return pathways. The primary photochemical reaction is the homolytic cleavage of a carbon-carbon bond shown in the top equation. Here the asterix represents an electronic excited state, the nature of which will be defined later.

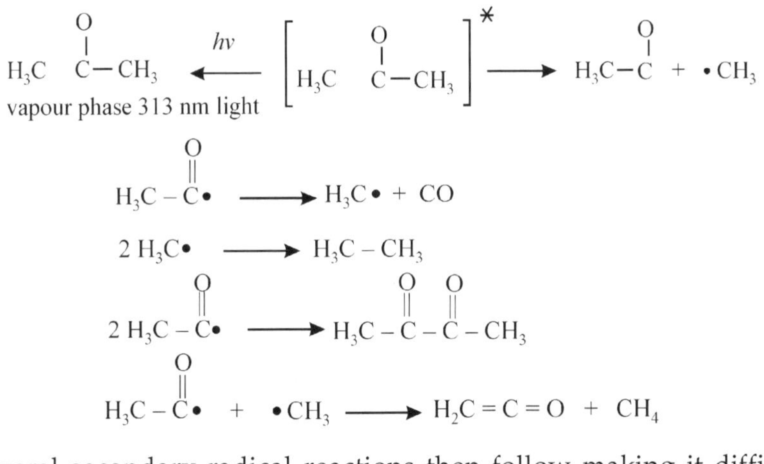

Several secondary radical reactions then follow making it difficult to assign a quantum yield to the primary reaction. The biacetyl product, formed in the third reaction, may itself be excited by light or accept excitation energy from an excited acetone molecule, further complicating this process. By comparison, the light induced chlorination of methane, or other alkanes, has a large quantum yield, often near 10^6, because of the secondary chain reactions that follow the primary cleavage of the Cl – Cl bond. Equations illustrating such halogenation reactions have been presented elsewhere in this text.

Mechanistic Background of Photochemical Reaction

Absorption of visible and/or ultraviolet light by a molecule introduces energy sufficient to break or reorganize most covalent bonds. From the relationship $E = hc / \lambda$, we see that longer wavelength visible light (400 to 800 nm) is less energetic (70 to 40 kcal/mole) than light in the accessible shorter wavelength (200 to 400 nm) near ultraviolet region (150 to 70 kcal/mole). Consequently, ultraviolet light is most often used to effect photochemical change. Care must also be taken to construct lamps and reaction vessels from glass that is transparent to the desired wavelength range. The low wavelength cut-off for some common glass typest. The light required for a photochemical reaction may come from many sources. Giacomo Ciamician, regarded as the "father of organic photochemistry", used sunlight for much of his research at the University of Bologna in the early 1900's. Depending on the compounds being studied and the information being sought, bright incandescent lamps (chiefly infrared and visible light), low, medium and high pressure mercury lamps (185 - 255 nm, 255 -1000 nm & 220 -1400 nm respectively), high intensity flash sources and lasers have all been used. In careful studies of specific chromophores, sources of monochromatic light may be desired.

Behaviour of the Electronic Excited States

Focus chiefly on the nature and behaviour of the electronic excited states formed when a photon is absorbed by a chromophoric functional group. As a rule, such excitation results in a change in molecular orbital occupancy, an increase in energy, and changes in local bonding and charge distribution.

Type of Glass	Wavelength Cut-off
Pyrex	< 275 nm
Corex	< 260 nm
Vycor	< 220 nm
Quartz	< 170 nm

We begin by considering the electronic excitation of a simple diatomic molecule such as Cl_2 or Br_2. Both absorb light, chlorine in the 300 to 380 nm region. and bromine in the 360 to 510 nm region. Both the ground (lowest energy electronic state) and excited states are shown as energy profiles populated by vibrational energy states (green lines) as well as rotational states.

The electron reorganization that occurs when the ground electronic state is excited by absorption of a photon takes place much more rapidly than any movement of the atom nuclei that eventually follow.

In other words, electron shifts, when viewed from the perspective of the nuclear coordinates, occur as if the heavier nuclei were fixed in place. This consequence of the Born-Oppenheimer approximation led James Franck and R. Condon to formulate the Franck-Condon Principle: Electronic transitions occur much faster than nuclei can respond.

Overall bonding in an excited state is usually lower than in the ground state. Thus, the X – X bond length is increased in the excited state. At normal temperatures essentially all molecules will exist in the ground vibrational state (zero level). The Franck-Condon principle requires that excitation occur by a vertical transition, shown by the red line, resulting in the population of higher vibrational levels in the excited state. Several events may then take place.

1. The vibrational energy may be lost as heat, relaxing the excited state to its zero vibrational level.
2. The excited state may return to the ground state by emitting a photon (light blue line). If this happens from the zero vibrational level the frequency or energy of the emitted light will be lower than that of the initially absorbed light. This radiative decay is called fluorescence if it takes place rapidly from the initial excited state. It is termed phosphorescence if it occurs slowly by way of other excited states.
3. If a higher vibrational level of the excited state is populated, either by the initial Franck-Condon transition or by collisional activation, the molecule may cleave into two X• atoms. Note that vibrational level 5 of the excited state is roughly coincident with bond breaking.

Organic Compounds

Virtually all organic compounds have more than two atoms, so the potential energy state diagram of X_2 must be adjusted for the increased number of bonding relationships. One way of doing this is to retain the energy coordinate while dispensing with the dimensional (r) coordinate. Each electronic state will have a group of vibrational (and rotational) states, depicted by light blue lines above each state marker. Transitions between electronic states often occur to higher vibrational levels which then relax to lower levels by collisional loss of heat (translational energy). Excited states may be classified as singlet or triplet based upon their electron spin angular momentum. The electrons in most non-metallic organic compounds are paired (opposite spins) in bonding and non-bonding orbitals, resulting in a net zero spin diamagnetic molecule for the ground state. Such states have a single energy state in an applied magnetic field, and are called singlets. Electronic states in which two electrons with identical spin occupy different orbitals (the Pauli exclusion principle) have a net spin of 1 (2 • 1/2) and are paramagnetic. In a magnetic field such states have three energy levels (+1, 0, –1) and are called triplets.

Molecular oxygen is a rare example of a triplet ground electronic state. The distinction between singlet and triplet states is important because photon induced excitation always leads to a state of the same multiplicity, i.e. singlet to singlet or triplet to triplet. Since most ground states are singlets, this means that the excited states initially formed by absorption of light must also be singlets. Internal conversion of excited states to lower energy states of the same multiplicity takes place rapidly with loss of heat energy (relaxation). Alternatively, an excited state may return to the ground state by emitting a photon (radiative decay). In the study of acetone described above, nearly 80% of the excited singlet states lose energy by internal conversion and about 3% by fluorescence.

Lower Energy Triplet State

Conversion of a singlet state to a lower energy triplet state, or vice versa, is termed intersystem crossing and is slower than internal conversion. Radiative decay from a triplet state is called phosporescence and is generally quite slow. The approximate timescales for these transitions are given in the following table.

Process	Transition	Timescale (sec)
Light Absorption (Excitation)	$S_0 \rightarrow S_n$	ca.10^{-15} (instantaneous)
Internal Conversion	$S_n \rightarrow S_1$	10^{-14} to 10^{-11}
Vibrational Relaxation	$S_n^* \rightarrow S_n$	10^{-12} to 10^{-10}
Intersystem Crossing	$S_1 \rightarrow T_1$	10^{-11} to 10^{-6}
Fluorescence	$S_1 \rightarrow S_0$	10^{-9} to 10^{-6}
Phosphorescence	$T_1 \rightarrow S_0$	10^{-3} to 100
Non-Radiative Decay	$S_1 \rightarrow S_0$	10^{-7} to 10^{-5}
	$T_1 \rightarrow S_0$	10^{-3} to 100

The non-radiative decay noted in the last row may take place by intermolecular energy transfer to a different molecule. This collisional process is termed quenching if the focus is on the initially excited species, or sensitization if the newly created excited state is of interest. Photochemical sensitization commonly occurs by a $T_1 + S_0 \rightarrow S_0 + T_1$ reaction, where the bold red-colored species is the sensitizer. The new triplet excited state may then undergo characteristic reactions of its own.

PHOTOCHEMISTRY REACTION

Photochemistry is concerned with reactions which are' initiated by electronically excited molecules. Such molecules are produced by the absorption of suitable radiation in the visible and near ultraviolet region of the spectrum. Photochemistry is basic to the world we live in. With sun as the central figure, the origin of life itself must have been a photochemical act. In the primitive earth conditions radiation from the sun was the only source of energy. Simple gaseous molecules like methane, ammonia and carbon dioxide must have reacted photochemically to synthesize complex, organic molecules like proteins and nucleic acids. Through the ages, nature has perfected her machinery), for the utilization of solar radiant energy for all photobiological phenomena and providing food for the propagation of life itself. Photobiology, the photochemistry of biological reactions, is a rapidly developing 'subject and helps the understanding of phenomena like photosynthesis, phototaxis, photo-periodism, photodynamic action, vision and mutagenic effects of light. The relevance of photochemistry also lies in its varied applications in science and technology. Synthetic organic photochemistry has provided methods for the manufacture 'of many chemicals which could not be produced by dark reactions. Moreover, greater efficiency and selectivity of these methods have an added advantage. *Some examples of industrially visible photochemical synthesis may mentioned here*:

- Synthesis of vitamin D_2 from ergosterol isolated from certain yeasts.
- Synthesis of cubanes which are antiviral agents.
- Industrial synthesis of caprolactam, the monomer of Nylon 6.
- Manufacture of cleaning solvents, insecticides and halogenated aromatics (used as synthetic intermediates) by photochlorination and production of hydrogen peroxide in industry as an antiseptic and as a fuel because its decomposition releases a great amount of energy.
- Synthesis of antioxidants by photosulphonation photo initiated polymerization and photo polymerization are used in photography, lithoprinting and manufacture of printed circuits for the electronic industry.

The light absorbed by dyes used for colouring the fabric initiates oxidative chain reactions in cellulose fibres. This causes the tendering of cotton. Similar depolymerising action is observed in plastic materials. Researches are going on to find suitable colourless chemicals which when added to dyed materials or plastics will take over the excited energy and divert it to non-destructive pathway. These are known as energy degraders or photostabilizers e.g., O-hydroxy-benzophenones.

MECHANISM OF PHOTOPRODUCTS

Thus decay at a real crossings provides a common mechanism for excited state radiationless transitions and for the generation of photoproducts. Although there are, in principle, at least three different ways of generating a photoproduct, via an adiabatic reaction, via decay at an avoided crossing and via decay at a real crossing, here we will deal exclusively with the latter type of process. Thus, the investigation of the mechanism of a photochemical reaction requires, as a primary step, the investigation of the structure and energetics of the low-lying real crossings for the system under investigation and the study of the ground state reaction paths which originates at this decay funnel with the methodology described in the section on computation methods.

The purpose of this section is to provide some background (by way of examples) to others who may wish to initiate theoretical work on photochemical methods. Thus, within the theoretical framework described in the previous sections, we hope that the case studies which we now discuss will give the reader some insight into the type of problems that may be encountered in some very different photochemical systems. Recent computational results do indicate some general features of surface crossings and of the related photochemical reaction paths. Here, we make an attempt to classify these features from a conceptual and chemical point of view.

These case studies will also serve to indicate that present theoretical methods and computational technology can go a long way towards a complete understanding of a photochemical reaction mechanisms.

Through the analysis of some selected case studies, we hope to establish the following ideas which appear to be general:

- The photochemistry of conjugated hydrocarbons can be rationalised by the common electronic and molecular structure of the surface crossing between a covalent excited state and the ground state;
- The photochemistry of azo-alkanes, and enones is dominated by intersections of n–π* and π–π states with the ground state as well as by the intervention of the triplet manifold;
- The photochemistry of protonated Schiff bases is also based on conical intersections; however, the excited state is ionic and corresponds to an intramolecular charge transfer state, thus the theoretical aspects of the problem are distinct from polyenes;
- The quantum yield in the radiationless decay and competitive photoproduct formation process in cyclohexadiene/cZc-hexatriene (1) system is controlled by competitive ground state relaxation paths which originate from a single conical intersection channel;
- All-trans hepta-2,4,6-trieniminium cation (2), a retinal protonated Schiff base model, may undergo trans cis isomerization at either of the double-bonds in position 2 and 4.

Thus, the photochemistry is dominated by the structure of the competitive excited state reaction paths leading to distinct conical intersection structures.

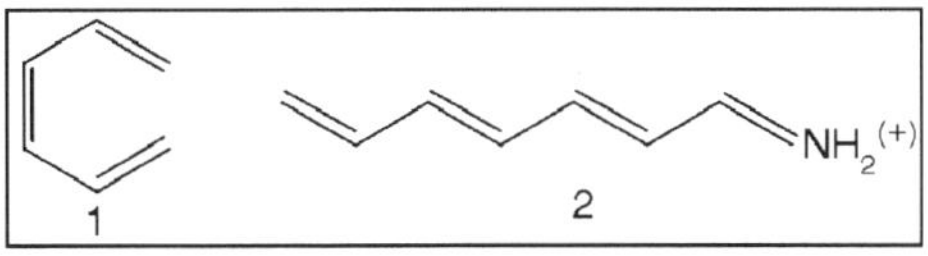

Conical Intersections of Conjugated Hydrocarbons

The application of different spectroscopic techniques to low temperature samples of"isolated" conjugated molecules has begun to provide very detailed information on the excited state dynamics of these organic systems and indicates that there is a small threshold energy to ultrafast radiationless decay. Use of the ab initio methods described in previous subsections suggest that the general mechanism which"triggers" the decay is a displacement of the electronically excited equilibrium structure towards a"critical" configuration where the excited and ground states cross at a conical intersection.

Molecular Geometry at the Point of Decay

The molecular geometry at the point of decay shows, in many examples, a"kink" located at a -$(CH)_3$- segment. In Figure we compare the structure of this -$(CH)_3$- segment for all-trans octatetraene (all-trans-OT), S_1 benzene and S_1 cyclohexadiene intersections. Comparison of these structures reveals common structural and electronic features.

Each structure contains a triangular arrangement of three carbon centres corresponding to a -$(CH)_3$- kink of the carbon skeleton in all-trans OT and benzene and to a triangular arrangement of the -CH_2 and -CH-CH_2 terminal fragments in cyclohexadiene. The electronic structure in each case corresponds to 3 weakly interacting electrons in a triangular arrangement (like H_3) which are loosely coupled to an isolated radical centre (this is delocalised on an allyl fragment in all-trans OT, benzene and cyclohexadiene).

This type of conical intersection appears to be a general feature of linear polyenes and polyene radicals. These intersections are located at the end of the excited state reaction path, i.e., the MEP on the S1 potential energy surface which has the general structure illustrated in Figure (for short polyenes, such as butadiene, it has the general structure illustrated in Figure).

The structure and energetics of the excited state decay path for six (n = 3...,8) all-trans conjugated hydrocarbons, three polyenes (butadiene, hexatriene and octatetraene) and three polyene radicals (allyl, pentadienyl and heptatrienyl), have been documented using the ab initio CAS-SCF method with the DZ+d basis set and an active space including all and * orbitals and electrons.

Conical Intersections of n- Excited States*

In other classes of organic molecules, the electronic structure of the lowest lying intersection changes. We have published detailed results on the olefin-carbonyl Paterno- Buchi system α,β-enones β,γ-enones, azo-compounds (diazomethane and cyclic diazoalkenes) and acylcyclopropenes photorearrangements. Whereas hydrocarbon photochemistry typically involves a low energy π-π*doubly-excited covalent state, the singlet photochemistry of carbonyl and azo-compounds is dominated by n to π* excitations.

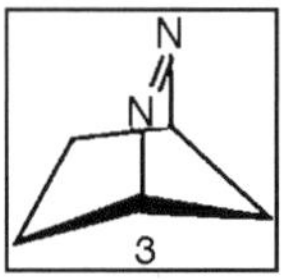

As an example of this class of system, we discuss some results on the photochemistry of diazabicyclo[2.1.1]hept-2-ene (DBH). The photochemistry of this system is remarkably complex because it involves a study of the ground state S0 surface as well as 1(n-π*), 3(n- π*), and 3(π-π *) surfaces and their crossings.

All the topological features suggested in Figure actually occur in practise, and a complete understanding of the photochemistry of this species involves a study of the evolution of singlet and triplet photoexcited DBH along a network of eighteen ground and excited state intermediates, seventeen transition structures and ten"funnels", where internal conversion (IC) or intersystem crossing (ISC) occurs. While the mechanistic photochemist specifies a mechanism in terms of a sequence of molecular structures that occur along various reaction paths, one can use theoretical computations as a complementary and powerful tool to investigate reaction mechanism. One can use theoretical computation to actually find a viable mechanism, determine the nature of the structures involved (intermediates, transition states, surface crossings etc), and discover whether they lie on the excited or ground state branch of the reaction path and whether they are on the triplet manifold (accessible via triplet sensitisation or intersystem crossing) or if they lie on the singlet manifold (via direct irradiation).

Companion Schematic Representation

The companion schematic representation of the diazenyl region of the computed potential surface, the intermediates are labelled in the same way. The accuracy of the methodology used in this study has been tested against other azoalkane spectroscopic data. For instance, the computed 0-0 singlet excitation energies are 84.0 kcal/mol [82.7 including zero point energy (ZPE) correction] for pyrazoline (experimental value 82 kcal/mol) and 73.7 kcal/mol for 2,3- diazabicyclo]oct-2-ene (DBO) (experimental value 76 kcal/mol). Second, the energy barriers for C-N bond cleavage of singlet-excited pyrazoline and DBO are 7.6 (6.4 including ZPE correction) and 11.4 kcal/mol, which compares with experimental values of 6-9 for a pyrazoline derivative and 8.6-10.2 kcal/mol for DBO derivatives.

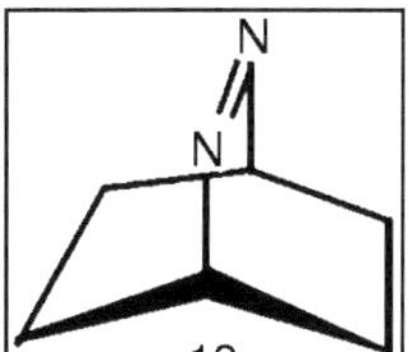

12

Three cyclic excited state species are reached following evolution from the Franck- Condon region: two metastable singlet (n-π*) and triplet (n-π*) species and a stable excited state 3(n-π*)-3(π-π*) intermediate. Structure can decay directly to S_0 (via the conical intersection labelled) or undergo ISC to generate. Structure can directly decay to the T_1 diazenyl biradical or undergo IC to generate the mixed 3(n-π*)- 3(π-π*) intermediate. Finally, the much more stable cannot be converted to the other excited state intermediates but can only react via either α C-N and β C-C cleavage. It is clear that the photochemistry of azo compounds is complex because of the delicate intertwining of the 3(n-π*), 3(π-π*), and 1(n-π*) states. The surface crossing region of the diazenyl biradicals is quite novel in that a four fold crossing occurs, i.e., the 1(n-π*)/S_0 crossing occurs at the same geometry as the 3(n-π*)/ 3(π-π*) crossing.

The diazenyl biradical exists in C-N-N bent forms or in a C-N-N linear form. The bent forms correspond to real biradical intermediates with three possible conformations (exo, endo, or exo-endo) and are generated by decay at the conical intersection corresponding to the linear form. Indeed the linear form corresponding to structure corresponds to an highly unstable configuration where the S_0, 3(π-π*), 3(n-π*) and 1(n-π*) states are degenerate and forms a multiple funnel. This is entered via alpha-cleavage by overcoming the S_1 or T_2 1/3(n-π*) transition structures shown in Figure.

Molecular and Electronic Structure of DBH

The molecular and electronic structure of DBH at the conical intersection. The origin of the four-fold crossing can easily be rationalised from the character of the two unpaired electrons in these structures. These two electrons can be considered almost uncoupled from each other, and since the coupling between the two radical centres is so small, the triplet and singlet states must be degenerate. Furthermore, one nitrogen atom is left with a singly occupied p-orbital and a lone-pair located along orthogonal axes in space.

The 1(n- π*) and 3(n-π*) states can be derived from the S_0 and 3(π-π*) states by swapping the relative occupancies of the singly occupied p-orbital and lone-pair. However this difference will not affect the energy and therefore all four states [1(n-π*), S_0, 3(n-π*) and 3(π-π*)] will be degenerate. This behaviour is consistent with the directions defined by the gradient difference and derivative coupling vectors at the multiple funnel (corresponding to"superimposed" S_0/S_1 and T_1/T_2 conical intersections) which indicate the type of molecular distortion required to lift the degeneracy. These vectors correspond to two"orthogonal" bendings of the N-N-C angle, which would split the degeneracy by increasing the coupling between the two radical centres. The decay channel for the triplet-sensitised photolysis also has an unusual surface topology which is indicated in Figure. In the Franck-Condon region, T_2 has (π-π*) character and lies ~34 kcal mol-1 above T_1 which has (n-π*) character.

As the structure of the molecule gets distorted from the Franck-Condon geometry, the 3(π-π*) and 3(n-π*) states become strongly mixed so that it becomes difficult to distinguish between the two triplet states, especially at structures where the C-N=N-C bridge is twisted. In other words, the electronic structures of the T_1 and T_2 states become a combination of (π-π*) and (n-π*) configurations. Near the triplet (n-π*) energy minimum there is a conical intersection between the (π-π*) and (n-π*) triplet states. The electronic structure of the T_1 and T_2 states in the vicinity of the intersection can be understood on the basis of the derivative coupling and gradient difference vectors. The derivative coupling vector involves an N-N-C bending, and the gradient difference vector involves twisting of the C-N=N-C bridge.

The N-N-C bending distortion causes the"pure" (n-π*) and (π-π*) states to cross. Thus on one side of the upper (T_2) cone is the (n-π*) state and on the other side is the (π-π*) structure (this structure corresponds to a steep T_2/T_1 intersection point). No stable (π-π*) minimum has been located on T_2. The orthogonal C-N=N-C distortion has the effect of producing"mixed" (n-π*) and (π-π*) states, i.e., states which can be represented by a mixture of (n-π*) and (π-π*) character. Thus decaying from the tip of the conical intersection in the direction of the gradient difference vector generates the mixed (n-π*)-(π-π*) minimum on the T_1 state (in this structure, the n and orbitals are strongly mixed so that the location of the two radical centres is not unambiguous).

These effects are typical of the presence of a conical intersection: as one moves in a circle centred on the conical intersection point, the wavefunction changes in a continuous fashion from (n-π*) to (n-π*)+(π-π*) to (π-π*) to (π-π*)-(n-π*) to -(n-π*). From the preceding discussion, a few of the complexities of the photochemistry that is typical of carbonyl and azo-compounds are apparent. Results on the olefincarbonyl Paterno-Buchi system α,β, -enones β,γ-enones, azo-compounds (diazomethane and cyclic diazoalkenes) and acylcyclopropenes photorearrangements show similar features. Here one encounters four-fold intersections as well as conical intersections and singlet triplet crossings. Thus the potential surfaces are more complex than in hydrocarbon photochemistry.

PHOTOPHYSICAL PHENOMENA OF FLUORESCENCE AND PHOSPHORESCENCE

The photophysical phenomena of fluorescence and phosphorescence have found varied applications in fluorescent tube lights. X-rays and TV screen as luminescent dials for watches, as optical brighteners in white dress materials, as paints in advertisement hoarding which show enhanced brilliancy by utilizing fluorescence, for detection of cracks in metal work, for tracing the course of river through caves, as micro analytical reagents and so on. Certain chemicals change their colour, that is, their absorption characteristics, when exposed to suitable radiations and reverse when the irradiation source is removed. These are known as photo chromic materials. A well known example IS the spiropyrans, used in photo chromic sunglasses. Another revolutionary application of electronically excited molecular system IS In Laser technology. Lasers are intense sources of monochromatic and coherent radiations. Lasers have provided powerful tools for the study of diverse phenomena ranging from moonquakes to Pico second processes of non-radiative decay of excitational energy in molecules. The intense and powerful beam of coherent radiations capable of concentration to a tiny point used for eye· surgery, cutting metals, boring diamonds, as military range finders and detectors and many such applications. The advent of tunable dye; lasers has increased' the possibility of their application in science and technology.

A further impetus to the study of photochemical reactions has been provided by the energy crisis. This has initiated researchers into the conversion and storage of solar energy, processes which plants carry out so efficiently. Solar energy provides a readily available source of energy, especially in those countries which lie between the tropics of cancers and capricorn. In these areas, the daily incident energy per square kilometre is equivalent to 3000 tonnes of coal. If suitable photochemical reactions are discovered and devices for proper utilization of this abundant source of energy perfected, half of the world's energy problem might be solved. Solar batteries working as the principle of photogalvanic effects are one such device.

The fundamental study of excited states of molecules is by exciting itself. The short lived energy states with nano and pico-seconds reactions kinetics have led to the proper understanding of chemical reactions, modes of energy transfer and the intricate structure of matter.

Flash photolysis and pulsed laser photolysis are newer tools for the study of higher energy states. Now it is possible to excite individual vibronic levels or isotopically substituted compounds by using appropriate beams from tunable dye lasers. Photochemical processes are also the basis of undesirable effects, such as degradation of polymers and the formation of smog, and of leisure activities, such as photography. Without photochemical processes the world is simply a warm, sterile, rock. Photocatalysis has opened many avenues of further researches as far as its applications part is concerned. The photocatalysis has emerged as a probable solution to some of the problems like energy crsis, environmental pollution wastewater treatment etc.

Semiconductor particulate system can provide a low cost and convenient way of treating several undesirable chemicals. The principle of such a treatment lies in initiating an oxidation or reduction process at the semiconductor surface. For example, H_2S, which is a by-product in the coal and petroleum industry, car) be oxidized to sulphur at CdS semiconductor surface.

A quantum yield of 50% has been reported for the reaction between sulphids anion and photogenerated valence band holes In CdS suspensions. Similarly, photocatalytic transformation of CN to SCN has been carried out in presence of rhodium-loaded CdS particulate system. Photocatalysis can be used to eliminate pollutants from the environment. Chloral hydrate is a toxic compound, which, is used for the synthesis of insecticides. Tanaka *el al.* reported the photocatalytic degradation of chloral hydrate in aqueous semiconductor suspension via the formation of OH radicals and utilizating these OH radicals for oxidizing chloral hydrate:

$$CCl_3CH(OH)_2 + 4\ OH \rightarrow 2CO_2\ H+ + 2\ H20$$

Photocatalysis has been used for the degradation of pesticides like alrazine5 and also as a bactericide for speclrocci. Nehara *et* al. made usc of irradiated titania semiconductor photocatalyst slurries in aqueous media for pnotoxidative degradation of the pesticides permet~riri.

- It has been shown by Domenech *et al.s* that, in prese!1ce of 2nO, Hg(ll) can be photocatalytically eliminated from aqueous solutions. Muneer et *al.9* inves'Cigated the photocatalytic degradation of an industrial pollutant like methyl vinyl ketone in aqueous solt.:tion using suspended TiO_2 and TiO_2immobilized on glass surface. The lw:) oxidizing species OH and O_2 are the primary species utilized in photocat::llytic degradati"on process. These oxidation reactions resulted in the depletion of O_2 and methyl vinyl ketone and in the formation of CO_2 and other semioxidized products in solution.

Herrmann *et al. 10* reported heterogeneous photocatalysis as an emerging technology for waste water treatment. It may also prove useful in recovery of some transition metals from industrial effluel'lts. observed photocatalytic dcgraclaLion of waste water pollutants involving TiO_2 mediated oxidation of some polynuclear aromatic hydrocarbons.

Recently Osawa and SunakarP_2 reported photo-degradation of polyurethane and polyvinyl chloride. Ahmed and Attia13 used certain aerogel materials for photocatalytic detoxification of cyanide in waste waters. Recently, Osunda and Osunal8 *et al. 14* have investigated photoreduction of manganese oxides in sea water. The photocatalysis can also prove to be useful in recovery of one costly metals from aqueous sulutlons, even if present in traces. Photocatalytic deposition of silver on TiO_2 powder was reported by Harrmann *et al.*

It has been advocated and predicted that hydrogen will be fuel of future and any newer method for efficient photocatalytic production of 1/2 will be a well-come addition in solving the existing problem of energy crisis. The field of heterogeneous photocatalysis has already gmwn out of its, infancy and has now emerged as a major field of research.

The recent developments of ultrafine semiconductor part:cles have added some newer dimensions. 1S·20 The ability of such semiconductors to carry. out redox processes with great efficiency and selectivity than in the homogenous solutions has made them more impol'tant in the conversion and storage of solar energy, in the mineralization of chemical pollutants and also for the treatment of some dreadful diseases. The dye molecules as light collectors in a solar cells (dye sensitiz;cd solar cells or D.S.S. cell) has been successfully used by great field.

Photochemical Reaction of Alkene Isomerization

A photochemical reaction occurs when internal conversion and relaxation of an excited state leads to a ground state isomer of the initial substrate molecule, or when an excited state undergoes an intermolecular addition to another reactant molecule in the ground state.

The cis-trans photochemical isomerization of stilbene is a reaction of the first kind. Both cis and trans-stilbene undergo $\pi \rightarrow \pi^*$ electron excitation by absorption of uv light.

Whereas isolated double bonds require 180 nm light for such excitation, conjugation with the phenyl substituents lowers the transition energy to about

300 nm, a more easily achieved source. The molar absorptivity of the cis-isomer is less than that of the trans-isomer because steric crowding of the ortho sites causes the phenyl groups to twist slightly out of coplanarity.

The stability of the stereoisomers of stilbene is due to a 62 kcal/mole barrier to rotation about the double bond produced by the π-bond.

This bonding is absent in the $\pi \rightarrow \pi^*$ excited state. Both the initial S_1 states formed from the cis and trans ground states are slightly twisted (the cis by 25° & the trans by 13°) with the C = C double bond being lengthened by about 4.5%. These local S_1 states quickly relax to a common lower energy twisted configuration ($\theta \cong 90°$). Non-radiative internal conversion of this S_1 twisted state leads to the transition state region of S_0, which decays equally to the ground states of the cis and trans isomers.

This simple configurational isomerization about a single double bond is referred to as a One-Bond-Flip (OBF) event. A small proportion (6%) of the trans-S_1 state fluoresces back to the trans-isomer, but there is less than 0.1% fluorescence from the cis-S_1 state. Triplet states may also be formed, but there is no observable phosphorescence in solution, and non-radiative decay from such states results in similar cis-trans isomerization. The quantum yield of trans to cis isomerization decreases in viscous solvents, accompanied by an increase in fluorescent decay. Freezing the solutions to a rigid glass halts the isomerization and results in maximum fluorescence efficiency.

Stilbene

cis

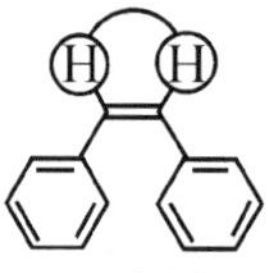

$\lambda_{max} = 280$ nm

Dihedral Angle θ

trans

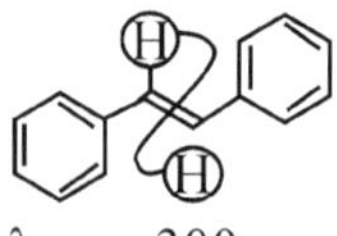

$\lambda_{max} = 300$ nm

Inspection of the cis-S_1 local minimum near $\theta = 0°$ shows that only 70% of the molecules in this state relax to the lower energy twisted S_1 state. The remaining 30% undergo an electrocyclic rearrangement to an isomeric 4a, 4b-dihydrophenanthrene (DHP) S_1 state. Molecules occupying this new excited state then relax to either DHP or cis-stilbene ground states. Over time, DHP accumulates and may be coverted to phenanthrene by mild oxidation with air or iodine. Substituted phenanthrenes thus become available from trans-stilbene precursors prepared by Wittig or Grignard procedures.

Another minor product from the photolysis of stilbene has been identified as 1,2,3,4-tetraphenylcyclobutane (distilbene). Unlike the previously described unimolecular isomerizations, this compound is formed by a bimolecular reaction between an electronically excited stilbene and a ground state stilbene molecule.

The dimer accumulates slowly, irradiation of a 0.07 M solution of trans-stilbene in benzene producing 27% (as two stereoisomers) after two months of exposure. As expected, higher stilbene concentrations increase the rate of dimer formation. Thus, a 0.56 M solution of trans-stilbene in ethyl acetate yielded 11% dimer in four hours of irradiation. Mercury lamps were used as the uv light source in all these cases.

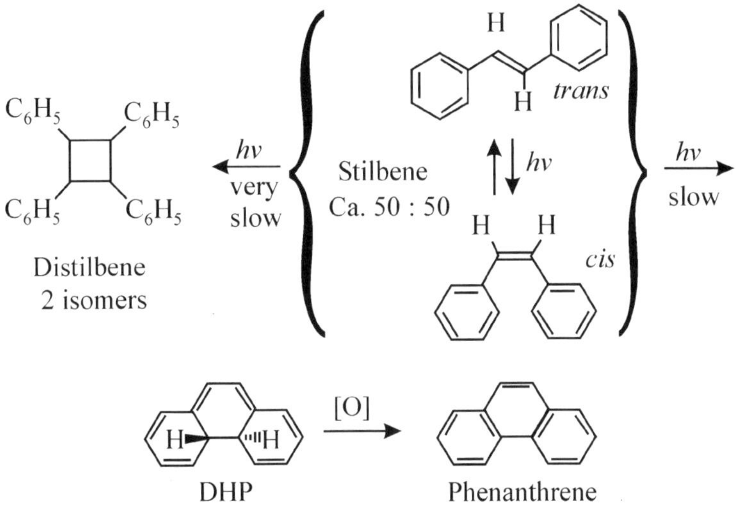

Electron donating substituents on the benzene rings facilitate the dimerization, as does restricting the ability of the double bond to isomerize or achieve orthogonally twisted excited states. The stilbene reactions described above have been attributed to singlet excited states. Triplet excited states exist, but their formation by intersystem crossing is inefficient. In order to study the behaviour of triplet excited states it is often necessary to generate them by energy transfer from a higher triplet excited state of a suitable sensitizer molecule. Spin conservation requires that spin exchange take place during the collisional energy transfer. Thus, a sensitizer triplet (Z_t), generated from sensitizer molecule Z_s, reacts with a ground state stilbene molecule (M_s) in the following manner:

$$Z_t(\uparrow\uparrow) + M_s(\uparrow\downarrow) \rightarrow Z_s(\uparrow\downarrow) + M_t(\uparrow\uparrow).$$

The following diagram illustrates important features of this sensitization reaction. The ideal sensitizer (Z) absorbs light preferentially with respect to the substrate (M), and undergoes efficient intersystem crossing to a triplet excited state (T_1). This energetic state then serves to activate a substrate molecule to a lower energy triplet state by collisional exothermic energy and spin exchange, returning the sensitizer to its ground state.

A few of their findings are presented in the table on the right, the same photostationary cis:trans ratio being observed from either isomer as the starting point. The unexpected change in steady state isomer distribution with the triplet energy of the sensitizer could not be rationalized as a single classical energy transfer. All sensitizers having a greater triplet energy than 60 kcal/mole act by rapid collisional vertical energy transfer to the first encountered stilbene isomer.

Table. Photosensitized Stilbene Isomerization

Sensitizer	Triplet Energy	Cis:Trans Ratio
Benzophenone	69 kcal/mole	60:40
Benzil	53 kcal/mole	85:15
Pyrene	47 kcal/mole	90:10
Eosin	43 kcal/mole	0:100

The initial cis and trans triplets undergo fast, and in the case of trans reversible, conversion to a lower energy twisted triplet, which then decays to cis and trans-stilbene at rates that favor cis by a factor of 1.5. As the triplet energy of the sensitizer drops below 57 kcal/mole, two changes occur.

First, the efficiency of energy transfer to cis-stilbene diminishes and the trans isomer is selectively activated, resulting in a greater [cis]/[trans] photostationary state. These competing excitations and subsequent decay to cis and trans ground states lead to remarkable variations in isomer ratios.

Finally, the very low energy triplet state of eosin is unable to effect any electronic excitation of stilbene, and simply catalyzes thermal equilibration, which strongly favors the trans-isomer (trans is 6 kcal/mole more stable than cis) These sensitized isomerizations do not give any significant amount of the electrocyclic rearrangement or dimerization reactions observed from singlet excited states.

Carbonyl Compounds of Ketones

Conjugated ketones are often good sensitizers, thanks to the efficiency of intersystem crossing from the $n \rightarrow \pi^*$ singlet to the triplet. To consider the bonding structure of the carbonyl group itself. In the case of the simple compound formaldehyde, the Lewis formula consists of two C – H sigma bonds, a C – O sigma bond, a C = O pi bond and two non-bonding electron pairs. Two Lewis structures, differing in the hybridization of oxygen, may be drawn, The structure on the left is a common representation in which an sp^2 oxygen replaces one of the CH_2 groups of an ethylene molecule.

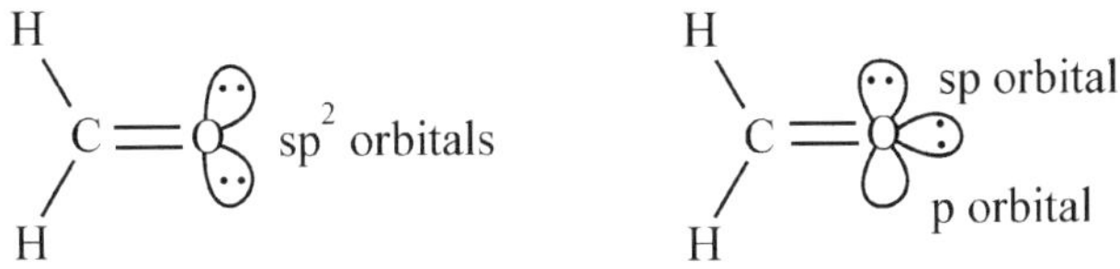

sp^2 Oxygen sp Oxygen

Lewis Structures for Formaldehyde

However, based on the principle that stable molecules will adopt the strongest bonding possible, the right hand structure becomes an attractive alternative. An sp^2 – sp sigma bond should be stronger and shorter than a sp^2 – sp^2 sigma bond, and the shorter bond distance will enhance the pi-bonding. Double bonds are of course shorter and stronger than equivalent single bonds. The average values given in the following table indicate that C = C is 13% shorter and 76% stronger than a C – C bond, whereas C = O is 15% shorter and over 100% stronger than a C – O bond, possibly reflecting the sp hybridization of the oxygen. An important difference between these models is found in the nature of the non-bonding electron pairs on oxygen. In the sp^2-oxygen model these occupy very similar (degenerate) orbitals, but in the sp-oxygen model one pair is in a relatively low energy sp-orbital and the other in a higher energy p-orbital. Molecular orbital calculations clearly show that the latter model is a better representation than the former.

Bond Length, Å	C–C, 1.54	C=C, 1.34	C–O, 1.44	C=O, 1.22
Bond Energy, kcal/mole	C–C, 84	C=C, 146	C–O, 86	C=O, 177

Electronic Excitations of a Carbonyl Group

CLASSIFICATION AND DESIGNATIONS OF DYES

The most authoritative compilation covering the constitutions, manufactures. and other colouring data is the publication of Colour Index, which is edited jointly by the Society of Dyers and Colourists.

In the colour index a dual,classification system is employed to group dyes according to area of usage and chemi~al constitution.

Because of ease of synthesis of azo, disazo, and polyazodyes, and their wide range of applications, azo dyes comprise the largest chemical class in numbers, monetary value, and tonnage produced.

- *Thiazine Dyes*: The presence of a thiazine rmg In Cl sulfur Blue 9 was conclusively proved. The thiazine ring is the fundamental chromophore that acsounts for the high colour value of both the sulfur dye and methylene blue. The dye Cl Basic blue 9 was first reporten in 1876. This is a basic dye powders, and liquids, coricentration varies from 6 to 100%. The concentrations, form, and purity of a dye is determined largley by the use for which it is int~nded.

Application of Dyes Compounds

Aromatic azo compounds which are also known as direct dyes, despite of their poor wet fastness properties, still represent an important class of dye for use on cellulose fibre because of their ease of applications and low cost. Adsorption ahd adsorption processes are important fields of study in chemistry.

They form a basis fur understanding phenomena such a heterogeneous catalysis, Chromatographic analysis, dycing of textiles, and clarification of various efnuents. The dyeing of cotton with direct dyes depends on the chemical nature of dye and auxiliaries. The substanlivity of dyes depends on the Istructure of dye molecule and the residual valency forces. Methylene blue Methylene blue has been widely used as a titration indicator, and for the, evaluation of photophysical phenomena of the spectral properties of dye are also discussed by Koizumi *et al.* Thiazine is not important in dyes as such, but it is a part of some reactive dyes.

Synthesis: The method of synthesis for methylene blue described in reference is still the stepwise method of choice for thiazine dyes. N,NDimethyl-p-phenylene diamine, CaH $12N_2$, reacts with sodium thiosulphate to form the thiosulfonic acid which condenses with N,N-dimethylaniline C8HIIN, in the presence of sodium dichromate.

Elimination of Organic Substances

The dyeing of cotton with dyes also depends on the diffusion of dye in the pores of celluiose. Activated carbon finds particular applications in the clarifications of effluents, including the removal of colouring matter from various types of solution and elimination of organic substances from portable wastc waler. Adsorption of methylene blue, a cationic organic dye stuff commonly used for tracer studies in water research, on activated carbon.

Ecological and toxicological association of dye stuff manufacturing industry have been identified and assessed the risk to health caused by colourants and their intermediate. More than 4'000 dyes have been analysed and showed acute toxicity values land the most toxic ones are cationic classes,

In 1970's the major dye stuff manufacturers agreed to phase out the manufacture of benzidine derivative dyes and pigments.

Ascorbic acid was determined which was used in the preparation of vitamins by titration with 3Fe (CN)6SO_4, HPO_4, or HCl using ferrain triphenylmethane or thiazine dyes (methylene blue) as indicators.

FUNDAMENTAL IMPORTANCE OF SURFACE PHOTOCHEMISTRY

It is of fundamental importance in physics and chemistry to analyse and understand the dynamics of molecules adsorbed to a surface. This interaction between adsorbate and substrate is at the heart of the catalytic properties of surfaces for mediating and accelerating particular chemical reactions. It is crucial to understand the dynamics of excited states of surface adsorbed molecules. From the analysis of this dynamics we can infer important information about the properties of the adsorbate-substrate chemical bond.

It is well known that the techniques of valence- and core-level spectroscopy (UPS/XPS) can be employed to acquire detailed information about the electronic structure and thus the chemical state of surface-adsorbate complexes. In an experiment performed by Bauer et al molecular oxygenwas adsorbed on a Pt(111) surface. The amplified Ti:sapphire laser systemwas operated at a 1 kHz repetition rate. A55 fs duration laser pulse (800 nm centralwavelength) of on-target fluence of 10μJ cm^{-2} was used to excite the adsorbed oxygen.

The probe pulse was generated through capillary phasematched high-harmonic generation at a duration of less than 25 fs. Because of the extended phase-matched conversion length for the capillary-generated harmonics, the spectrum consists of only 3-5 harmonics (23rd-31st) at photon energies from 34.5 to 46.5 eV. Filtering using a 200 nmthickness Al-film (for removing the fundamental light) and a multilayer mirror for beam steering and focusing resulted in a further decrease ofEUV-bandwidth. Half of the energy of the EUV pulse arriving at the target was contained in the 29th harmonic (43.5 eV) with low contributions of the neighbouring orders.

A time-of-flight electron spectrometre was used to measure the photoelectron energies. The platinum surface was kept at a temperature of –195 °C. In this case, it is known from the literature that chemisorbing molecular oxygen prefers two different configurations on the surface, peroxo $\left(O_2^{2-}\right)$or superoxo $\left(O_2^{-}\right)$The likelihood for an adsorbed molecule to be found in either of these configurations depends on the coverage, with the superoxo state being dominant at high coverage and the peroxo state at low coverage. In the experiment, a distinct peak at 6 eV below the Fermi level appeared for time delays between 0 and 5 ps. A rapid buildup of this peak on a timescale of a few hundred femtoseconds could be observed. According to earlier UPS studies a peak at 6 eV indicates the presence of either atomic oxygen or peroxo configuration molecular oxygen adsorbed to the Pt surface while it is absent for the superoxo state. In the study of Bauer et al, this peak is only transiently visible, disappearing for pump-probe time delays longer than 5 ps. So it was possible to monitor the structural change of an adsorbed molecular species after laser excitation directly in the time domain.

By monitoring the photoelectron distribution at the Fermi level it was shown that the change in molecular bonding structure is preceded by the thermalization of an initially created hot-electron distribution. It is the time scale of the energy transfer to the lattice that matches the dynamics of the structural rearrangement of the oxygen molecules on the surface.

Solid State Materials

Many materials in the solid phase exhibit an important property: the atoms are arranged in a regular manner. The unit cell is the smallest part of the solid consisting of one or more atoms which is repeated in three dimensions according to the lattice structure of the crystal. This lattice structure gives rise to the characteristic diffraction pattern (narrow reflection peaks) that arises when x-rays are scattered off a crystal. This diffraction pattern not only reveals the lattice structure but also contains information about the unit cell. One of the main benefits of x-rays is their capability of resolving the structure of solid material.

For that reason it is not astonishing that many experiments using ultrafast x-rays focused on the study of time-resolved structural dynamics in solids. Beyond the fact that x-rays are well suited to study the solid phase, this particular state of matter has intrinsically interesting physical and chemical properties. Since many atoms are packed into a small space, interactions between particles govern the electronic and structural behaviour of solids. Processes can be explained by employing statistical methods, since the typical number of equal particles in a crystal is very large. These statistical processes give rise to collective phenomena such as ferromagnetism and superconductivity, where electron correlations play a dominant role.

In general, the solid state provides for a large variety of structural and electronic phase transitions. X-rays, due to their short wavelength and short optical cycle, are ideally suited to resolve small-scale spatial structures and to eventually resolve correlated electron dynamics on the natural time-scale of electronic motion.

Extended reviews on the field of time-resolved spectroscopy in solids can also be found in the literature. The experiments that illuminate solid-state dynamics with atomic spatial and temporal resolution. The same methods will be used to study an ultrafast structural phase-transition. Ultra fast x-rays can be used to learn about the interaction between the electronic and the lattice structure of solids.

PHOTOPRODUCT MOLECULAR STRUCTURE

Features such as excited state intermediates and funnels are conveniently optimised, using gradient optimisation methods, as critical points on the potential energy surface associated with the photochemically relevant excited state (usually the first singlet or triplet excited state). The computation of the excited state potential energy surface per se can be carried out using standard quantum chemical methods. However, in excited state chemistry, it is clear that the knowledge of the molecular structure of the funnel appears to be of vital importance for the rationalisation and prediction of the observed photoproduct distribution. We expect the photoproduct molecular structure to be related to the molecular structure of the decay channel more or less in the same way in which the structure of a thermal product is related to that of the corresponding transition state.

Similarly, the detailed knowledge of the energetic stability of the decay channel relative, for instance, to the excited state equilibrium structure of the reactant is expected to be related to the excited state lifetime. In other words, excited state energy barriers may control the time taken by the system to reach the decay channel. Thus, the new feature that occurs in the quantum chemistry of photochemical reactions is the characterisation of the conical intersection and its relation to other features on the ground and excited state potential energy surface.

Computational Approach to Photochemistry

The remainder of this tutorial is divided into three parts. The first two parts are theoretical while the third illustrates the application of these theoretical concepts via some case studies drawn mainly from our own work. Our objective is to outline a computational approach to photochemistry.

We aim for a complete description of what happens along the reaction co-ordinate from absorption to photoproduct formation. We shall show how this can be achieved by mapping of the photochemical reaction path computed by following the MEP from the excited state intermediate (or from the Franck-Condon structure) to the ground state photoproduct through a conical intersection.

This method (pathway approach), discussed previously, pays attention to local details and properties like slopes, saddle points, barriers and funnels (such as conical intersections) and has an intimate connection to the approach using the motion of wavepackets or semiclassical trajectories on potential surfaces to describe ultrafast photochemical processes.

This description is becoming increasingly important because of recent advances in femtosecond spectroscopy and ultrafast laser techniques. The first theoretical subsection is conceptually oriented.

We shall discuss the special"features" occurring when more than one energy surface is involved in the chemical reaction (e.g., avoided and real crossings) as well as the general structure of the"photochemical reaction path" that connects the excited state reactant and the photoproducts through the funnel. The second theoretical subsection is more practically oriented. Here we shall illustrate the computational tools and strategies which are being used to compute a photochemical reaction path.

This discussion will include the computation of the excited state branch of the reaction path, how to study the branching at a conical intersection and computation of the"competing" ground state relaxation paths and a brief discussion of semi-classical trajectories.

We will focus on the special techniques that are required for the study of excited state processes.

In principle these can be implemented in a variety of computational algorithms as long as they can produce analytical gradients and hessians and give a balanced description of the energetics. It is not our purpose to discuss the details of particular algorithms that have been implemented. Rather we will focus on the conceptual background that is necessary to use such methods effectively. Thus we will limit ourselves mainly to some general remarks about current quantum chemical methods and algorithms that are suitable for computational organic photochemistry.

Finally, in the last subsection, we illustrate a few general results, via case studies, which have been obtained in the field of mechanistic organic photochemistry and compare them with modern (time resolved) and traditional experimental data.

We shall concentrate on the following points:

- The funnel structure;
- The existence of chemically or stereochemically distinct competing paths, i.e., funnels, on the excited state energy surface;
- The reaction path branching, i.e., the competing ground state relaxation paths, at a specific funnel.

Our objective is to illustrate how the observed photoproduct stereochemistry and distribution in a photochemical organic reaction must depend on radiationless decay via a conical intersection (i.e., a real surface crossing).

POTENTIAL ENERGY SURFACE OF MOLECULAR SYSTEM

The way the energy of a molecular system varies with small changes in its structure is specified by its potential energy surface (PES). A potential energy surface is a mathematical relationship linking molecular structure and the resultant energy. The concepts of energy surfaces for molecular motion, equilibrium geometries, transition structures and reaction paths depend on the Born-Oppenheimer approximation to treat the motion of the nuclei separately from the motion of the electrons. Minima on the potential energy surface for the nuclei can then be identified with the classical picture of equilibrium structures of molecules (i.e., reactant, product and intermediates); saddle points can be related to transition states and reaction rates. Minima, maxima and saddle points can be characterised by their first (i.e., the gradient) and second (i.e., the Hessian) derivatives of the energy.

If the Born-Oppenheimer approximation is not valid, for example in the vicinity of surface crossings, non-adiabatic coupling effects (that couple nuclear and electronic motion) need to be taken in account to correctly describe the motion of the molecular system. This is done, for instance, when one needs to describe a jump between two different PES. In this case, one uses semi-classical theories and the surface-hopping method which we discuss subsequently. We now discuss in some detail how the region where non-adiabatic effects become important can be characterised topologically.

"Non-Crossing Rule" and Conical Intersections

In photochemistry one must deal with a new type of potential surface feature (surface crossings and conical intersections), and we now introduce this subject. In diatomic molecules the PES of two states (e.g., the ground state and the first excited state) will only intersect if the states have a different (spatial or spin) symmetry. However, this statement is not true in polyatomic systems. Rather the correct statement is: two PES of a polyatomic molecule can in principle intersect even if they belong to states of the same symmetry and spin multiplicity. The preceding sentence leaves open the question of whether such intersections actually occur in polyatomic systems. We now give a quantitative analysis of this situation.

If we suppose we have all but two of the solutions for the electronic part of the Schrödinger equation, and $\phi_1$andϕ_2 are any two functions which, together with the known solutions, constitute a complete orthonormal set (the two missing solutions correspond to the two states whose energies are E1 and E_2 respectively, and whose crossings we are interested in), then it must be possible to express each of the two remaining electronic eigenfunctions (which describes the states we want to examine) in the form $\Psi' = c_1\phi_1 + c_2\phi_2$ The resulting secular equation is then,

$$\begin{bmatrix} H_{11} - E & H_{12} & Tc_1 \\ H_{21} & H_{22} - E & \perp c_2 \end{bmatrix} = 0$$

and we can write down the expressions for the energies E_1 and E_2 of the two states as

$$E_1 = \frac{1}{2}\left[(H_{11} + H_{22}) - \sqrt{(H_{11} - H_{22})^2 + 4H_{12}^2}\right]$$

$$E_2 = \frac{1}{2}\left[(H_{11} + H_{22}) - \sqrt{(H_{11} - H_{22})^2 + 4H_{12}^2}\right]$$

where the matrix elements are defined as

$$H_{11} = \langle \phi_1 | H | \phi_1 \rangle$$

$$H_{22} = \langle \phi_2 | H | \phi_2 \rangle$$

$$H_{12} = \langle \phi_1 | H | \phi_1 \rangle = H_{21}$$

Now, in order to have degenerate solutions (i.e., an unavoided crossing) the discriminant must vanish, and it is necessary to satisfy two independent conditions,

$$H_{11} = H_{22}$$

$$H_{12}\,(= H_{21}) = 0$$

This requires the existence of at least two independently variable nuclear coordinates. In a diatomic molecule there is only one variable co-ordinate - the interatomic distance - so the non-crossing rule can be stated as: For states of different (spatial or spin) symmetry, H_{12} is always zero and the two surfaces cross when H_{11} H_{22}.

This is possible for a suitable value of the single variable co-ordinate. Otherwise, if the two states have the same symmetry, they will not intersect. However in a system of three or more atoms (N is the number of atoms) there are enough degrees of freedom for the rule to break down: the two conditions can be simultaneously satisfied by choosing suitable values for two independent variables, while the other n-2 degrees of freedom (n = 3N – 6) are free to be varied without leaving the crossing region.

If we denote these two independent co-ordinates by x1 and x2, and take the origin at the point where H_{11} H_{22} W and H_{12} (H_{21}) 0, in the hypothesis of the first order (i.e., linear) approximation, the secular equations may be cast in the form,

$$\begin{bmatrix} \bar{H}_{11}-E & \bar{H}_{12} \\ \bar{H}_{21} & \bar{H}_{22}-E \end{bmatrix}\begin{bmatrix} c_1 \\ c_2 \end{bmatrix} = \begin{bmatrix} W+h_1x_1-E & lx_2 \\ lx_2 & W+h_2x_1-E \end{bmatrix}\begin{bmatrix} c_1 \\ c_2 \end{bmatrix} = 0$$

$$\left(\text{i.e.,} \bar{H}_{11} = W + hx_1, \text{etc}\right)$$

or,

$$\begin{bmatrix} W+E(m+k)x_1-E & lx_2 \\ lx_2 & W+(m-k)x_1-E \end{bmatrix}\begin{bmatrix} c_1 \\ c_2 \end{bmatrix} = 0$$

where,

$$m = \frac{1}{2}(h_1+h_2), k = \frac{1}{2}(h_1-h_2).$$

The eigenvalues are,

$$E = W + mx_1 \pm \sqrt{k^2x_1^2 + l^2x_2^2}$$

Equation is the equation of an elliptic double cone (i.e., with different axes) with vertex at the origin (it will be a circular cone only for the case k = l). For this reason, such crossing points are called conical intersections. Indeed, if we plot the energies of the two intersecting states against the two internal co-ordinates x_1 and x_2 [whose values at the origin satisfy the two conditions H_{11} H_{22} and H_{12} (H_{21}) 0], we obtain a typical double cone shape.

Now let us inquire into the physical meaning of the two conditions H_{11} H_{22} and H_{12} (H_{21}) 0.

If we consider the basis $(\phi_1 \text{ and } \phi_2)$ of the secular equation as the diabatic components of the adiabatic electronic eigenfunction (a diabatic function describes the energy of a particular spin-coupling or atomic orbital occupancies, while the adiabatic function represents the surface of the real state), the crossing condition (real or avoided) is fulfilled when the two diabatic components ϕ_1 and ϕ_2 cross each other, and this happens when H_{11} H_{22}, i.e., the energy of the two diabatic potentials (H_{11} is the energy for the diabatic function ϕ_1, and H_{22} is the energy for the diabatic function) is the same.

At the crossing of the diabatic functions (H_{11} H_{22}), the expressions for the energies of the two real states become

$$E_1 = H_{11} - H_{12}$$
$$E_2 = H_{11} + H_{12}$$

and the energy gap between the two real states is $E_2 = H_1 - 2H_{12}$ Thus, if the off-diagonal (resonance) term H_{12} is not zero, the crossing will be avoided and the potential surfaces of the two real states will"split". The energy separation at an avoided crossing thus depends on the magnitude of H_{12}. H_{12} will be zero (and the crossings will be unavoided) when the two electronic states have a different (spatial or spin) symmetry.

However, in general, H_{12} is not generally zero for states of the same symmetry (which will generate avoided crossings). This is the noncrossing rule. Anyway, as we have seen above, this rule is true only for diatomic molecules, and in a polyatomic system one can always have unavoided (i.e., real) crossings for suitable values of a pair of independent co-ordinates (x_1 and x_2), which will simultaneously satisfy Equations. In conclusion the most general statement for unavoided crossings is: for a polyatomic system two states (even with the same symmetry) will intersect along an n-2 dimensional hyperline (i.e., a line in more than 3 dimensions) as the energy is plotted against the n internal nuclear co-ordinates [the two dimensions referred to above are the two independent variable (i.e., x_1 and x_2) defined previously].

Theoretical investigations of surface crossings have required new theoretical techniques based upon the mathematical description of conical intersections and we now briefly review the central theoretical aspects. For two geometric variables, two surfaces of the same multiplicity intersect as a double cone. If one moves in the plane spanned by the two directions x_1 and x_2 (the so-called"branching space") the degeneracy is lifted. In n dimensions the degeneracy persists along an n-2 dimensional hyperline (called"intersection space"): if we move from the apex of the cone along any of the remaining n-2 internal co-ordinates defining the intersection space, the degeneracy is not lifted. This n-2 dimensional space is a hyperline consisting of an infinite number of conical intersection points. It can be demonstrated that these two directions are given as the gradient difference vector,

$$x_1 = \frac{\partial(E_1 - E_2)}{\partial Q}$$

and the gradient of the interstate coupling vector

$$x_2 = \left\langle C_1^t \left(\frac{\partial H}{\partial Q} \right) C_2 \right\rangle .$$

The vector g(Q) is the coupling term that gives the magnitude of the coupling between the Born-Oppenheimer states described by C_1 and C_2 as a function of the nuclear motion along Q.

The Surface Crossing and Photochemical Reactivity

To understand the relationship between the surface crossing and photochemical reactivity, it is useful to draw a parallel between the role of a transition state in thermal reactivity and that of a conical intersection in photochemical reactivity. In a thermal reaction, the transition state (TS) forms a bottleneck through which the reaction must pass, on its way from reactants (R) to products (P). The motion through the TS is described by a single vector, the transition vector x_1 (i.e., the eigenvector related to the imaginary vibrational frequency). A transition state separates the reactant and product energy wells along the reaction path. An accessible conical intersection (CI) also forms a bottleneck that separates the excited state branch of the reaction path from the ground state branch.

The crucial difference between conical intersections and transition states is that, while the transition state must connect the reactant energy well to a single product well via a single reaction path, an intersection is a"spike" on the ground state energy surface, and thus it may connect the excited state reactant to two or more products (P_1 and P_2) on the ground state via a branching of the excited reaction path (in the plane x_1 and x_2) into different ground state relaxation valleys. The branching is possible even in the first order approximation because of the elliptic nature of the double cone; however in the case of an elliptic cone the branching will occur at most along two directions.The nature of the products generated following decay at a surface crossing will depend on the ground state valleys (relaxation paths) that can be accessed from that particular structure. Different topological situations are possible for unavoided crossings between surfaces. One can have intersections between states of different spin multiplicity (an n-1 dimensional intersection space in this case, since the interstate coupling vector vanishes by symmetry), or between two singlet surfaces or two triplets (and one has an n-2 dimensional conical intersection hyperline in this case).

We have encountered situations where both types of intersection occur at the same geometry. These three various topological possibilities are summarised in Figure. Notice that for the examples shown in Figure, the gradient of both the surfaces at the crossing is not zero. A conical intersection is just a Jahn-Teller like degeneracy that occurs without symmetry. One might ask if a Renner-Teller like degeneracy (i.e., the gradients of both surfaces go to zero at the degeneracy) can occur without having its origin in the symmetry of the states.

This situation is shown in Figure and is characterised by the fact that the gradients of both states is zero (i.e., they are real minima). Thus this situation is a"touching" rather than a crossing. The topography of the potential energy surfaces in the vicinity of a conical intersection can also be characterised by the relative orientation of the two potential surfaces, as discussed by Ruedenberg et al.

In this review we will use Ruedenberg's terminology: peaked, sloped and intermediate as shown in Figure. Often the chemically relevant conical intersection point is located along a valley on the excited state potential energy surface (i.e., a peaked intersection). Figure illustrates a two-dimensional model example that occurs in the photochemical trans cis isomerization of octatetraene. Here two potential energy surfaces are connected via a conical intersection. This intersection appears as a single point (C_I) since the surfaces are plotted along the branching space (x_1, x_2).

The intermediate M* is reached by relaxation from the Franck- Condon region (FC), and it is separated from the intersection point by a transition state (TS). In this case (a peaked type of intersection) the molecular structure of the intersection and the reaction pathway leading to it can be studied by computing the MEP connecting FC to M* and M* to CI using the standard intrinsic reaction co-ordinate (IRC) method.

However, there are situations where there is no transition state connecting M* to the intersection point. In such situations, mechanistic information must be obtained by locating the lowest lying intersection point along the n-2 intersection space of the molecule. The practical computation of the molecular structure of a conical intersection energy minimum will be illustrated in the next subsection. This technique provides information on the structure and accessibility of the intersection point which controls the locus and efficiency of internal conversion.

Nonadiabatic events (transition from the excited state to the ground state at the conical intersection) pose a serious challenge because the non-adiabatic transition is rigorously quantum mechanical without a well-defined classical analogue. At a simple level of theory (we return to a better treatment subsequently) the probability of a surface hop is given as $P = (\exp)[-(\pi/4)\xi]$ where the Massey parametre is,

$$\xi = \frac{\Delta E(Q)}{\hbar Q \cdot g(Q)}.$$

Thus this simple theory predicts that radiationless transitions will occur when the energy gap $\Delta E(Q)$ is small and the scalar product between the velocity vector and the non-adiabatic coupling $Q \cdot g\ Q$ is large.

$$Q = \frac{\partial Q}{\partial t} \text{and}\, g(Q)$$

and g(Q) is defined in Equation. The motion to ground state photoproducts following decay via internal conversion at a conical intersection channel requires a study of the possible ground state relaxation process.

A new method (called initial relaxation direction (IRD) method) to locate and characterise all the relaxation directions that originate at the lower vertex of the conical intersection cone, has been recently implemented, and will be illustrated in detail in the next section.

The MEP starting along these relaxation directions defines the ground state valleys which determine the possible relaxation paths and ultimately the photoproducts which can be generated by decay.

Although this information is structural (i.e., nondynamical), it provides insight into the mechanism of photoproduct formation from vibrationally cold excited state reactants such as those encountered in many experiments where slow excited state motion or/and thermal equilibration is possible (in cool jets, in cold matrices and in solution).

When such structural or static information is not sufficient (i.e., the excited state may not decay at the minimum of the conical intersection line, or the momentum developed on the excited state branch of the reaction co-ordinate may be sufficient to drive the ground state reactive trajectory along paths that are far from the ground state valleys), a dynamics treatment of the excited state/ground state motion is required.

These techniques will be also illustrated in the next subsection.

The S_1/S_0 Conical Intersection of Benzene

We now give an example of the way in which the topological features just discussed occur in practical problems. In S1 benzene there is a ~3000 cm^{-1} threshold for the disappearance of S1 fluorescence. This observation is assigned to the opening of a very efficient, radiationless decay channel (termed"channel 3") leading to the production of fulvene and benzvalene via a prefulvene intermediate.

Ab initio CAS-SCF (complete active space SCF) calculations show that the general surface topology of the excited state energy surface is consistent with that shown in Figure.

Thus the observed energy threshold, which is reproduced by multi-reference MP2 (Møller-Plesset 2) computations corresponds to the energy barrier which separates S1 benzene from an S1/S0 conical intersection point.

A molecular species has only a transient existence in the region of a conical intersections.

Thus, the molecular structure can only be derived from theoretical computations.

The optimised conical intersection structure for S1 benzene is shown in Figure. The structure contains a triangular arrangement of three carbon centres corresponding to a -(CH)3- kink of the carbon skeleton. The electronic structure corresponds to 3 weakly interacting electrons in a triangular arrangement which are loosely coupled to an isolated radical centre (this is delocalised on an allyl fragment).

This type of conical intersection structure appears to be a general feature in conjugated systems and has been documented in a series of polyene and polyene radicals. We will illustrate this point in the last subsection.

The electronic origin of this feature can be understood by comparison with H_3 where any equilateral triangle configuration corresponds to a point on the D_0/D_1 conical intersection (this is an example of Jahn-Teller degeneracy) in which the three H electrons have identical pairwise interactions. We now discuss the $-(CH)_3-$ kink electronic structure and coupling involved in photoproduct formation after decay back to the ground state.

In the conical intersection surface topology, the two geometrical distortions that lift the degeneracy (x_1 and x_2).

By examining the molecular structure of the conical intersection, its electronic distribution and the directions indicated by the x_1 and x_2 vectors, we can derive information on the photochemical reaction path and on the possible coupling patterns involving the three unpaired electrons of the kink and leading to the final photoproducts.

Three different pairings of two of the three electrons of the kink are possible. The gradient difference vector x_1, which is almost parallel to the S_1 transition vector, predicts a relaxation towards the pre-fulvene diradical in the positive direction (1-5 pairing) and a planar ground state benzene in the negative direction.

The other two couplings are described by the non-adiabatic coupling vector x_2 which is the other geometrical co-ordinate shown in Figure. It describes the simultaneous double bond re-construction which occurs upon relaxation. This direction corresponds to localising the bonds in either the 1-6 or 5-6 positions (1-6 and 5-6 pairings in the positive and negative direction of x_2 respectively).

A "circuit" of the conical intersection changes the coupling in the triangular arrangement of the three carbon centres corresponding to the -$(CH)_3$- kink of the carbon skeleton. This discussion is more general than it appears.

For the conical intersection geometry that has been optimised on the S_1 surface for the problem of cyclohexadiene/hexatriene photochemical interconversion, one again sees the three different pairings of two out of three electrons.

COMPUTATIONAL INVESTIGATION OF PHOTOCHEMICAL REACTION

The practical computational investigation of photochemical reaction mechanisms. During the last decade or so, the speed of the computers has grown considerably and the computational investigation of realistic models of organic compounds is becoming a standard practice. Current applications range from the investigation of the mechanism of synthetically useful reactions to the study of short lived organic intermediates detected in the interstellar medium. For thermal reactions, standard state-of-the-art ab initio quantum chemical methods are already capable of providing a complete description of what happens at the molecular level during bond-breaking and bond-forming processes. In particular, it is possible to compute the transition structure which connects a reactant to a product and the associated energy barrier with almost chemical accuracy (ca. 1 kcal mol-1 error).

Furthermore the reaction path, i.e., the progression of the molecular structure towards the transition state and the product, can be determined, in a completely unbiased way, by computing the minimum energy path (MEP) connecting the reactant to the product on the 3N-6 dimensional potential energy surface of the system. A detailed understanding of the reaction pathway in the excited state manifold will increase our ability to design new and to control known photochemical reactions.

As an example, the conversion of light into chemical energy in plants and animals involves extended conjugated molecules - carotenoids and retinals - bound in protein complexes. The use of such extended systems in optical data storage and processing technology is now being investigated. Photobiological systems exploit the ability of these chromophores to undergo cis-trans isomerization and to transduce radiative energy into thermal energy on picosecond or shorter timescales. Recent advances in time-resolved spectroscopy (e.g., the use of ultrafast laser pulses) has provided a powerful tool to monitor reaction dynamics on the femtosecond timescale and made direct observation of these processes possible, increasing our understanding of the excited state structures and dynamics for model systems. Ultrafast (femtosecond) radiationless decay has been observed, for example, for simple dienes, cyclohexadienes, hexatrienes, and in both free and opsin-bound retinal protonated Schiff bases.

However a complete understanding of molecular dynamics on multiple electronic states is required to interpret these laser experiments with confidence and to understand the principles involved in the design of optical devices. Until recently, reaction path computations were mainly limited to the investigation of thermal reactions and thus to reactions occurring on a single potential energy surface. Photochemical processes, where the reactant resides on an excited state potential energy surface and the products accumulate on the ground state, could not be easily investigated. In photochemistry, the reaction path must have at least two branches: one located on the excited state and the other located on the ground state energy surface.

The main difficulty associated with such computations lies in the correct definition and practical computation of the"funnel" region where the excited state reactant or intermediate is delivered to the ground state. Thus, while the progression on excited state energy surface (i.e., the excited state"branch" of the reaction path) may be investigated with the same methods used for thermal reactions, there was no general way of defining the"locus" where the excited state branch of the reaction path was connected to the ground state branch. During the last decade, computational tools have been developed and strategies discovered to explore electronically excited state reaction paths. The goal of such computational approaches, in the study of photochemical mechanisms, is the complete description of what happens at the molecular level from energy absorption to product formation. This review will focus on some of these new theoretical tools, with case studies to show how they can be applied. We shall begin with some simple ideas that are the main focus of the theoretical study of excited state processes.

A very schematic view of the course of a photochemical reaction is given in Figure. Following light absorption, the system is promoted to an excited state $\left(R \xrightarrow{+hv} R^*\right)$ Photoproduct formation can then occur by adiabatic reaction $\left(R \longrightarrow R^{\cdot *}\right)$ on the excited state (a photochemical process) followed by emission $\left(P^{\cdot *} \xrightarrow{-hv} P^{\cdot}\right)$ or by internal conversion to the ground state (a photophysical process). However, the most common mechanism involves a nonadiabatic radiationless decay process which either regenerates the reactant R (a photophysical process) or generates new products P or P' (a photochemical process). Whether a photochemical reaction occurs, thus depends upon the relative rates of photochemical processes that generate new molecular structures versus competing photophysical processes that convert between electronic states at the same nuclear geometry. The competition between photochemical and photophysical processes may occur via two different mechanisms: branching at a same decay channel or competition between two different decay channels.

Understanding the mechanism of this non-adiabatic radiationless decay is central to explaining excited state processes. There are two possible mechanisms. When real surface crossings exist and are accessible, the Landau-

Zener model (which we will discuss in more detail subsequently) provides a semi-classical model for fast radiationless decay. By 'accessible', we mean that there is a reaction co-ordinate with a sufficiently low energy barrier that leads from the initial excited state geometry to the crossing region. In this case, internal conversion can take place within a single vibrational oscillation through, or near, the surface crossing $\left(R^{*} \longrightarrow P \, or \, R^{*} \longrightarrow R\right)$ and radiationless decay occurs on a scale of ps (picosecond) to fs (femtosecond). If surface crossings are not present, or are present but not easily accessible, the process of radiationless decay is better described as the transformation of electronic energy into a manifold of vibronic states associated with the lower electronic state. This process is governed by the density of vibrational states and Franck-Condon factors (overlap of ground and excited state vibrational wavefunctions) according to the Fermi Golden rule formalism.

The Fermi Golden rule type decay occurs at a local minimum on the excited state (which might be either an avoided crossing, as shown in Figure, or the minima R* or P'*). This process is much slower than decay at a surface crossing and typical internal conversion rates for aromatic hydrocarbons are found to be 105-106 s-1.

Recently it has been shown that certain photochemical radiationless reactions are extremely fast: For example, the cis to trans isomerization of the retinal chromophore in the vision process occurs in ca. 200 fs. This demonstrates that these reactions are likely to occur via real surface crossings since they can be faster than processes such as fluorescence and internal conversion via avoided crossings or at local minima which take place on a s (microsecond) to ns (nanosecond) timescale.

Recent complementary theoretical computations have shown that low-lying intersections (real crossings) between the photochemically relevant excited state and the ground state occur with a previously unsuspected frequency. Such crossings, i.e., conical intersections in the case of two singlet (or two triplet) states, or singlet-triplet intersections, provide a very efficient"funnel" for radiationless deactivation (internal conversion and intersystem crossing) and, in turn, prompt photoproduct formation.

To summarise, the decay probability (i.e., the internal conversion rate) at an avoided crossing or a local excited state minimum is controlled by the interaction between the vibrational energy levels of the ground and excited state potential energy surfaces by using the Fermi Golden Rule, and thus radiationless decay and fluorescence can occur on competitive timescales. On the other hand, radiationless decay at a conical intersection implies that the internal conversion process can approach 100% efficiency so that any observed retardation in the internal conversion or reaction rate (i.e., the competition with fluorescence) must reflect the presence of some excited state energy barrier which separates R* from the intersection structure.

Finally, in the case where the radiationless decay leads to a chemical reaction, the molecular structure at the intersection must be related to the structure of the photoproducts.

The traditional view of deactivation of an electronically excited intermediate by internal conversion, mainly due to the work of Van der Lugt and Oosteroff on the ringopening of cyclobutene, was formulated in terms of avoided crossing funnels.

Thus internal conversion rates were predicted to be slow as in aromatic hydrocarbons because of the finite gap at the avoided crossing (energy gap law). Because it was impossible to compute real reaction paths in the 1960s, the real nature of the funnel was missed.

The relation between an avoided crossing (a section of a cone along R- P) and the double cone topology of a real conical intersection. In two dimensions, the Van der Lugt and Oosteroff model is refined by replacing the"avoided crossing" with an"unavoided crossing", i.e., a conical intersection.

The Van der Lugt and Oosteroff model reaction avoided crossing path $R \longrightarrow P$ is replaced by a path involving a real surface crossing $\left(R \longrightarrow PI \longrightarrow P\right)$ In the subsequent discussion we will use the acronym CI (in bold) to refer to conical intersections, while the acronym CI (plain text) is used for Configuration Intersection. Teller was the first to point out that in a polyatomic molecule the non-crossing rule, which is rigorously valid for diatomics, fails.

Rather, two electronic states, even if they have the same symmetry, are allowed to cross at a conical intersection. Accordingly, radiationless decay from the upper to the lower intersecting state can occur within a single vibrational period when the system travels in the vicinity of such intersection points.

In the field of photochemistry, Zimmerman and Michl were the first to suggest, independently, that certain photoproducts originate from internal conversion at a conical intersection.

Zimmerman and Michl used the term"funnel" for this feature. We can now suggest a theoretical basis for the computational modeling of photochemical reactions.

We shall call this method the pathway approach, following the suggestion of Fuss et al.

According to this approach, the excited state motion is determined by the structure of the relevant excited and ground state potential energy surfaces. In simple terms, information on the excited state lifetime and on the type of photoproducts generated is obtained by following the detailed relaxation and reaction paths of the molecule along the potential energy surfaces from the Franck-Condon (FC) point (i.e., vertically excited geometrey), or excited state intermediate, to the ground state.

This approach is part of a more general way of considering photochemistry which is already employed in one recent textbook: it follows the pathway on the potential energy surfaces and pays attention to local details such as slopes, barriers, saddle points, collecting funnels, etc.

One key element of the pathway approach is the existence of low lying real crossings or excited state products preceded by a transition state which control the rate of transformation or decay of the excited state reactant.

This feature has been suggested by experimental observations. Experiments on isolated molecules in cold-matrices, expanding-jets and in solution have revealed the presence of thermally activated fast radiationless decay channels in polyenes, such as hexatrienes and octatetraenes, and in aromatic compounds, such as benzene, azulene and azoalkanes.

In particular, recent spectroscopic low-temperature investigations of isolated polyene molecules have provided evidence that photoinduced double-bond trans cis isomerization may occur via a non-adiabatic reaction path where the excited state intermediate decays to the ground state at a highly twisted molecular geometry.

The original suggestions of Teller, Zimmerman and Michl have now been fully verified by recent computational results, which provide a particularly clear illustration of the application of the pathway approach to the study of organic photochemistry. In Figure we illustrate the results of two different experiments on all-trans octa- 1,3,5,7-tetraene (all-trans OT).

(a) Matrix Isolated Conditions and

(b) Expanding Cool-jet.

The first experiment is due to Kohler and co-workers who recorded the fluorescence lifetime of S1 (2Ag) all-trans OT as a function of the temperature. In this experiment the all-trans OT molecules are isolated in a molecular cavity of frozen nhexane and do not interact with each other. From Figure, one can see that, at temperatures above 200 K, the fluorescence lifetime drops dramatically indicating fast decay of the excited state molecules to the ground state.

This event was assigned to the opening of a thermally activated efficient radiationless decay channel with a barrier height of ~1500 cm-1 (4.3 kcal mol-1).

The second experiment is due to Christensen, Yoshihara, Petek and co-workers, who reported the fluorescence decay rate of S_1 all-trans OT molecules measured in free jet expansion as a function of the excitation energy. These authors propose that (under isolated conditions in a cool-jet) trans cis motion in all-trans OT is responsible for the observed radiationless decay channel on S1 (2Ag) which opens up at ~2100 cm-1 (~6 kcal mol-1) excess energy.

These experimental results can be rationalised using the potential energy profiles. The fluorescence lifetime decreases slowly and almost linearly by increasing the S_1 excess vibrational energy until an energy threshold is reached and a dramatic decrease in excited state lifetime is observed. Quantum chemical computations of the S_1 reaction path of all-trans OT have revealed that the energy threshold corresponds to a transition state which connects an excited state intermediate to a conical intersection funnel.

6

Organic Chemistry

INTRODUCTION

Organic Chemistry is the study of the compounds of carbon, their reactions and their preparation. It is a fundamental course for the life sciences and chemical engineering. Traditionally, it is presented as a description of a large number of compounds classified by structure, and a few hundred typical reactions that will show how they can be prepared, and how they behave with respect to one another. This constitutes a very large amount of empirical information that is usually committed to memory as a sort of mental handbook, supplemented by actual handbooks, and by laboratory practice with a relatively small number of important or illustrative general reactions. It is unusually difficult to assimilate this mass of information because of the lack of a general pattern (only empirical rules) and heuristic aids. Nevertheless, organic chemists become quite skilled in the use of this gigantic amount of information, and can work wonders in the laboratory with processes of which they have no fundamental understanding, but a wonderful empirical mastery. In fact, a fundamental understanding, were it generally possible, would be of little help to them in their practical endeavors, even if it could be brought to a more functional level.

However, a fundamental understanding is intellectually much more satisfying than a collection of empirical or semi-empirical rules. Just what goes on in a chemical reaction is fully known in principle, but predicting what will happen in any particular case is not possible, for more reasons than the difficulties of numerical calculation. Digital computers have brought much computing power to bear, but even this is much too feeble for the complexities of organic chemistry. Even if the results for a particular case were known, they would be only numbers giving no understanding: each problem would be unique. This might be technologically useful, but very boring from an intellectual point of view.

The great variety of organic compounds, and the enormous amount of investigation that has been done on them, can be appreciated in no better way than by a look at Beilstein's handbook of organic chemistry. The fourth edition, which appeared in the 1920's, covers work up to 1910, and later work is quoted in supplements. Several suggestions are made in this article about compounds to look up, and the exercise is highly recommended. Proper use of Beilstein requires a knowledge of German, which was once a sufficient reason for all chemistry postgraduates to learn to read the language. Similar references exist in English, but they are not of the standard of Beilstein. Incidentally, a *Handbuch* in German was not one you could hold in your hand (all of Beilstein now seems to weigh about a ton), but one that is to be kept "at hand" for reference. Among the sciences, chemistry uniquely requires a reference like Beilstein.

The qualifier "organic" comes from the times when all organic chemicals were thought to be produced by organisms. In 1828, Wöhler made urea, H_2N-CO-NH_2, by heating its isomer ammonium cyanate, NH_4OCN, showing that "life force" was not necessary for making "organic" compounds. Etymologically, the name comes from Greek organon, a "tool," via "organisms," which are collections of tools (organs). The Greek adjective organikos means "serving as an instrument," which is not what the "organic" in organic chemistry means.

Carbon alone gives us the giant molecules of diamond and graphite, the hollow balls of buckminsterfullerenes, and nanotubes. For information on these subjects, and all the lore of carbon, including oxides, gems and fuels.

Hydrogen and oxygen play important roles in organic chemistry, in addition to carbon. Hydrocarbons are composed of carbon and hydrogen only, while carbohydrates join carbon with hydrogen and oxygen in the atomic ratio 2:1 as in water. These compounds include fuels and important biological substances such as sugars, cellulose and starch. Many additional compounds involve only C, H and O. With the addition of nitrogen, phosphorus and sulphur, most of the important biological substances are included, such as the amino acids, proteins, and many others. The halogens, F, Cl, Br and I, are important in many reactions, including those of synthesis. These 10 atomic species: C, H, O, N, P, S, F, Cl, Br and I, are enough to explain nearly all of organic chemistry. Petroleum is a major source of aliphatic hydrocarbons (those not involving the benzene ring) and coal is a major source of aromatic hydrocarbons (those which do). From these sources most of the organic compounds of non-biological importance can be synthesized.

The *formula* expresses the atomic constitution of a substance. The *empirical* formula merely states the ratio of the atoms, as CH_2O for acetic acid. This says that the ratio of carbon, hydrogen and oxygen atoms is as 1:2:1 in the molecule.

From the atomic weights, the proportions by weight are found to be 12/30, 2/30 and 16/30 or 6:1:8. More useful is the *molecular* formula, which gives the numbers of each atom in one molecule. For acetic acid, this is $C_2H_4O_2$. The *molecular weight* is 2x12 + 4x1 + 2x16 = 60. 60 grams of acetic acid contains 6.023 x 10^{23} molecules. The *structural* formula suggests the way in which the atoms are connected. This is CH_3COOH in the present case. The carbon of the methyl radical -CH_3 is connected to the carbon of the carboxyl radical -COOH by a single bond. We are supposed to recognize these structural elements from these abbreviations. Finally, the *graphic* formula explicitly shows the bonds between atoms, but does not usually show the spatial arrangement of the atoms. A *stereographic* formula shows the arrangement of the atoms in space as a perspective drawing, a stereopair, or an actual model. Examples of all kinds of formulas except the empirical will be found in this article. Familiarity with formulas and chemical equations is a basic skill.

Two substances with the same molecular formula but different structures are called *isomers*. Isomers are distinct substances with different properties. Two substances with the same chemical properties but different structures are called *metamers*, and are rare enough to be a curiosity. Two substances with structures that are mirror images of each other are called *stereoisomers*. This can happen, for example, when four different groups are bonded to a carbon. An interchange of two groups results in a molecule that cannot be superimposed on the original, but is a mirror image of it. Such molecules are called *chiral*, or "handed," and exist in different forms. A molecule with more than one chiral carbon can exhibit multiple stereoisomers. Stereoisomers usually have identical chemical properties, however. Molecules differing only in *conformation* are the same molecule, except that there may be rotation about certain bonds. Proteins, for example, are very flexible, and their conformation is important to their function.

Molecular models are a powerful aid to visualization, especially since they can be handled and moved to show the possibilities of molecular configurations. The best ones are correctly scaled with accurate angles and bond distances, the atoms represented by (truncated) spheres that show the spatial extent of electron density, and colored to show the different species. Such model sets still exist (a search of the Fisher catalog did not produce any photos) but are probably expensive. Photographs of such models are included on this page. There are many less expensive alternatives that may give a degree of satisfaction, generally using sticks and balls. The stereopair for free fusion is an excellent, but little-used, technique of illustration that would be very useful for organic chemistry.

Examples of structural formulas are shown at the left. The full structural formula shows each bond. Double bonds are represented by two lines, and triple bonds by three. The formula is usually abbreviated, as shown in the middle. The arrangement of the hydrogens is evident in H_3C or CH_3, and it is clear that the bond is with the carbon, whether the H_3 is written before or after the C. The carboxyl radical is clearly meant by COOH, with a double C=O bond followed by -OH. Sometimes double bonds are shown for clarity even in an abbreviated formula. At the right is the Lewis structural formula, where the dots represent valence electrons. Each C contributes 4 dots, each H one dot, and each O six dots. The dots are arranged in a stable molecule so that each atom kernel, represented by its chemical symbol, is surrounded by eight dots. The *kernel* is the nucleus together with all the electrons out to the last completed noble gas shell of 2 or 8 electrons. The remaining electrons are the *valence* electrons, equal in number to the charge of the kernel in electronic units.

The carbon kernel consists of the nucleus of charge +6 and the two 1s electrons, so its charge is +4. The oxygen kernel consists of the nucleus of charge +8 and the two 1s electrons, so its charge is +6. The hydrogen kernel consists of the proton of charge +1. The *formal charge* on each atom is found by starting with the charge of the kernel and subtracting one for each electron that "belongs" to the atom. This includes one of the two electrons in each bond, and any valence electrons that are not bonded, called *lone pairs*. If this is done for each atom in the Lewis formula, we find that the formal charge of each atom is zero. The usual signed valence of inorganic chemistry (H = +1, O = -2) that works for ionic compounds means nothing here.

An *ion* is an atom with fewer or more electrons than necessary for electrical neutrality. We can extend the concept to refer to an assembly of atoms that is not electrically neutral, which we'll call a *radical*. For example, OH^- is the *hydroxyl* radical. It has a kernel of charge +7 and 8 electrons, 6 from O, 1 from H, and 1 to give it a negative charge. Write the Lewis formula for the hydroxyl radical. The oxygen will be surrounded by 8 electrons, the proton by 2, so both will be happy and the radical will be stable. If a proton comes up, it can stick easily to one of the three electron pairs that are free, and make H_2O, a well-known stable molecule. There are still two free pairs, and another proton could stick to one of them quite easily, forming H_3O^+, the hydrated proton. This is certainly what happens to any odd protons floating about. A fourth proton for the remaining free pair would give an excessive charge for such a small molecule, which is not stable considering the alternatives, so H_4O^{++} is hypothetical. In principle, though, it would work. Any free pair is a target for a proton, though unattractive to a neutral hydrogen atom.

A *free radical* is a neutral atom or molecule with an "unsatisfied valence," or an odd unpaired electron that could engage in some arrangment of lower energy when encountering another molecule. A simple example is the H atom, a proton and an electron. Should it encounter another free radical, combination is certain, because in that way the total energy can be lowered. If it finds an atom to which it can bind more strongly than the atom's current engagement, it can steal the atom away, leaving another free radical in its wake.

Inorganic chemistry is characterized by ionic reactions in water solution. If we dissolve silver nitrate in water, we get solvated Ag^+ and NO_3^- ions in solution. Now if we add salt, Na^+ and Cl^- are added to the solution. It happens that if silver and chlorine ions meet, they form AgCl molecules that ionize very little and are insoluble in water because they clump together. The silver chloride precipitates until either silver or chlorine runs out. Similarly, if a gas is evolved a reaction will go to completion. Usually, however, we have an equilibrium between reactants and products with both present at the same time. Inorganic reactions also occur in the solid state, but the nature of these reactions is much less well-known.

Because organic compounds usually do not ionize, or even dissolve in water, they seem unreactive. This, however, is not actually so. Gasoline burns quickly with the release of a great deal of heat in internal combustion engines, for example. Instead of an ionic reaction, we are dealing with a free radical reaction in this case. Suppose methane and chlorine are mixed in a vessel. In the absence of light or a catalyst, there is no reaction although one would be expected on energy grounds. These reagents would love to rearrange themselves as methyl chloride and hydrogen chloride. When the vessel is exposed to light, the reaction is quick, forming mainly CH_3Cl until either the chlorine or the methane is used up (other chloromethanes are formed in smaller amounts). The mechanism of this reaction is: first the formation of free chlorine radicals by photochemical *homolysis*: $Cl_2 \rightarrow 2Cl.$, where the. represents an unpaired electron. Now, $CH_4 + Cl. \rightarrow HCl + H_3C.$, so a free methyl radical is produced when the chlorine grabs a hydrogen. Then, $H_3C. + Cl_2 \rightarrow CH_3Cl + Cl.$ and the chlorine free radical is recovered. The C-H bond is only a little less stable than the H-Cl bond, but still the chlorine has a good chance of stealing the hydrogen. Every photolysis, the splitting of Cl_2 by light, is the start of a chain reaction that ends only when two free radicals encounter each other and combine. If the heat produced in the reaction is enough to create free radicals by itself, the chain reaction may branch by *thermolysis* and proceed even more rapidly. Free radical chain reactions are almost always involved in rapid reactions, and are much more common that might be supposed.

Returning to equilibria, we might review a few points that are treated in general chemistry. The ionization of acetic acid is an example of a chemical equilibrium. In water, CH_3COOH "! $CH_3COO^- + H^+$. The equilibrium between the three species is expressed by $[Ac^-][H^+]/[HAc] = 1.753 \times 10^{-5} = K$, where the [HAc] is the concentration of acetic acid in moles per litre, and so forth. In 1M acetic acid (60g per litre, about 6%, like household vinegar), the hydrogen ion concentration x will be the solution of $x^2 = K$, since the hydrogen ion and acetate ion concentrations will be equal in this case. Then, $x = 4.3 \times 10^{-3}$, or pH = 2.4, since pH = -log $[H^+]$. Also, $[H^+][OH^-] = 1 \times 10^{-14}$ in aqueous solution, where the concentration of water is about constant (55.6 mol/litre) and is figured into the equilibrium constant. The pH of water is 7. In water, either the hydrogen ion concentration can be large, or the hydroxyl ion concentration can be large, but not both at the same time. These ions often have an important effect on reactions, and even on the structure of dissolved molecules. If you are rusty, it would be a good idea to review equilibrium and solutions.

Historical Highlights

At the very beginning of the nineteenth century chemists generally thought that compounds from living organisms were too complicated in structure to be capable of artificial synthesis from non-living things, and that a 'vital force' or vitalism conferred the characteristics of living beings on this form of matter. They named these compounds 'organic', and preferred to direct their investigations toward inorganic materials that seemed more promising.

Organic chemistry received a boost when it was realized that these compounds could be treated in ways similar to inorganic compounds and could be created in the laboratory by means other than 'vital force'. Around 1816 Michel Chevreul started a study of soaps made from various fats and alkali. He separated the different acids that, in combination with the alkali, produced the soap. Since these were all individual compounds, he demonstrated that it was possible to make a chemical change in various fats (which traditionally come from organic sources), producing new compounds, without 'vital force'. In 1828 Friedrich Wohler first manufactured the organic chemical urea (carbamide), a constituent of urine, from the inorganic ammonium cyanate NH_4OCN, in what is now called the Wohler synthesis. Although Wohler was, at this time as well as afterwards, cautious about claiming that he had thereby destroyed the theory of vital force, most have looked to this event as the turning point.

A great next step was when in 1856 William Henry Perkin, while trying to manufacture quinine, again accidentally came to manufacture the organic dye now called Perkin's mauve, which by generating a huge amount of money greatly increased interest in organic chemistry. Another step was the laboratory preparation of DDT by Othmer Zeidler in 1874, but the insecticide properties of this compound were not discovered until much later.

The crucial breakthrough for the theory of organic chemistry was the concept of chemical structure, developed independently and simultaneously by Friedrich August Kekule and Archibald Scott Couper in 1858. Both men suggested that tetravalent carbon atoms could link to each other to form a carbon lattice, and that the detailed patterns of atomic bonding could be discerned by skillful interpretations of appropriate chemical reactions.

The history of organic chemistry continues with the discovery of petroleum and its separation into fractions according to boiling ranges. The conversion of different compound types or individual compounds by various chemical processes created the petroleum chemistry leading to the birth of the petrochemical industry, which successfully manufactured artificial rubbers, the various organic adhesives, the property-modifying petroleum additives, and plastics.

The pharmaceutical industry began in the last decade of the 19th century when acetylsalicylic acid (more commonly referred to as aspirin) manufacture was started in Germany by Bayer. The first time a drug was systematically improved was with arsphenamine (Salvarsan). Numerous derivatives of the dangerously toxic atoxyl were systematically synthesized and tested by Paul Ehrlich and his group, and the compound with best effectiveness and toxicity characteristics was selected for production.

Early examples of organic reactions and applications were serendipitous, such as Perkin's accidental discovery of Perkin's mauve. However, from the 20th century, the progress of organic chemistry allowed for synthesis of specifically selected compounds or even molecules designed with specific properties, as in drug design.

The process of finding new synthesis routes for a given compound is called total synthesis. Total synthesis of complex natural compounds started with urea, increased in complexity to glucose and terpineol, and in 1907, total synthesis was commercialized the first time by Gustaf Komppa with camphor.

Pharmaceutical benefits have been substantial, for example cholesterol-related compounds have opened ways to synthesis of complex human hormones and their modified derivatives.

Since the start of the 20th century, complexity of total syntheses has been increasing, with examples such as lysergic acid and vitamin B12. Today's targets feature tens of stereogenic centers that must be synthesized correctly with asymmetric synthesis.

Biochemistry, the chemistry of living organisms, their structure and interactions in vitro and inside living systems, has only started in the 20th century, opening up a brand new chapter of organic chemistry with enormous scope.

Classification of Organic Substances

Description and Nomenclature

Classification is not possible without having a full description of the individual compounds. In contrast with inorganic chemistry, in which describing a chemical compound can be achieved by simply enumerating the chemical symbols of the elements present in the compound together with the number of these elements in the molecule, in organic chemistry the relative arrangement of the atoms within a molecule must be added for a full description. One way of describing the molecule is by drawing its structural formula. Because of molecular complexity, simplified systems of chemical notation have been developed. The latest version is the line-angle formula, which achieves simplicity without introducing ambiguity. In this system, the endpoints and intersections of each line represent one carbon, and hydrogens can either be notated or assumed to be present by implication. Some disadvantages of chemical notation are that they are not easily described by words and they are not easily printable. These problems have been addressed by describing molecular structures using organic nomenclature.

Because of the difficulties arising from the very large number and variety of organic compounds, chemists realized early on that the establishment of an internationally accepted system of naming organic compounds was of paramount importance. The Geneva Nomenclature was born in 1892 as a result of a number of international meetings on the subject.

It was also realized that as the family of organic compounds grew, the system would have to be expanded and modified. This task was ultimately taken on by the International Union on Pure and Applied Chemistry (IUPAC). Recognizing the fact that in the branch of biochemistry the complexity of organic structures increases, the IUPAC organization joined forces with the International Union of Biochemistry and Molecular Biology, IUBMB, to produce a list of joint recommendations on nomenclature.

Later, as the numbers and complexities of organic molecules grew, new recommendations were made within IUPAC for simplification. The first such recommendation was presented in 1951 when a cyclic benzene structure was named a cyclophane. Later recommendations extended the method to the simplification of other complex cyclic structures, including heterocyclics, and named such structures *phanes*.

For ordinary communication, to spare a tedious description, the official IUPAC naming recommendations are not always followed in practice except when it is necessary to give a concise definition to a compound, or when the IUPAC name is simpler (viz. *ethanol* versus *ethyl alcohol*). Otherwise the *common* or trivial name may be used, often derived from the source of the compound. In summary, organic substances are classified by their molecular structural arrangement and by what other atoms are present along with the chief (carbon) constituent in their makeup, whilst in a structural formula, hydrogen is implicitly assumed to occupy all free valences of an appropriate carbon atom which remain after accounting for branching, other element(s) and/or multiple bonding.

Hydrocarbons and Functional Groups

Classification normally starts with the hydrocarbons: compounds which contain only carbon and hydrogen. Other elements present themselves in atomic configurations called functional groups which have decisive influence on the chemical and physical characteristics of the compound; thus those containing the same atomic formations have similar characteristics, which may be: miscibility with water, acidity/alkalinity, chemical reactivity, oxidation resistance, and others.

Some functional groups are also radicals, similar to those in inorganic chemistry, defined as *polar* atomic configurations which pass during chemical reactions from one chemical compound into another without change.

Some of the elements of the functional groups (O, S, N, halogens) may stand alone and the *group* name is not strictly appropriate, but because of their decisive effect on the way they modify the characteristics of the hydrocarbons in which they are present they are classed with the functional groups, and their specific effect on the properties lends excellent means for characterisation and classification.

Referring to the hydrocarbon types below, many, if not all of the functional groups which are typically present within aliphatic compounds are also represented within the aromatic and alicyclic group of compounds, unless they are dehydrated, which would lead to non-reacting co-optional groups.

Reference is made here again to the organic nomenclature, which shows an extensive (if not comprehensive) number of classes of compounds according to the presence of various functional groups, based on the IUPAC recommendations, but also some based on trivial names. Putting compounds in sub-classes becomes more difficult when more than one functional group is present. Two overarching chain type categories exist: Open Chain aliphatic compounds and Closed Chain cyclic compounds. Those in which both open chain and cyclic parts are present are normally classed with the latter.

Aliphatic Compounds

The aliphatic hydrocarbons are subdivided into three groups, homologous series according to their state of saturation: paraffins alkanes without any double or triple bonds, olefins alkenes with double bonds, which can be mono-olefins with a single double bond, di-olefins, or di-enes with two, or poly-olefins with more. The third group with a triple bond is named after the name of the shortest member of the homologue series as the acetylenes alkynes. The rest of the group is classed according to the functional groups present.

From another aspect aliphatics can be straight chain or branched chain compounds, and the degree of branching also affects characteristics, like octane number or cetane number in petroleum chemistry.

Aromatic and Alicyclic Compounds

Cyclic compounds can, again, be saturated or unsaturated. Because of the bonding angle of carbon, the most stable configurations contain six carbon atoms, but while rings with five carbon atoms are also frequent, others are rarer. The cyclic hydrocarbons divide into alicyclics and aromatics (also called arenes). Of the alicyclic compounds the cycloalkanes do not contain multiple bonds, whilst the cycloalkenes and the cycloalkynes do.

Typically this latter type only exists in the form of large rings, called macrocycles. The simplest member of the cycloalkane family is the three-membered cyclopropane.

Aromatic hydrocarbons contain conjugated double bonds. One of the simplest examples of these is benzene, the structure of which was formulated by Kekule who first proposed the delocalization or resonance principle for explaining its structure. For "conventional" cyclic compounds, aromaticity is conferred by the presence of 4n + 2 delocalized pi electrons, where n is an integer. Particular instability (antiaromaticity) is conferred by the presence of 4n conjugated pi electrons.

The characteristics of the cyclic hydrocarbons are again altered if heteroatoms are present, which can exist as either substituents attached externally to the ring (exocyclic) or as a member of the ring itself (endocyclic). In the case of the latter, the ring is termed a heterocycle. Pyridine and furan are examples of aromatic heterocycles while piperidine and tetrahydrofuran are the corresponding alicyclic heterocycles. The heteroatom of heterocyclic molecules is generally oxygen, sulfur, or nitrogen, with the latter being particularly common in biochemical systems.

Rings can fuse with other rings on an edge to give polycyclic compounds. The purine nucleoside bases are notable polycyclic aromatic heterocycles. Rings can also fuse on a "corner" such that one atom (almost always carbon) has two bonds going to one ring and two to another. Such compounds are termed spiro and are important in a number of natural products.

Polymers

One important property of carbon in organic chemistry is that it can form certain compounds, the individual molecules of which are capable of attaching themselves to one another, thereby forming a chain or a network. The process is called polymerization and the chains or networks polymers, while the source compound is a monomer. Two main groups of polymers exist: those artificially manufactured are referred to as industrial polymers or synthetic polymers and those naturally occurring as biopolymers. Since the invention of the first artificial polymer, bakelite, the family has quickly grown with the invention of others. Common synthetic organic polymers are polyethylene or polythene, polypropylene, nylon, teflon or PTFE, polystyrene, polyesters, polymethylmethacrylate (commonly known as perspex or plexiglas) polyvinylchloride or PVC, and polyisobutylene an important artificial or synthetic rubber also the polymerised butadiene, a rubber component. The examples are generic terms, and many varieties of each of these may exist, with their physical characteristics fine tuned for a specific use.

Changing the conditions of polymerisation changes the chemical composition of the product by altering chain length, or branching, or the tacticity.

With a single monomer as a start the product is a homopolymer. Further, secondary component(s) may be added to create a heteropolymer (co-polymer) and the degree of clustering of the different components can also be controlled. Physical characteristics, such as hardness, density, mechanical or tensile strength, abrasion resistance, heat resistance, transparency, colour, etc. will depend on the final composition.

Biomolecules

Biomolecular chemistry is a major category within organic chemistry which is frequently studied by biochemists. Many complex multi-functional group molecules are important in living organisms. Some are long-chain biopolymers, and these include proteins, DNA, RNA and the polysaccharides such as starches in animals and celluloses in plants.

The other main classes are amino acids (monomer building blocks of proteins), carbohydrates (which includes the polysaccharides), the nucleic acids (which include DNA and RNA as polymers), and the lipids.

In addition, animal biochemistry contains many small molecule intermediates which assist in energy production through the Krebs cycle, and produces isoprene, the most common hydrocarbon in animals. Isoprenes in animals form the important steroid structural (cholesterol) and steroid hormone compounds; and in plants form terpenes, terpenoids, some alkaloids, and a unique set of structural hydrocarbons called biopolymer polyisoprenoids present in latex sap which is the basis for making rubber.

Buckyballs

Buckminsterfullerenes, also known as Buckyballs, are among the types of compounds engineered by organic chemists that have generated the most interest. The discovery of their unique electronic properties due to their spherical structure has stimulated new research into related fields such as carbon nanotubes.

Others

Organic compounds containing bonds of carbon to nitrogen, oxygen and the halogens are not normally grouped separately. Others are sometimes put into major groups within organic chemistry and discussed under titles such as organosulfur chemistry, organometallic chemistry, organophosphorus chemistry and organosilicon chemistry.

Characteristics of Organic Substances

Organic compounds are generally covalently bonded. This allows for unique structures such as long carbon chains and rings. The reason carbon is excellent at forming unique structures and that there are so many carbon compounds is that carbon atoms form very stable covalent bonds with one another (catenation). In contrast to inorganic materials, organic compounds typically melt, boil, sublimate, or decompose below 300 °C. Neutral organic compounds tend to be less soluble in water compared to many inorganic salts, with the exception of certain compounds such as ionic organic compounds and low molecular weight alcohols and carboxylic acids where hydrogen bonding occurs.

Organic compounds tend to dissolve in organic solvents which are either pure substances like ether or ethyl alcohol, or mixtures, such as the paraffinic solvents such as the various petroleum ethers and white spirits, or the range of pure or mixed aromatic solvents obtained from petroleum or tar fractions by physical separation or by chemical conversion. Solubility in the different solvents depends upon the solvent type and on the functional groups if present.

Solutions are studied by the science of physical chemistry. Like inorganic salts, organic compounds may also form crystals. A unique property of carbon in organic compounds is that its valency does not always have to be taken up by atoms of other elements, and when it is not, a condition termed unsaturation results. In such cases we talk about carbon carbon double bonds or triple bonds. Double bonds alternating with single in a chain are called conjugated double bonds. An aromatic structure is a special case in which the conjugated chain is a closed ring.

Molecular Structure Elucidation

Organic compounds consist of carbon atoms, hydrogen atoms, and functional groups. The valence of carbon is 4, and hydrogen is 1, functional groups are generally 1. From the number of carbon atoms and hydrogen atoms in a molecule the degree of unsaturation can be obtained. Many, but not all structures can be envisioned by the simple valence rule that there will be one bond for each valence number. The knowledge of the chemical formula for an organic compound is not sufficient information because many isomers can exist. Organic compounds often exist as mixtures. Because many organic compounds have relatively low boiling points and/or dissolve easily in organic solvents there exist many methods for separating mixtures into pure constituents that are specific to organic chemistry such as distillation, crystallization and chromatography techniques. There exist several methods for deducing the structure of an organic compound. In general usage are (in alphabetical order):

- Crystallography: This is the most precise method for determining molecular geometry; however, it is very difficult to grow crystals of sufficient size and high quality to get a clear picture, so it remains a secondary form of analysis. Crystallography has seen especially extensive use in biochemistry (for protein structure determination) and in the characterization of organometallic catalysts, which often possess significant molecular symmetry.
- Elemental analysis: A destructive method used to determine the elemental composition of a molecule. See also mass spectrometry, below.
- Infrared spectroscopy: Chiefly used to determine the presence (or absence) of certain functional groups.
- Mass spectrometry: Used to determine the molecular weight of a compound and from mass spectrum analysis its structure. High resolution mass spectrometry can often identify the precise formula of a compound through knowledge of isotopic masses and abundances; it is thus sometimes used in lieu of elemental analysis.
- Nuclear magnetic resonance (NMR) spectroscopy identifies different nuclei based on their chemical environment. This is the most important and commonly used spectroscopic technique for organic chemists, often permitting complete assignment of atom connectivity and even stereochemistry given the proper set of spectroscopy experiments (e.g. correlation spectroscopy).

- Optical rotation: Distinguishes between two enantiomers of a chiral compound based on the sign of rotation of plane polarized light. If the specific rotation of an enantiomer is known, the magnitude of rotation also gives the ratio of enantiomers in a mixed sample, though HPLC with a chiral column also can supply this information.
- UV/VIS spectroscopy: Used to determine degree of conjugation in the system. While still sometimes used to characterize molecules, UV/VIS is more commonly used to quantitate how much of a known compound is present in a (typically liquid) sample.

Additional methods are provided by analytical chemistry.

Organic reactions

Organic reactions are chemical reactions involving organic compounds. While pure hydrocarbons undergo certain limited classes of reactions, many more reactions which organic compounds undergo are largely determined by functional groups. The general theory of these reactions involves careful analysis of such properties as the electron affinity of key atoms, bond strengths and steric hindrance. These issues can determine the relative stability of short-lived reactive intermediates, which usually directly determine the path of the reaction. An example of a common reaction is a substitution reaction written as:

$$Nu^- + C\text{-}X \rightarrow C\text{-}Nu + X^-$$

where X is some functional group and Nu is a nucleophile.

There are many important aspects of a specific reaction. Whether it will occur spontaneously or not is determined by the Gibbs free energy change of the reaction. The heat that is either produced or needed by the reaction is found from the total enthalpy change. Other concerns include whether side reactions occur from the same reaction conditions. Any side reactions which occur typically produce undesired compounds which may be anywhere from very easy or very difficult to separate from the desired compound.

Synthetic Organic Chemistry

Synthetic organic chemistry is an applied science as it borders engineering, the "design, analysis, and/or construction of works for practical purposes". Organic synthesis of a novel compound is a problem solving task, where a synthesis is designed for a target molecule by selecting optimal reactions from optimal starting materials.

Complex compounds can have tens of reaction steps that sequentially build the desired molecule. The synthesis proceeds by utilizing the reactivity of the functional groups in the molecule. For example, a carbonyl compound can be used as a nucleophile by converting it into an enolate, or as an electrophile; the combination of the two is called the aldol reaction. Designing practically useful syntheses always requires conducting the actual synthesis in the laboratory. The scientific practice of creating novel synthetic routes for complex molecules is called total synthesis.

There are several strategies to design a synthesis. The modern method of retrosynthesis, developed by E.J. Corey, starts with the target molecule and splices it to pieces according to known reactions. The pieces, or the proposed precursors, receive the same treatment, until available and ideally inexpensive starting materials are reached. Then, the retrosynthesis is written in the opposite direction to give the synthesis. A "synthetic tree" can be constructed, because each compound and also each precursor has multiple syntheses.

CHEMICAL BONDS

Organic chemistry (and all other chemistry at that) is completely described by the quantum mechanics of nuclei and electrons interacting by electrostatic forces. The small contributions of the magnetic interactions of orbital currents and spin magnetic moments is of interest in spectroscopy, but of no consequence in chemistry. Charges of like sign repel one another, so electrons are repelled by electrons and nuclei are repelled by nuclei, but electrons and nuclei attract one another strongly and at large distances. The classical forces are $F = z_1z_2(e^2/r^2)$, where F is the force in dynes, e the magnitude of the electronic charge (4.803×10^{-10}) in esu, r the distance between the charges z_1e and z_2e. For electrons, $z = -1$.

The description of matter by means of classical mechanics, with point particles interacting by the electrostatic force just given, in accordance with Newton's laws of motion, is impossible. Classically, our world cannot exist. Quantum mechanics must be used instead, and it gives a full and accurate description of matter, on the level of chemistry. It is a good enough approximation to consider the heavy nuclei as occupying definite positions, and to provide an electric field in which the electrons move, subject to their mutual repulsion. The motion of the nuclei can be described classically, but the electrons are a different matter. The electrons occupy most of the volume in a molecule. The volume that an electron occupies depends on the attractive electric field. A nucleus draws the electrons neutralizing its charge closely around it, in a sphere of about 0.1 nm radius. All atoms are about the same size, since z electrons are attracted by a nuclear charge of ze, so that more electrons means stronger attraction, so the electrons huddle more closely.

The motion of the electrons is described by a *wave function* that is a solution of the Schrödinger equation with the electrostatic potentials of nuclear attraction and electronic repulsion in the Hamiltonian. In this way, an electron "feels" all of the region in which it moves. Generally, we take as a first approximation a single electron moving in the average field of all the other charged particles. These approximations are necessary for finding solutions in a practical case, but are not fundamental. In a particular *stationary state* the electron is described by a wave function called an *orbital*, to which corresponds an energy. That is, an electron "occupying" the state has the energy corresponding to the orbital. In any problem, we can find (in principle) many states, with energies from some minimum upwards. Then we "assign" electrons to the states to determine the overall state of the atom or molecule. The states themselves are dependent on which other states are occupied, and which are not, so we must adopt some kind of iterative approach (called the *self-consistent field*).

An atom or molecule is usually electrically neutral: it contains equal amounts of negative and positive charge. If this is not true, very strong forces are exerted on other charged atoms or molecules and something vigorous occurs. When salt is dissolved in water, Na^+ and Cl^- ions are formed in large numbers. If they were not very well mixed, extraordinary things would happen. Without the Cl^-, the Na^+ ions would instantly rush to the limits of the solution, like a charge on a metal sphere, and a powerful spark would attract electrons from the air.

Not only are the ions well mixed, but each is surrounded by an atmosphere of polar water molecules, the positive hydrogens clustered around a chlorine ion, the negative unbonded electrons of the oxygens clustered around a sodium ion. These micelles spread the ionic charge over a larger volume, and the ionic charges are distributed to screen one another well. An applied electrostatic field will cause the ions to drift in the appropriate directions, the sodium to the cathode (-), the chlorine to the anode (+). We also note that the sodium ions do not behave anything like sodium metal, and the chlorine ions do not behave anything like chlorine gas.

The energy of an isolated system is constant. However, if a collection of nuclei and electrons can rearrange themselves to give a lower energy, and the excess energy can be carried away somehow, we have a *chemical reaction*. In most practical cases, systems are in thermal contact, so that the criterion for stability is a minimum of the *free energy* $a = u - Ts + Pv$, and not just a minimum of the *internal energy* u. Let's simply talk of u instead here, letting it refer to whatever thermodynamic potential that is appropriate. Therefore, if we bring two systems into contact, they may rearrange themselves to form a new system of lower energy, dissipating the excess energy by collision or by breaking into two or more parts with kinetic energy. This is the *only* reason for a chemical reaction. All binding energy in molecules is electrostatic. A molecule is stable if its energy is less than that of any other configuration accessible to it. When different molecules come together, there may be rearrangements of smaller energy, and a *reaction* may occur.

For a reaction to occur, the reactants must be brought together physically, and in such an orientation that the reaction may proceed, rather than repulsion. This means, generally, that there are only two reactants (unless by some means we can bring more than two reactants to bear at the same time) and they must be properly oriented so that they attract. Some of the kinetic energy of the molecules may be used to attain a favorable configuration. Two free hydrogen atoms, for example, are each electrically neutral and quite happy. They exert no forces on each other until they approach closely, so that their electrons overlap. With the nuclei at a certain distance apart, the Schrödinger equation gives two orbitals, one of low energy (the bonding orbital) where the two electrons are between the nuclei, and one of high energy (the antibonding orbital) where the two electrons are on the opposite sides of the nuclei. One electron of the two available put in the bonding orbital gives a stable system, H_2^+. We can put the second electron in the same orbital, provided its spin is opposite to the spin of the electron already there. Since the spin angular momenta are opposite, the net spin angular momentum is 0 (a *singlet* state). This is the stable H_2 molecule. If we happened to have a third electron, it could go nowhere but in the antibonding orbital, so the H_2^- ion would have about the binding energy of H_2^+. H_2 in the *triplet* state, where the electron spins are in the same direction, would not be bound at all. To a (good) approximation, the spins have only a bookkeeping significance.

These things are illustrated at the right in an energy-level diagram. The energy ε is about 51 kcal/mol. The antibonding state is assumed to be as high above the zero level as the bonding state is below it. The *Pauli Principle* is that no two electrons may occupy the same state, since the wave function must change sign if the coordinates of any two electrons are interchanged. The "state" is assumed to include the spin. Electrons are exactly the same, and can be identified only by the quantum numbers specifying a state. An organic chemistry textbook can be happy saying in one place that "electrons tend to pair," and in another that "electrons repel." The statement that "electrons tend to pair" is not only wrong, it is misleading. The two electrons in H_2 are in the same state because all the other possibilities give higher energy. They actually would rather not be so close together, and their mutual repulsion decreases the binding energy somewhat. They form a pair out of necessity, not out of desire for one another. When electrons are being added to the 2p levels in B, C and N the spins are parallel in the ground state. In O, F and Ne they are forced to double up.

An equally misleading statement is that "electrons tend to form octets." The only reason for this is that when the eight 2s and 2p levels are filled, it is quite a jump in energy to the next available state, 3s. When the 3p levels are filled, the next are the 4s, not the 3d, and after the 4p levels, the next are the 5s. It just happens that at Ne, A, Kr, Xe and Rn, which have just completed s^2p^6 "shells" of 8 electrons, there is an energy gap to the next s level. No energy advantage can be gained by promoting an electron from the filled shell in most cases, so a *kernel* with a noble-gas structure generally remains untouched. The charge on the kernel is equal and opposite to the charge on the additional *valence* electrons. Electrons have no "tendency" to form groups of 8; it just works out that way. Of course, this is just a manner of speaking, but it should not be allowed to hide the real reason. There is a search for lowest energy. These "rules" are typical of organic chemistry, ascribing nonexistent wills and desires to electrons and atoms as explanations of physical phenomena. The tetrahedral angle of carbon bonding does not result from any love of carbon for 109° 28', but simply from the fact that this angle puts equivalent bonds as far from each other as possible. When conditions are not the same at the ends of the bonds, the angles are not exactly tetrahedral.

In H_2, the pair of bonding electrons occupy the bonding orbital, staying as far away from each other as they can in the limited volume. They are mainly between the two protons, screening them from each other, and symmetrically disposed relative to the horizontal plane of symmetry. The molecule is *quadrupolar,* with positive charges on the ends and a negative charge in the middle. Its electrical field decreases rapidly with distance from the molecule. Both the molecule and its bond are described as *nonpolar,* and the bond is called *covalent*. Suppose that one of the protons is replaced by a chlorine atom. This would affect the bonding orbital by pulling the electrons closer to the increased charge, and away from the other proton. The chlorine atom would "like to add one electron to its octet" in the usual parlance, meaning only that this would be energetically favorable. Now one end of the molecule would have an increased positive charge, the other end a negative charge of equal and opposite amount. This is a *dipole,* whose external field is stronger and of longer range than a quadrupole field. The molecule would be *polar,* and the bond has no good name in organic chemistry, except to call it a polar covalent bond.

The bonds in many organic compounds can be considered independent of one another, so that the total bond energy, the heat of formation, is approximately the sum of the individual bond energies. A table of bond energies is shown at the left. In many cases, the energy of a bond is affected by neighboring bonds. We will see that the energy of a C-H bond is affected by how many other carbons are bonded to the carbon (more carbons makes the bond weaker), and that the C-OH bond in the carboxyl radical COOH is affected by the presence of the C=O nearby. Also, energies depending on the state of the substance are not included. The heat of evaporation of water, for example, is about 9.7 kcal/mol, and the heat of fusion is about 1.4 kcal/mol. These rather unusually large figures show the limits of these effects. The energies of bonds not in the table can be estimated by comparison, or can be found from tabulated heats of formation in handbooks.

If we imagine an electron taken from one hydrogen atom and transferred to the chlorine, what results would be the ions H^+ and Cl^- that would attract one another electrostatically. In HCl gas, this does not quite happen, but HCl dissolves in water to form the ions, each surrounded by water molecules, or *solvated*. In salt, NaCl, the electron in the bond is similarly attracted to the Cl, or would be if this molecule existed. In solution, we have sodium and chlorine ions, as in the case of HCl, and if the water is evaporated, we have a crystal of salt, which contains Na^+ and Cl^- ions in a cubic lattice. The salt crystal is the state of least energy, and is one huge molecule. Chemists speak of an *ionic* bond in this case, though there is really no bond at all, unless it is a polar covalent bond or an expression for the crystal binding.

The covalent radii of atoms making single bonds are shown at the right. 10Å = 1 nm. The C-H bond is 0.77 + 0.29 = 1.06Å in length. The C-C bond is 2 x 0.77 = 1.54Å long. The results are approximate, of course, but the marvel is that these values are relatively consistent. The C=C bond is 1.33Å, and the Ca"C bond is 1.20Å. The C=O bond is 1.24Å, and the N=O bond 1.18Å. Multiple bonds are shorter than single bonds. By means of the tables just given, the sizes and heats of formation of organic compounds can be estimated. A good set of molecular models also makes clear the spatial configurations.

Three possible structures can be drawn for the carbonate ion, CO_3^{-}. The kernels have charge 22, and there are 24 valence electrons. In each structure, there is a double bond with one oxygen, and single bonds to the others. The state of the ion is a linear combination of equal amounts of the three structures shown. The result is that the three oxygens are equivalent, and located at the corners of an equilateral triangle. The C-O bond length is 1.31Å, intermediate between the C-O and the C=O lengths. The ion is more stable than any one of the contributing structures, the result of having the freedom of making a linear combination of them to construct the actual state. In chemistry, this is called *resonance*, although there is no actual resonance involved. The name is derived from an early semiclassical model. Protons can adhere to any of the free pairs, two protons making the molecule neutral, which is carbonic acid, H_2CO_3. If the two protons carry away an oxygen, the result is CO_2 and a molecule of water.

Exactly the same thing occurs with the nitrate ion, NO_3^-, but here the kernel charge is +23 and there are 24 electrons, as before. Three possible structures of reasonable stability can be drawn as before, and the actual state is the linear combination of them. The nitrate ion is triangular, stable, and with an N-O bond length of 1.22Å.

The carboxyl group -COOH ionizes to $-COO^-$ and H^+ in water, as we have already seen with acetic acid. Two structures are possible for the ionized group, shown at the left. The actual state is a linear combination with equal weights, making the two oxygens equivalent. A bond picture is shown in the diagram; the reader may want to construct the Lewis structures. Resonance in these structures makes the acetate ion more stable, and increases the probability that the -COOH will ionize. In chloroacetic acid, $CH_2ClCOOH$, the chlorine pulls electrons towards it, and away from the oxygen in the -OH group. This makes it easier for water to pull off the hydrogen, so chloroacetic acid is a stronger acid than acetic, with $K = 1.396 \times 10^{-3}$. Dichloroacetic acid is still stronger, at $K = 5 \times 10^{-2}$, and trichloroacetic acid, $K = 0.13$, is as strong as sulphuric acid.

Another form of bonding is shown at the left for SO_2. The kernel charge is +18, and there are 18 electrons, so the molecule is neutral. The 18 electrons can be distributed in two ways so that each atom has a completed octet. In each way, one of the oxygens is bonded by a pair of electrons donated by the sulphur. The two structures resonate so that the oxygens are equivalent and the molecule is symmetric. Note that each Lewis structure has a formal charge of +1/2 on the S, and -1/2 on the O. In the actual molecule, the S will have a formal charge of +1/2, and each oxygen a formal charge of -1/4. The oxygens pull the electrons towards themselves, leaving the sulphur slightly positive. This type of bond is called a "semi-polar double bond," or a "coordinate covalent bond," neither name being particularly descriptive or fortunate. Although the electrons "donated by the sulphur" are distinguished in the figure, electrons arrange themselves for the lowest energy, and cannot remember to what atoms they belong.

ORGANIC COMPOUNDS

Carbon atoms can join to each other to form chains and rings of any desired complexity. A few examples are shown at the right. In them, carbon makes four bonds at tetrahedral angles (109° 28'). We assume that all the bonds not shown in the figure are with hydrogen atoms, so that all these molecules are *hydrocarbons*. Two major classes are the molecules without rings, which form tree-like branching molecules, and those with rings. Of course, the two classes may be combined in any way. Only the simpler structures are commonly found, however. The compounds are named according to the number of carbon atoms in them. The branched molecules can also be named by the IUC system, in which the longest chain of carbons gives the basic name, and the side chains are considered as substituents. The carbons of the longest chain are given serial numbers so that the smallest numbers appear in the name. For example, 2-methylpropane has a methyl group (CH_3) attached to carbon 2 of the propane chain.

All compounds like those shown in the figure are called *paraffins* or *alkanes*. The acyclic paraffins have the molecular formula C_nH_{2n+2} (no matter how they are branched), and the *cycloparaffins*, C_nH_{2n}. A series of compounds differing only by CH_2 groups is called a *homologous series*. The first three cyclic paraffins are planar, and the bond angles are considerably changed from the tetrahedral value, which makes them less stable than if they had tetrahedral angles. The angle 108° is shown for cyclopentane, but the molecule is actually not planar and the actual angles are close to the tetrahedral value. Cyclohexane has the tetrahedral bond angles, and is not planar. It exists in two conformations, called *boat* and *chair*, depending on whether two ends are both tipped in the same direction, or opposite directions. The cycloparaffins are not very important compounds, though interesting ones.

Carbons with three hydrogens attached are called *primary*, with two hydrogens *secondary*, with one hydrogen tertiary, and when attached only to carbon, *quaternary*. Primary hydrogens are more strongly bound than secondary, and secondary more than tertiary. Free radicals attack tertiary hydrogen most effectively, secondary hydrogens less effectively, and primary hydrogens least effectively. Straight-chain hydrocarbons without branches are called *normal*. Normal butane, for example, may be written n-butane. Usually, if the "n" is omitted, the paraffin is considered to be normal. There is only one structure for methane, ethane and propane, but all higher paraffins have *isomers* with the same molecular formula but different structures. Pentane has 3 isomers, but dodecane (12 carbons) already has 355 isomers.

The paraffin chains are not actually straight lines, but zigzag ones as each carbon maintains tetrahedral bond angles. They can rotate freely about any bond, so they represent more a plate of spaghetti than a pile of rods. All the paraffins have about the same chemical properties. They do not react with any of the common reagents, which gave them the name "paraffin" from Latin *parum*, "slight" and *affinis*, "affinity." They do react readily with free radicals, which displace the hydrogens, notably in the reaction of burning. They are colorless and odorless. They dissolve in organic (nonpolar) solvents, but not in water. The melting and boiling temperatures increase with the number of carbon atoms, and are lower for the more compact molecules that do not get entangled so easily. At room temperature, methane to butane are gases, pentane to nonadecane (19 carbons) liquids, and eicosane and above solids. Eicosane, with 20 carbons, is a soft gel at room temperature, typical of petroleum jelly. Cetane, or n-hexadecane, with 16 carbons, melts at just below room temperature and boils at 287.5°C. Examples of paraffins are easy to find in daily life: natural gas (methane), gasoline, kerosene, lubricating oils, petroleum jelly and wax.

The primary source of paraffins is petroleum. Some high-quality crude oils consist almost entirely of acyclic paraffins. They can be separated by fractional distillation into fractions with small ranges of numbers of carbons. The *bubble tower* fractionating column was introduced in the 1920's, replacing the simple still and condenser. Straight fractionation yields naphtha (gasoline, boiling 40°C-180°C, 5-10 carbons), distillate (kerosene, boiling 180°C-230°C, 10-13 carbons), gas oil (fuel oil, boiling 230°C-400°C, 13-25 carbons), heavy oils (lubricating oils, boiling 400°C-500°C, 20-30 carbons) and bottoms (wax, tar and asphalt, more than 30 carbons). The predominant demand for motor fuels prompted a search for ways of increasing the amount of gasoline produced from a barrel of crude, which was originally only about 25% (it was then a waste product). In 1913, *cracking* of the heavier fractions by catalysis and heat was introduced, which doubled the gasoline yield. This scrambling of the structures introduced more branched paraffins, which burn more smoothly in an internal-combustion engine than straight chains. This alone boosted the octane rating from about 50 to over 70. Catalytic polymerization or *reforming* (catalytic cyclodehydrogenation), together with hydrogenation, adds additional compounds with high anti-knock value, such as "iso-octane." Isooctane is 2,2,4-trimethylpentane. The octane number of a fuel is the percentage of isooctane in a mixture with n-heptane that has the same anti-knock properties. Isooctane, then, represents a 100-octane fuel, n-heptane a 0 octane fuel. Isooctane melts at -107.4°C and boils at 99.2°C, while n-heptane melts at -90.6°C and boils at 98.4°C. These figures are typical of "gasoline," which must be liquid and volatile at ordinary temperatures.

Petroleum is the *only* cheap natural source of paraffin hydrocarbons, supplying ethylene and propylene, the raw material for plastics, alcohol, acetylene, phenol, detergents and other basic industrial chemicals. It is a waste to squander petroleum as a fuel, but because of its present cheapness this is its principal use. If anything, the parallel misuse of natural gas is even worse. When petroleum becomes scarce and expensive (and it will, not far in the future and quite suddenly), the effect on the chemical industry will be far worse than the effect on fuel supplies. There are alternative fuels, but no alternative cheap source of paraffins.

Two carbon atoms can be joined by double or triple bonds, and this gives further prospects for molecules. Some important examples are shown at the left. A compound that contains double or triple bonds between carbons is called *unsaturated*, while those with only single bonds are *saturated*. Just as saturated compounds are called *alkanes*, those with double bonds are *alkenes* and those with triple bonds *alkynes*. Aliphatic compounds with multiple bonds between carbons are, in general, called *olefins*. The most important are the alkene ethylene and the alkyne acetylene, which are important starting points for making other organic compounds because of the activity of the double bonds, which also make *polymerization* possible. The *thermoplastics* we see every day are an example. Ethylene polymerizes into a saturated compound called polyethylene, or PE. This is made in two forms, high-density HDPE and low-density LDPE. Propylene polymerizes to polypropylene, PP, which is stronger than PE. If one hydrogen is replaced by a chlorine to form ethylene chloride, more commonly called vinyl chloride, the result is the saturated polymer polyvinyl chloride, or PVC. If a benzene ring is used instead of chlorine, the result is polystyrene, PS. Plastic articles usually carry a recycling symbol indicating the polymer used by a number in a triangle, plus the symbols given above. HDPE is 2, PVC is 3, LDPE is 4, PP is 5 and PS is 6.

The addition of oxygen to our toolbox gives further possibilities. We can base a series of compounds on a fundamental compound, such as water, HOH. If an H is replaced by any paraffin, denoted by R, we get ROH, which is an *alcohol*. The simplest alcohol is CH_3OH, methanol. We can make alcohols by sticking one or more OH, *hydroxyl*, groups on any of the paraffins. $(CH_2OH)_2$ (1,2 dihydroxyethane) is glycol, famous from car antifreezes. $(CH_2OH)(CHOH)(CH_2OH)$ (1,2,3-trihydroxypropane) is glycerol or glycerine. Mannitol has 6 hydroxys, with 3 more CHOH groups added to glycerol. The OH makes these molecules soluble in water if the R part is small enough. The H can even come off as H^+, and ionic reactions can occur. The essential thing here is the -OH group, which is called the *functional group* of the alcohols, and is responsible for their particular properties. An alcohol never lets go of the O, however.

If both of the hydrogens in HOH are replaced by paraffin groups, which may be the same or different, the result is an *ether*. The simplest ether is CH_3OCH_3, methyl ether, a gas. Ethyl ether, $(C_2H_5)_2O$, a volatile liquid, is the familiar ether that was used as a general anesthetic, and is a useful solvent. It boils at 34.6°C and is very inflammable. On long standing, or if the bottle is exposed to sunlight, explosive peroxides can form. The vapour explodes in concentrations of 1.85% to 36.5%, and the ignition temperature is only 180°C. Ether is more hazardous than gasoline.

The convenient abbreviations Me = CH_3 for the methyl group, and Et = C_2H_5 for the ethyl group, will often be used in what follows.

Alcohols and ethers are both derived from water, HOH, but they act very differently. In alcohols, the OH group may donate a hydrogen: ROH $\rightarrow$ RO^- + H^+. Then it is a Brönsted-Lowry acid, or proton donor, and its anion RO^- a base, or proton acceptor. MeOH is methanol, and MeO^- is the methoxide anion, a strong base. The lone pairs of electrons on the O may attract the H from another molecule, forming a *hydrogen bond*. The hydrogen bond is what gives water its peculiar properties, such as high melting and boiling temperatures. The lighter alcohols share this peculiarity: even MeOH is a liquid. Higher alcohols become less and less like water as their alkyl parts dominate.

None of this can happen with an ether, ROR′, so there is no acid-base behaviour, and no hydrogen bonding, even with the lightest memeber, MeOMe. Indeed, methyl ether is a gas, and ethyl ether a very volatile liquid. With no hydrogen, there is no easy point of chemical attack in an ether, and they are as inert to ionic reactions as paraffins.

Carbon can form a double bond with oxygen, to make the *carbonyl* group =C=O, in which the carbon has two free valences. The basic compound is HCHO, formaldehyde, where the two free valences are satisfied by hydrogens. Then we can add a hydrocarbon R to make the series of compounds RCHO, which are called *aldehydes*. A second hydrocarbon R′, that may be different from R or the same, then gives the compounds R(CO)R′, called *ketones*. The reason the two kinds of compounds are distinguished is that the CHO group of an aldehyde behaves somewhat differently than the CO group of a ketone, just as the OH of an alcohol behaves differently from the O of an ether. Further examples are CH_3CHO, acetaldehyde (a gas), and CH_3COCH_3, acetone or dimethyl ketone (a liquid). Methyl ethyl ketone, called MEK, is a popular solvent, as is acetone.

The carbonyl and hydroxyl groups can be combined into the *carboxyl* group, (C=O)OH or COOH. The two groups modify each other's behaviour considerably. The H comes off more easily than in an alcohol, leaving a COO^- ion in which the oxygens are equivalent (a case of resonance, mentioned above, which is the reason for the behaviour), and a H^+ ion. They are stronger acids than the alcohols. Conversely, their bases, such as $MeCOO^-$, the acetate ion, are weaker. They will form salts with cations, such as MeCOONa, sodium acetate. Compounds containing the COOH group are called *organic acids*, of which CH_3COOH, acetic acid, is a familiar example. The simplest organic acid is HCOOH, formic acid (found in ants, *formicae*). HOOC-COOH is oxalic acid. HOOC-CH_2-COOH is malonic acid.

Cyclohexane, C_6H_{12}, is a typical paraffin, containing only single bonds. We have mentioned above that it is not a planar molecule, and has two conformations. The very different compound C_6H_6, called benzene, was first found in the liquids obtained by distilling coal. In German, it is known as benzol. Benzine is an impure benzene that can be used as a motor fuel. It is a colorless, volatile liquid with a characteristic odor and density 0.88. It is carcinogenic. Faraday studied benzene in 1825, but it was known to Schelenz in 1785. Benzene is found in some petroleums, in addition to coal tar. It has only half as much hydrogen, and is a planar molecule of high stability. The fewer hydrogens suggest that it is unsaturated, but it does not act like any of the unsaturated hydrocarbons. It is the basis of a large number of compounds, called *aromatic* compounds from the pleasant aroma of benzene and of many compounds containing the benzene ring, including many flavorings. The best traditional structural formula, the Kekulé formula, is shown at the upper left. It features alternating double and single bonds, called *conjugated double bonds*. (As usual, hydrogen is not shown explicitly.) A space-filling model is shown at the left. However, benzene does not behave like linear molecules with conjugated double bonds in any way. There are six electrons in addition to those required for the single bonds, and these six electrons are free to move in circles above and below the plane of the molecule. This mobility, similar to the "resonance" we have encountered above, allows a large binding energy, which makes benzene very stable. This is indicated by the hexagon at the right, where a carbon and hydrogen are understood at each vertex, and the circle represents the six ring electrons. A hexagonal skeleton is often used to represent a benzene ring.

Substituting a methyl group for a hydrogen gives toluene, also an aromatic liquid. Toluene is not carcinogenic and you can safely smell it. Its odor resembles that of benzene, but is not as pleasant. A second methyl group could go onto any one of three vertices to make distinct compounds. These vertices are denoted by ortho, meta and para, which are abbreviated o-, m- and p-. Xylene has two methyl groups, and three isomers, o-xylene, m-xylene and p-xylene. In the figure, m-xylene is shown. The functional groups OH and COOH can be added to the benzene ring, producing *phenols* and *aromatic acids*. Adding an OH to toluene gives a *cresol*. Phenol was discovered in 1834 by Runge, who named it *carbolic acid*. In 1841, Laurent obtained it in pure form, calling it *acide phénique*. In the same year, Gerhardt named it phenol. The OH in a phenol acts differently from the OH in an alcohol, since the attraction of the benzene ring for electrons makes it easier for phenol to ionize as an acid. In fact, it is known popularly as benzoic acid. The group BzO^- resulting from this ionization is called the *phenoxy* group (Bz represents a benzene nucleus). There can be more than one OH group, as in resorcinol and hydroquinone. These can be named systematically as m-dihydroxybenzene and p-dihydroxybenzene. If the benzene ring is not adjacent to the OH group, the compound acts like an alcohol, and is called an aromatic alcohol. For example, $Bz(CH_2)OH$, benzyl alcohol. The COOH groups behave similarly, making stronger acids than when attached to an alkane. Again, more than one group can appear on a benzene nucleus. Terephthalic acid has two COOH groups in the para position. In the meta position, the compound is called isophthalic acid, and in the ortho position, phthalic acid. Mellitic acid has six carboxyl groups, hemimellitic acid three.

Phenol is a colorless solid, melting at 40.9°C and boiling at 181.8°C, with a characteristic odor suggesting disinfection. It is an excellent antiseptic, but is also corrosive to tissues and poisonous, so it has largely been replaced by other compounds, some of them related to phenol. It is found in wood and coal smoke, and with formaldehyde gives the preserving power of smoking. The name comes from the Greek fainos, "shining," because it was found in the distillate from making illuminating gas. Benzol is not phenol, but the German name for benzene. Benzene itself has a similarly tortuous etymology, being originally from Arabic *luban jawi*, the "frankincense of Java," through "benjoin" after dropping the article lu-, then to the aromatic "gum benzoin" and finally to benzene. Gum benzoin contains cinnamic acid, which is ethylene with Bz on one carbon and COOH on the other.

The benzene ring can also act as the R groups in ethers, aldehydes and ketones. These are called *aryl* radicals, Ar, as the R were alkyl radicals. Benzaldehyde, BzCHO, a colorless liquid smelling like almonds, is an example. Adding an OH in the para position, and OMe (methoxy) in the meta position gives *vanillin*, a very popular flavoring. Benzene rings can also fuse, as in naphthalene (mothballs), anthracene and phenanthrene. The typical inertness of benzene disappears as more rings are fused. The limit is reached in graphite, which consists of sheets of fused benzene rings. Benzene, and some of the fused ring compounds, are powerful carcinogens, and contact with them should be avoided. Other aromatic compounds have no carcinogenic properties at all.

We can take a closer look at naphthalene, which forms many useful compounds. The carbons are not all equivalent, as in benzene. They are numbered as shown in the diagram. Carbons 1, 4, 5 and 8 are called á-carbons or 1-carbons, carbons 2, 3, 6 and 7 are called â-carbons or 2-carbons. The bonds of the other two carbons are all involved in the naphthalene core, so substitutions cannot take place at these locations. An -OH substitution can make two phenol-like molecules, á naphthol (1-naphthol) or â naphthol (2-naphthol), with closely similar but not identical properties. á-naphthol smells faintly of phenol, but â-naphthol is odorless. â-naphthol is triboluminescent. Both naphthols irritate the nose, have a burning taste, and crystallize in the monoclinic system. The melting points are 96°C and 122°C, respectively. Their densities are about 1.22. The melting point of naphthalene itself is 80.2°C, and it boils at 218°C; its density is 1.1517. From alcoholic solution, it crystallizes in colorless plates. Naphthalene has a strong characteristic odor, and is not carcinogenic. Naphthalene is not only found in coal tar, but also in some petroleums, such as that from Puente Hills, California.

We have now looked at many carbon compounds that can be made with C, H and O only, as well as at the functional groups OH, CO, and COOH. We have met the alkanes, alkenes, alkynes, and aromatics, and have become acquainted with alcohols, ethers, aldehydes, ketones and acids. These building blocks can be put together in limitless ways. We have not even considered the compounds of biological importance, such as sugars, amino acids, fats and oils, starch and cellulose. For the biological compounds, the reader is advised to refer to Stryer. We have not even considered the halogens: fluorine, chlorine, bromine and iodine, that can replace hydrogens in any of the compounds so far considered. Rings containing nitrogen (heterocyclics) have not been mentioned, nor the functional groups -NO_2 (nitro), -NH_2 (amino), -Ca"N (cyanide or nitrile), =C=N- (imine), and many others. Compounds in which S replaces O are yet to be mentioned.

ORGANIC REACTIONS

The reactions of inorganic chemistry usually take place in aqueous solution, where the water pulls apart the reagents into ions and allows them to move and interact freely. Occasionally reactions occur in fused reagents, between gases, or in the solid state where exchanges with the gaseous state can take place. The reactions are generally fast, and often go to completion. In organic chemistry, there are often other solvents than water, since most of the compounds are not soluble in water and do not form ions. Even where molecules are mobile, as in liquids and gases, reactions are often slow and incomplete. Even when a reaction is very exothermic, the reactants may not react. For a reaction to occur, the reagents must be able to try out various alternatives to see which ones will lead to a reduction in free energy, so that the reaction may proceed. A reaction must have a definite *mechanism* that permits it to proceed with reasonable speed. The reaction path may be *reversible*, so that the products can react to produce the reagents as well as the reagents can react to produce the products. This situation is well-known in chemistry, and is expressed by the law of mass action and equilibrium constants. An organic reaction may follow several paths, with different probabilities and different products. Often the particular products are a clue to the reaction mechanism.

In the rest of this section, some reaction mechanisms will be discussed from a theoretical point of view in an effort to find out what is going on.

Organic chemistry has a very different practical side, however. The best conditions for a particular reaction have been empirically determined, and a definite procedure prescribed for it. An organic chemistry review book lists 258 named reactions. This "cookbook" approach is very practical and effective, but tends to obscure basic principles. The reader is referred to texts on organic chemistry for the practical details of reactions. One is struck by the fact that discussions of organic reactions involve practically no mathematics or fundamental theory, and instead are based on qualitative theories and empirical rules. In principle, every question could be answered by numerical calculation on the basis of quantum mechanics, but this procedure is impossibly complicated besides being unilluminating. The wonder is that the empirical approach of organic chemistry is so useful and illuminating. The reader is warned, however, that this is a very complex and confusing subject, with an appallingly large literature.

Free-Radical and Ionic Reactions

If we drop sodium metal in water, the vigorous reaction evolves hydrogen gas and produces sodium and hydroxide ions: $2Na + 2HOH \rightarrow 2Na^+ + 2OH^- + H_2$. If we drop sodium metal in EtOH, a milder reaction has this result: $2Na + 2EtOH \rightarrow 2Na^+ + 2EtO^- + H_2$ (Note: Et = ethyl). The ethoxide ion, EtO^- is produced. If we evaporate the remaining alcohol, we get crystals of EtONa, sodium ethoxide. When dropped in water, EtONa is hydrolyzed to make EtOH, Na^+ and OH^-. The solvent in any reaction using EtONa should be EtOH, not water. This reaction can be imagined for any alcohol, so we have available in principle any alkoxyl ion we desire.

We have already mentioned that a mixture of methane and chlorine gases does not react in the dark, though the reaction is strongly favored energetically. If a chlorine molecule is split by absorbing light, however, we now have free-radical Cl. (the dot represents an electron available for a bond) and a reaction mechanism for producing methyl chlorides. Probability makes MeCl the predominant product. Using this rapid chain reaction makes alkyl chlorides available to us, and alkyl chlorides are more subject to chemical attack than the alkanes. The C-H bond is tight and nonpolar; there is no place to gain an electrical hold on it. Only the free-radical attack is successful, since Cl. can tear the H away from the C to form HCl. Now we can make other compounds by *substitution*, where the Cl is replaced by some group of our choosing.

Nucleophilic Substitution

When one of the hydrogens of methane is replaced by chlorine to make chloromethane, the carbon-chlorine bond becomes slightly polar, the carbon aquiring a net charge +ä and the chlorine a net charge -ä This creates a dipole, with a rather long-range electrostatic field. A group with negative charge is attracted to the carbon, and this group could be OH^-. It is not necessary for the attracted group to be negatively charged, since a neutral group could be polarized by the field and still attracted. It is necessary that this group be a strong base, eager to donate an unbonded pair of electrons to make a bond. Such a group that seeks out a positive charge is called *nucleophilic*. The number of unbonded pairs, and the number available for nucleophilic attack, is shown at the right for the atoms of the first period.

The importance of nitrogen and oxygen is evident. When the nucleophile approaches the carbon, electrons are repelled by its charge onto the chlorine atom, which becomes even more negative and independent. In the final stage, the OH can bond to the carbon by means of a lone pair of electrons on the oxygen, while the chlorine drifts away taking a pair of electrons with it. The net reaction is $OH^- + CH_3Cl \rightarrow CH_3OH + Cl^-$. This reaction is called *nucleophilic substitution* and denoted S_N2. The S means substitution, the N nucleophilic, and the 2 means that the rate depends on the collision of two species, and so is proportional to the product of their concentrations. This is a *type mechanism* that describes a family of similar reactions. From stronger to weaker, some important nucleophiles, or bases, are NH_2^-, EtO^-, OH^- and CH_3COO^-. Suppose we have some ethoxide anion, EtO^-. This anion is strongly nucleophilic, so when ethyl bromide, EtBr is available, it may attack the positive carbon bound to the bromine. It donates its free electron pair, and the bromine goes off with the displaced electron pair, in accordance with the general mechanism of the S_N2 reaction.

This is shown schematically in the diagram at the left. The products are ethyl ether, EtOEt and a bromine ion. If we used MeO^- instead, we would get MeOEt, methyl ethyl ether. It is clear that, in principle, we now have a means of synthesizing any alkyl ether we may want. If we use the cyanide (nitrile) ion CN^- instead, we obtain EtCN.

Now we have succeeded in lengthening the carbon chain by one carbon. If we can replace the nitrogen, we will have a propyl compound. Since there is a large variety of nucleophilic groups, we can make a large variety of compounds. Water will not work in this reaction, because HOH is too weak a base (it is a fairly strong base, actually, but not strong enough). F^- will not work either, since it is too strongly solvated and will not donate its unbonded pairs, although it has three. Groups containing nitrogen work very well, since nitrogen is willing to donate its unbonded pair to make a new bond. NH_3, in particular is a very strong base, forming the ammonium ion NH_4^+ if protons are available. In the substitution reaction, ammonia yields *amines*, such as $EtNH_2$, primary ethylamine. The nitrogen can be further attacked in the same way, until $(Et)_4NBr$, tetraethylammonium bromide, is formed. Now the nitrogen has no unbonded pairs left. These amines are bases, forming, for example, ions like $EtNH_3^+$, ethylammonium, that form salts.

Elimination

However, the ethyl bromide also contains hydrogens, and the ethoxide anion could pick one off the neutral carbon that is not bound to the bromine and go off as EtOH, releasing an electron pair that then makes another carbon-carbon bond, again displacing the bromine on the other end. The net result in this case is a molecule of ethyl alcohol, a molecule of ethylene, and a bromine ion. This second reaction is called an *elimination,* denoted E2. The elements of HBr have been eliminated from the ethyl bromide. By means of this reaction, we can synthesize ethylene, an important source of further compounds, as well as further alkenes. The double bond will now be the point of attack. Another kind of elimination is based on quaternary amines, such as $CH_3CH_2N(CH_{23})_3$, where a nucleophile, say OH^-, picks off one of the hydrogen atoms on the CH_3 group. This creates a double bond between the carbons, and releases an electron pair to the electrophile nitrogen, which now happily goes its way as $N(CH_3)_3$, trimethyl amine (which smells like rotting fish). The result is ethylene, water and the amine. This is a general reaction for creating a double bond in whatever you attach to the amine, called *Hofmann elimination*. This reaction is an example of one of the many named reactions in organic chemistry, which are an organic chemist's stock-in-trade. The mechanism of the reaction may not be understood, but it still works.

Carbonium Ions

There is another way to perform a substitution, which more closely resembles an inorganic ionic reaction. If an alkane should ionize like MeCl $\rightarrow Me^+ + Cl^-$ to form a *carbonium* ion Me^+, this ion could then react quickly with any anion around, such as OH^- in water, to form MeOH and the ions of HCl. Methane will not form a carbonium ion even with all the blandishments of polar water, but tertiary carbons (those bound to only one hydrogen) hold their hydrogens more weakly, and may be induced to form a carbonium ion, such as $(Me)_3C^+$ (tertiary butyl carbonium ion), which then rapidly forms tert-butyl alcohol if it finds any OH^- around. The rate of this reaction depends only on the concentration of the carbonium ion, so it is effectively monomolecular. This kind of substitution reaction is denoted S_N1. Carbonium ions are quite rare, so this reaction is also rare.

Electrophilic Addition

An unsaturated molecule such as ethylene can undergo reactions in which a pair of electrons is removed from the double bond and is used to attach new groups to the two carbons. Such reactions are called *additions*. When X-Y is added to $H_2C{=}CH_2$, the product is $XH_2C\text{-}CH_2Y$. Of course, the addition can occur across any C-C double bond, not just the one in ethylene. If X-Y is H_2, the reaction is called *hydrogenation*. This is an exothermic reaction, as we can see by comparing the heats of formation of ethane and ethylene, and deducting the energy required to dissociate the H_2. Using the table of bond energies given above, the heat of formation of ethane is 84 + 6 x 98 = 672 kcal/mol. The heat of formation of ethylene is 150 + 4 x 98 = 542, to which we must add the 102 kcal/mol required to break the H-H bond, for a total of 644 kcal/mol. The hydrogenation of ethylene is exothermic to the amount of 28 kcal/mol, so it is energetically favored.

However, if you mix ethylene and hydrogen, nothing will happen even if you wait forever. There is no mechanism that will lead to the desired final state of ethane from this initial state. Even light will not work, since it requires 4.4 eV to dissociate hydrogen and produce free radicals, and this is more than ordinary daylight can provide. If we had free radicals, however, they would certainly be able to pick apart the double bond, and this is one mechanism for the addition reaction.

An ionized proton, H^+, however, actively seeks out electrons where it can find them, and when it does, it will form a bond of considerable strength, since the proton is small. The proton, and similar electron-seekers such as NH_4^+, are called *electrophiles*. They will attack the large electron density in a double bond, and will muscle in to share the bounty. A proton will go right ahead and make a new C-H bond, leaving the other carbon with a positive charge (since it has effectively lost an electron). This carbon will then woo any nucleophiles that happen to be around in its search for neutrality. HBr will add to ethylene to form $H_3C\text{-}H_2Br$, ethyl bromide. The mechanism of this reaction is shown at the right. Even Br_2 will add in this way, since it ionizes slightly to form $Br^+ + Br^-$. To see this, you must be in the dark, since light easily dissociates bromine to make free radicals with much greater probability. The dissociation into ions is called *heterolysis*, while dissociation into free radicals is called *homolysis*. Either way we have addition to the double bond, in the first case by *electrophilic attack*, and in the latter by a free-radical reaction.

Sulphuric acid, $HOSO_3H$ (written this way to exhibit the hydrogen sulphate nucleophilic anion) also adds across the double bond in ethylene to form ethyl hydrogen sulphate, an ester that is hydrolyzed in water to form ethanol and sulphuric acid (recall that esterification is a reversible reaction).

This reaction is the basis for the industrial process that makes ethanol from "cracked" petroleum, which contains ethylene. The demand for alcohol is so large that it can no longer be satisfied by alcohol from fermentation.

An alcohol can be dehydrated by a strong acid by electrophilic attack by the H^+ on the oxygen of the -OH group of the alcohol, to add the proton and make an *oxonium* ion. This oxonium ion is then attacked by the nucleophile (the anion of the acid) which picks off a hydrogen from the end farthest from the oxygen, and electron pairs then cascade onto the HOH at the other end, releasing it as the amine was released above. The result, if ethanol was dehydrated, is water, acid and ethylene. We shall see that ethanol can be made from ethylene, so we can move easily from one to the other, depending on what is required. This is an example of addition followed by elimination. Electrophilic attack by something larger than a proton forms a positively-charged bridge structure between the two carbons, which is easily disrupted by the approach of a nucleophile. Since the double bond draws electrons away from the carbons, they may fall victim to nucleophilic attack at the beginning. This makes a negatively charged carbon that will attract a positive ion, and again the addition is completed. In alkenes, this reaction usually does not occur, since the carbons are not positive enough to be attractive to a nucleophile. It does occur, however, for the C=O double bond, where the oxygen sucks electrons away from the carbon.

Boron, with its lack of valence electrons, is a strong electrophile, although not positively charged. Diborane, B_2H_6 can add to the double bonds in six molecules of ethylene to form two molecules of triethylene boron (or ethylene borane). This molecule hydrolyzes in acidic water to form ethane and boron hydroxide, or in alkaline hydrogen peroxide to form ethyl alcohol and boron hydroxide. The boron attacks the double bond, and bonds to one carbon, while the proton released bonds with the other carbon. This is yet another way of making alcohol out of petroleum.

PROTEINS ARE BUILT FROM A REPERTOIRE OF 20 AMINO ACIDS

Amino acids are the building blocks of proteins. An *α-amino acid* consists of a central carbon atom, called the *α carbon,* linked to an amino group, a carboxylic acid group, a hydrogen atom, and a distinctive R group. The R group is often referred to as the *side chain.* With four different groups connected to the tetrahedral α-carbon atom, α-amino acids are *chiral;* the two mirror-image forms are called the l isomer and the d isomer.

Only l amino acids are constituents of proteins. For almost all amino acids, the l isomer has *S* (rather than *R*) absolute configuration. Although considerable effort has gone into understanding why amino acids in proteins have this absolute configuration, no satisfactory explanation has been arrived at. It seems plausible that the selection of l over d was arbitrary but, once made, was fixed early in evolutionary history.

Amino acids in solution at neutral pH exist predominantly as *dipolar ions* (also called *zwitterions*). In the dipolar form, the amino group is protonated (-NH_3^+) and the carboxyl group is deprotonated (-COO^-). The ionization state of an amino acid varies with pH. In acid solution (e.g., pH 1), the amino group is protonated (-NH_3^+) and the carboxyl group is not dissociated (-COOH). As the pH is raised, the carboxylic acid is the first group to give up a proton, inasmuch as its pK_a is near 2. The dipolar form persists until the pH approaches 9, when the protonated amino group loses a proton.

Twenty kinds of side chains varying in *size, shape, charge, hydrogen-bonding capacity, hydrophobic character,* and *chemical reactivity* are commonly found in proteins. Indeed, all proteins in all species—bacterial, archaeal, and eukaryotic—are constructed from the same set of 20 amino acids. This fundamental alphabet of proteins is several billion years old. The remarkable range of functions mediated by proteins results from the diversity and versatility of these 20 building blocks.

Let us look at this set of amino acids. The simplest one is *glycine,* which has just a hydrogen atom as its side chain. With two hydrogen atoms bonded to the α-carbon atom, glycine is unique in being *achiral. Alanine,* the next simplest amino acid, has a methyl group (-CH_3) as its side chain.

Larger hydrocarbon side chains are found in *valine, leucine,* and *isoleucine. Methionine* contains a largely *aliphatic* side chain that includes a *thioether* (-S-) group. The side chain of isoleucine includes an additional chiral centre; only the isomer shown in figure is found in proteins. The larger aliphatic side chains are *hydrophobic*—that is, they tend to cluster together rather than contact water. The three-dimensional structures of water-soluble proteins are stabilized by this tendency of hydrophobic groups to come together, called *the hydrophobic effect*. The different sizes and shapes of these hydrocarbon side chains enable them to pack together to form compact structures with few holes. *Proline* also has an aliphatic side chain, but it differs from other members of the set of 20 in that its side chain is bonded to both the nitrogen and the α-carbon atoms. Proline markedly influences protein architecture because its ring structure makes it more conformationally restricted than the other amino acids.

Three amino acids with relatively simple *aromatic side chains* are part of the fundamental repertoire. *Phenylalanine,* as its name indicates, contains a phenyl ring attached in place of one of the hydrogens of alanine. The aromatic ring of *tyrosine* contains a hydroxyl group. This hydroxyl group is reactive, in contrast with the rather inert side chains of the other amino acids discussed thus far. *Tryptophan* has an indole ring joined to a methylene (-CH_2-) group; the indole group comprises two fused rings and an NH group. Phenylalanine is purely hydrophobic, whereas tyrosine and tryptophan are less so because of their hydroxyl and NH groups. The aromatic rings of tryptophan and tyrosine contain delocalized p electrons that strongly absorb ultraviolet light.

A compound's *extinction coefficient* indicates its ability to absorb light. Beer's law gives the absorbance (*A*) of light at a given wavelength:

A = ε clBeer's Law

where is the extinction coefficient [in units that are the reciprocals of molarity and distance in centimeters (M^{-1} cm^{-1})], *c* is the concentration of the absorbing species (in units of molarity, M), and *l* is the length through which the light passes (in units of centimeters). For tryptophan, absorption is maximum at 280 nm and the extinction coefficient is 3400 M^{-1} cm^{-1} whereas, for tyrosine, absorption is maximum at 276 nm and the extinction coefficient is a less-intense 1400 M^{-1} cm^{-1}. Phenylalanine absorbs light less strongly and at shorter wavelengths. The absorption of light at 280 nm can be used to estimate the concentration of a protein in solution if the number of tryptophan and tyrosine residues in the protein is known.

Two amino acids, *serine* and *threonine,* contain aliphatic *hydroxyl groups.* Serine can be thought of as a hydroxylated version of alanine, whereas threonine resembles valine with a hydroxyl group in place of one of the valine methyl groups. The hydroxyl groups on serine and threonine make them much more *hydrophilic* (water loving) and *reactive* than alanine and valine. Threonine, like isoleucine, contains an additional asymmetric centre; again only one isomer is present in proteins.

Cysteine is structurally similar to serine but contains a *sulfhydryl,* or *thiol* (-SH), group in place of the hydroxyl (-OH) group. The sulfhydryl group is much more reactive. Pairs of sulfhydryl groups may come together to form disulfide bonds, which are particularly important in stabilizing some proteins, as will be discussed shortly.

We turn now to amino acids with very polar side chains that render them highly hydrophilic. *Lysine* and *arginine* have relatively long side chains that terminate with groups that are *positively charged* at neutral pH. Lysine is capped by a primary amino group and arginine by a guanidinium group. *Histidine* contains an imidazole group, an aromatic ring that also can be positively charged.

With a pK_a value near 6, the imidazole group can be uncharged or positively charged near neutral pH, depending on its local environment. Indeed, histidine is often found in the active sites of enzymes, where the imidazole ring can bind and release protons in the course of enzymatic reactions. The set of amino acids also contains two with *acidic side chains: aspartic acid* and *glutamic acid*. These amino acids are often called *aspartate* and *glutamate* to emphasize that their side chains are usually negatively charged at physiological pH. Nonetheless, in some proteins these side chains do accept protons, and this ability is often functionally important. In addition, the set includes uncharged derivatives of aspartate and glutamate—*asparagine* and *glutamine*—each of which contains a terminal *carboxamide* in place of a carboxylic acid.

Seven of the 20 amino acids have readily ionizable side chains. These 7 amino acids are able to donate or accept protons to facilitate reactions as well as to form ionic bonds.

Amino acids are often designated by either a three-letter abbreviation or a one-letter symbol. The abbreviations for amino acids are the first three letters of their names, except for asparagine (Asn), glutamine (Gln), isoleucine (Ile), and tryptophan (Trp). The symbols for many amino acids are the first letters of their names (e.g., G for glycine and L for leucine); the other symbols have been agreed on by convention. These abbreviations and symbols are an integral part of the vocabulary of biochemists.

How did this particular set of amino acids become the building blocks of proteins? First, as a set, they are diverse; their structural and chemical properties span a wide range, endowing proteins with the versatility to assume many functional roles. Second, as noted in figure many of these amino acids were probably available from prebiotic reactions. Finally, excessive intrinsic reactivity may have eliminated other possible amino acids. For example, amino acids such as homoserine and homocysteine tend to form five-membered cyclic forms that limit their use in proteins; the alternative amino acids that are found in proteins—serine and cysteine—do not readily cyclize, because the rings in their cyclic forms are too small.

Proteins are the workhorses of biochemistry, participating in essentially all cellular processes. Protein structure can be described at four levels. The primary structure refers to the amino acid sequence. The secondary structure refers to the conformation adopted by local regions of the polypeptide chain. Tertiary structure describes the overall folding of the polypeptide chain. Finally, quaternary structure refers to the specific association of multiple polypeptide chains to form multisubunit complexes.

Proteins Are Built from a Repertoire of 20 Amino Acids

Proteins are linear polymers of amino acids. Each amino acid consists of a central tetrahedral carbon atom linked to an amino group, a carboxylic acid group, a distinctive side chain, and a hydrogen. These tetrahedral centres, with the exception of that of glycine, are chiral; only the l isomer exists in natural proteins. All natural proteins are constructed from the same set of 20 amino acids. The side chains of these 20 building blocks vary tremendously in size, shape, and the presence of functional groups. They can be grouped as follows:

- Aliphatic side chains—glycine, alanine, valine, leucine, isoleucine, methionine, and proline;
- Aromatic side chains—phenylalanine, tyrosine, and tryptophan;
- Hydroxyl-containing aliphatic side chains—serine and threonine;
- Sulfhydryl-containing cysteine;
- Basic side chains—lysine, arginine, and histidine;
- Acidic side chains—aspartic acid and glutamic acid; and
- Carboxamide-containing side chains—asparagine and glutamine. These groupings are somewhat arbitrary and many other sensible groupings are possible.

Primary Structure

The amino acids in a polypeptide are linked by amide bonds formed between the carboxyl group of one amino acid and the amino group of the next. This linkage, called a peptide bond, has several important properties. First, it is resistant to hydrolysis so that proteins are remarkably stable kinetically. Second, the peptide group is planar because the C-N bond has considerable double-bond character.

Third, each peptide bond has both a hydrogen-bond donor (the NH group) and a hydrogen-bond acceptor (the CO group). Hydrogen bonding between these backbone groups is a distinctive feature of protein structure. Finally, the peptide bond is uncharged, which allows proteins to form tightly packed globular structures having significant amounts of the backbone buried within the protein interior. Because they are linear polymers, proteins can be described as sequences of amino acids. Such sequences are written from the amino to the carboxyl terminus.

Secondary Structure

Polypeptide Chains Can Fold into Regular Structures Such as the Alpha Helix, the Beta Sheet, and Turns and Loops Two major elements of secondary structure are the α helix and the β strand. In the β helix, the polypeptide chain twists into a tightly packed rod.

Within the helix, the CO group of each amino acid is hydrogen bonded to the NH group of the amino acid four residues along the polypeptide chain. In the β strand, the polypeptide chain is nearly fully extended. Two or more β strands connected by NH-to-CO hydrogen bonds come together to form β sheets.

Tertiary Structure

Water-Soluble Proteins Fold into Compact Structures with Nonpolar Cores

The compact, asymmetric structure that individual polypeptides attain is called tertiary structure. The tertiary structures of water-soluble proteins have features in common:

- An interior formed of amino acids with hydrophobic side chains and
- A surface formed largely of hydrophilic amino acids that interact with the aqueous environment. The driving force for the formation of the tertiary structure of water-soluble proteins is the hydrophobic interactions between the interior residues. Some proteins that exist in a hydrophobic environment, in membranes, display the inverse distribution of hydrophobic and hydrophilic amino acids. In these proteins, the hydrophobic amino acids are on the surface to interact with the environment, whereas the hydrophilic groups are shielded from the environment in the interior of the protein.

Quaternary Structure

Polypeptide Chains Can Assemble into Multisubunit Structures. Proteins consisting of more than one polypeptide chain display quaternary structure, and each individual polypeptide chain is called a subunit. Quaternary structure can be as simple as two identical subunits or as complex as dozens of different subunits. In most cases, the subunits are held together by noncovalent bonds.

CATALYTIC HYDROGENATION

Hydrogenation of olefins is an important reaction, in petroleum refining and other industrial processes. It will proceed *catalytically* in the presence of an active metal surface. Ni, Pt or Pd are often used, in "black" colloidal form. Free bonds on the metal do the job of dissolving the double bond when the olefin is adsorbed on its surface, acting like free radicals. Hydrogen is dissociated in the same way. The molecules can diffuse on the metal surface, and when they meet the hydrogens (protons) prefer to bond with the adsorbed olefin rather than with the metal. The hydrogenated molecule is then freed to go on its way.

Addition to the Carbonyl Group

The C=O double bond appears in aldehydes, ketones and acids, so it is very important. Unlike the C=C bond, it is polarized, with the O end negative and the C end positive, just like the C-Cl bond we met above. Nucleophiles will add to the C, and electrophiles to the O, and both kinds of reactions will be common with the C=O bond. For example, when chloral, trichloroacetaldehyde, Cl_3C-CHO, is treated with water, OH^- will attack the C and stick to it, while H^+ will attack the O and stick to it, so that we have two OH groups on the same carbon. In this case, we get chloral hydrate ("knockout drops"), which is quite stable, but in most cases the product is not stable and exists only in solution.

If we mix formaldehye, HCHO, and ammonia, NH_3, $NH_3^+CH_2O^-$ will be formed. The charge distribution on this molecule is as indicated, which easily persuades the molecules to polymerize. Four of these polymerize to a curious molecule called hexamethylenetetramine, also called urotropine, shown at the right, where the three-dimensional structure is suggested. This was the first organic molecule whose structure was determined by X-ray diffraction, in 1923. Its symmetry is tetrahedral, with the carbons at the vertices of a regular octahedron.

The bond angles are tetrahedral, and the bond lengths agree with the covalent radii. This molecule forms colorless cubic crystals, and is soluble in water because of the unbonded electrons on the nitrogens. It irritates the skin, burns readily, is a urinary antiseptic and diuretic, and dissolves uric acid in cases of kidney stone and gout. It was used in an alkaline solution with phenol and glycerine as an antidode to phosgene, ($COCl_2$), which is closely related to formaldehyde. A picture of a space-filling model is shown at the left. Two nitrogens (blue) marking 3-fold axes, can be seen. When it is nitrated, electrophilic attack by the NO_2^+ on the nitrogens cleaves the molecule at the nitrogens and adds a nitro. The fragments reform to make cyclotrimethylenetrinitramine, with a ring of alternating N and C, a nitro at each N and H_2 at each C. This is a powerful explosive, also called *cyclonite* or *RDX*, which is easily detonated with mercuric fulminate while being more powerful than TNT. It is notable as not being an nitrate ester, but on the other hand it has N-N bonds, which are also explosive.

The proton from HCl can mount an electrophilic attack on the O atom of dimethyl ketone, forming OH there and making the carbon atom positive. This resembles a carbonium ion, and is reactive enough to attract an electrophilic attack by the unbonded electrons of an alcohol, say ethanol, which become bonded to the carbon of what was the C=O group. Now the positive charge on the O of the alcohol OH group migrates down to the other O as the OH group ionizes. Now this oxygen can be attacked by a proton, and after it adds and H, HOH separates readily. Now we are left with $(CH_3)_2COEt$ with a + charge on the central carbon. This carbonium-like group can now attract a second alcohol OH, and now Cl^- ion takes away its hydrogen and departs as HCl. The result is $(CH_3)_2C(OEt)_2$, acetal, with two ether-like oxygens. Since the HCl is restored, the net result is the addition of two OEt's across the carbon-oxygen double bond.

The C=O double bond can also be catalytically hydrogenated like the C=C double bond, but the reaction is more sluggish, since it is not as favored energetically. The addition of hydrogen is called *reduction* in organic chemistry, like the addition of electrons in inorganic chemistry. An aldehyde or ketone is reduced to an alcohol in this way. An oxidizing agent such as the permanganate ion, MnO_4^- (Mn +7), can add an oxygen to the carbon atom of the carbonyl group of RCHO and leave it there by becoming manganate, MnO_3^- (Mn +5). Now we have $RCOO^- + H^+ + MnO_3^-$, and the aldehyde has been reduced to a carboxylic acid.

Reactions of the Carboxyl Group

The carboxyl, COOH, group contains the C=O of a ketone and the OH of an alcohol, but the two groups interact so strongly that the reactions of the carboxyl group are distinct from those of ketones and alcohols. We have already mentioned that the carboxyl group ionizes more readily than the OH of an alcohol, and that resonance causes the two oxygens of COO^- (the carboxylate anion) to be equivalent, with a positive charge on the carbon and a negative charge on the oxygens.

An important reaction of the carboxyl group is *esterification*, whose mechanism is shown in the figure. When acetic acid and ethanol are mixed in an acidic solution, which can be aqueous since both are water-soluble, the ester ethyl acetate (with the characteristic aroma of bananas) and water are created. Both reagents ionize, the acid more than the alcohol, and the ethoxy group makes a nucleophilic attack on the carbon of the acetate ion. This releases an oxygen to form OH^-, which is then quickly protonated to form water. The reaction is reversible, so that ethyl acetate is *hydrolyzed* by water. Ethyl acetate is not an ionic compound, since the carbonium ion Et^+ does not exist. Esterification is not analogous to $NaOH + HCl \rightarrow NaCl + HOH$. NaCl is not hydrolyzed by water to sodium hydroxide and hydrochloric acid. An ester, therefore, bears no similiarity to an inorganic salt.

An *ester* is the compound formed by taking the H from an alcohol, and the OH from the carboxyl group of an acid, and joining the remainders. For example, $EtOH + CH_3COOH \rightarrow HOH + EtO\text{-}OCCH_3$. Ethyl alcohol and acetic acid yield the ester ethyl acetate (which smells like bananas). This might look like the H from the COOH combined with the OH from the alcohol, as in MeCOOEt, but that is not the case. The COOH can be induced to give up the OH by nucleophilic attack by the ethoxide anion on the carbon. This reaction is reversible, and does not go to completion unless water is removed. It goes very slowly indeed unless a catalyst is present, such as a strong acid or base.

A similar thing happens in the nitration of glycerol, $(CH_2OH)_2CHOH$, with nitric acid, HO-NO_2. The result is $(CH_2ONO_2)_2CHONO_2$, an ester called glyceryl trinitrate or nitroglycerine. The ONO_2 or NO_3 groups make the substance explosive. Methyl nitrite, or nitromethane, CH_3NO_2, is a nonexplosive gas, while methyl nitrate, CH_3ONO_2, an ester of methanol and nitric acid, is an explosive liquid. Nitration is carried out in a mixture of concentrated nitric and sulphuric acids. The sulphuric acid takes up any water produced, as well as acting as a catalyst. In the mixture, nitric acid is very little dissociated, and the nitronium ion, NO_2^+ is formed that reacts readily with the ionized glycerol. Schönbein discovered this method of nitration when making guncotton in 1845, and it was used by Sobrero in 1846 to produce the ester glyceryl trinitrate, or nitroglycerine.

Other nucleophiles add to the carboxyl group equally readily as EtO^-. For example, ammonia adds to the C=O carbon in ethyl acetate in a typical nucleophilic addition. Then the leaving of EtO^- reestablishes the double bond, producing acetamide, $Me(CO)NH_2$. Further reaction with ammonia adds another NH_2, producing urea, $CO(NH_2)_2$. The amides are like carboxylic acids, but with an NH_2 group instead of OH. The group -(C=O)-(NH)- is called a *peptide* link, which joins the amino acids in proteins. Carboxylic acids will not succumb to nucleophilic attack on the C of the COOH group. They simply form the stable carboxylate ion and throw a proton at the hungry nucleophile. Ammonia and acetic acid give ammonium acetate, which is an ionic salt and not an ester.

Organometallic Compounds

Metal atoms will bond covalently to organic groups to form organometallic compounds. We don't include ionic compounds like lead acetate, $Pb(CH_3COO)_2$, in this category. Tetraethyl lead, $Pb(Et)_4$, is a typical organometallic compound. In 1849, Frankland found that by combining an alkyl halide RX with powdered zinc in ether, a stable compound RZnX was produced in which the carbon attached to the Zn acquired a negative charge and so could be attacked by electrophilic reagents. You will recall that in RX the carbon attached to the X acquires a negative charge and is exposed to nucleophilic attack. The new organometallic compound made many additional reactions possible. The negative carbon is also a nucleophile, and can mount nucleophilic attacks itself.

In 1901, Victor Grignard found that Mg was even better than Zn for making these compounds, which are now called *Grignard reagents*. Bromine is the best halogen to use, since Cl is less reactive. A typical Grignard reagent, then, is EtMgBr, made by mixing ethyl bromide and zinc powder in pure ether. The reagent can be crystallized, but it is generally used in the same solution in which it was prepared. A Grignard reagent such as EtMgBr is readily hydrolyzed by water, since the nucleophilic carbon attracts the electrophilic H^+ of HOH to give C_2H_6 + Mg(OH)Br.

To see how this could be useful, consider the reaction of EtMgBr with formaldehyde. The Et adds to the carbon of the formaldehyde by electrophilic addition to the C=O double bond, and the MgBr to the oxygen at the other end, making C_3H_7OMgBr. This product can be hydrolyzed, as just explained, to C_3H_7OH, propyl alcohol, and Mg(OH)Br. We have added CH_2 to the carbon chain, and this is a general method of ascending a homologous series.

By using a ketone instead, we get a tertiary alcohol by the same process. If we start with dimethyl ketone and MeMgBr, we end up with 2-isobutanol, Me(CCH_3OH)Me. Methaldehyde instead of dimethyl ketone gives 2-propanol. If we start with a carboxylic ester, such as ethyl acetate, we first get dimethyl ketone (by rearrangement of the addition product that eliminates EtO and recreates the double bond) and EtOMgBr. A further attack by EtMgBr produces a Grignard reagent that will hydrolyze to tertiary butanol.

Grignard reagents even attack the positive carbon in CO_2. CO_2 + EtMgBr $\rightarrow$ $EtCOO^-$ + $MgBr^+$ $\rightarrow$ EtCOOMgBr, which hydrolyzes to EtCOOH, propionic acid. To avoid further reaction of the desired acid product, the reaction is carried out by pouring the fresh Grignard reagent on powdered solid CO_2. Then the addition of water creates the acid before the slow second reaction can take place.

EtMgBr will react with $PbCl_2$ to make tetraethyl lead: 4EtMgBr + $2PbCl_2$ $\rightarrow$ $Pb(Et)_4$ + 4MgClBr + Pb. This is not the industrial process, which uses EtCl and PbNa alloy instead. Tetraethyl lead is a liquid, which was added to motor fuels so that ethyl free radical would be released at the proper time to smooth out combustion in Otto cyle engines. Incidentally, Diesel engines prefer a fuel that ignites immediately upon injection, so straight-chain hydrocarbons are the best Diesel fuel, while branched hydrocarbons are preferred by Otto-cycle engines.

Reactions of Benzene

The benzene molecule is a strong fortress, symmetrical and tightly bound. The ring carbons and their hydrogens are unpromising targets. The one weakness is the six ring electrons, three on one side and three on the other, which may be captured by strong electrophiles. An electron pair may be donated to a Br^+ ion, to bond it with the molecule with the six hydrogens. If one of the hydrogens is then sacrificed to an electrophile, the bromine will have succeeded in muscling into the ring in place of a hydrogen. Note that the loss of the hydrogen re-establishes the stable ring electrons. The bromobenzene that results is now open to chemical attack of many kinds. This reaction is illustrated at the right, together with the usual means of obtaining positive bromine. The ferric bromide acts as a catalyst, since it is not consumed in the reaction. The reaction is best described as addition followed by elimination, not as a substitution, since the addition and elimination are consecutive, not simultaneous. An activation energy is required to attain the middle state, then a much smaller activation energy when the hydrogen is emitted.

A very important reaction makes use of aluminium chloride in the same way that ferric bromide was used in bromination. Methyl chloride will form a complex with aluminium chloride through the reaction MeCl + $AlCl_3 \rightarrow$ Me(+)-$AlCl_4$(-). The Me(+) is a powerful electrophile, like the corresponding carbonium ion, and can successfully attack the benzene ring, and add Me to it, producing methyl benzene, or toluene, BzMe (Bz = C_6H_5). This is called the *Friedel-Crafts* reaction. Compare with the Grignard reaction described above.

Benzene can also be nitrated by nitric acid in anhydrous sulphuric acid, in which the very electrophilic nitronium ion, NO_2^+, exists, making nitrobenzene. Toluene is easily nitrated to nitrotoluene, where the nitro group is *ortho* to the methyl. Further nitration results in trinitrotoluene or TNT, $Bz(NO_2)_3$, with the three nitros ortho and para to the methyl. This is not a nitrate ester, but is still quite explosive, like the other two explosive arrangments we have found, O-NO_2 and N-NO_2. Further additions to the benzene ring can be made after the first one, and are generally easier than the first one. The additions may be *directed* to a particular position. With toluene, the nitro goes *ortho*, but a second methyl will go *meta*, to form m-xylene.

Potassium permanganate will not oxidize benzene, but it will oxidize the methyl group in toluene, making a (C=O)OH while eliminating hydrogen. Even the methyl group is more readily attacked than the benzene nucleus. The result in this case is benzoic acid, BzCOOH. Nitrobenzene can be reduced (hydrogenated) to aminobenzene, or aniline, $BzNH_2$, while the benzene ring is unaffected. Chlorine free radicals will attack the benzene ring when they have fully conquered all easier targets. The result is 1,2,3,4,5,6-chlorocyclohexane, an aliphatic compound. There are many stereoisomers, since the chlorines and hydrogens can be above or below the ring *ad libitum*. Usually all the chlorines are on one side (*cis*), or chlorines and hydrogens alternate (*trans*). One of the stereoisomers is a powerful insecticide. This compound should not be confused with hexachlorobenzene, C_6Cl_6, which is aromatic. It is sometimes confusingly called benzene hexachloride.

Halobenzenes form Grignard reagents with magnesium, which render the benzene ring susceptible to electrophilic attack, and allow the addition of benzene rings by nucleophilic addition. For example, BzMgBr is formed the usual way by treating powdered magnesium with benzene in ether. OH^- will not attack BzCl as it attacked RCl, because no positively charged carbon exists. However, the reaction will go at the high temperatures and pressures of an industrial process, and phenol, BzOH, is formed. The OH group behaves differently when attached to the benzene nucleus than when attached to an alkane. Because of resonance in the BzO^- ion, which is not as strong as with the carboxyl group but still acting, the H is more easily ionized and phenol is a weak acid. When the H^+ leaves, the negative charge on the oxygen can be spread around the ring. The ionization constant of ethanol is only about 10^{-18}, but that of phenol is 1.3×10^{-10}.

Diazo Compounds

If we treat ethyl alcohol with nitrous acid, HO-N=O, we get the ester ethyl nitrite, EtO-N=O by the normal esterification reaction. With ethylamine, we get instead: $EtNH_2 + HO\text{-}N{=}O \rightarrow EtNH\text{-}N{=}O + H_2O$. The product rearranges by electrons moving from left to right to Et-N=N-OH and then ionizes as Et-$N{=}N^+ + OH^-$, forming a *diazonium cation*. This has two resonating forms, the one shown, and Et-N^+a"N. The diazonium cation is unstable, decomposing to Na"N and a carbonium ion. In this case, the carbonium ion forms EtOH. The word "azo" refers to nitrogen (the French name for nitrogen is *azote*), since all the other good words for nitrogen are already taken.

There is an aromatic amine, aminobenzene, ususally called *aniline*, $BzNH_2$. When we treat it with nitrous acid and hydrochloric acid, we get benzenediazonium, BzN^+a"N, as the chloride. This ion is stabilized by having several resonance structures that spread the charge over the benzene nucleus, so it is a reasonably stable molecule. It is a strong electrophile, so it can attract OH^-, Cl^-, CN^- and other anions, then eliminate N_2 and tack the anions onto the benzene nucleus to get phenol, chlorobenzene and benzonitrile, respectively. Aniline is prepared from benzene by nitration with HNO_3 in H_2SO_4 to make nitrobenzene, followed by reduction with H_2 and Ni catalyst, or by chemical reduction by Sn in HCl.

Benzenediazonium will add phenoxide, BzO^-, but to the outer nitrogen and form the stable molecule Bz-N=N-Bz-OH, p-hydroxyazobenzene. This is called a *coupling reaction*. The *azo* group -N=N- is stabilized by having a benzene nucleus on each end, and less triple bond character. The result of this reaction has a bright orange color, and is the simplest of the *azo* dyes. The -N=N- group is the *chromophore*, responsible for the absorption of light, while the -OH is the polar *auxochrome* group, that binds the dye to the fiber, or to the mordant for nonpolar fibres. Methyl Red has an $N(Me)_2$ on one benzene ring, and COOH on the other. Methyl Yellow has only the methamine group. Methyl Orange has the methamine group on one ring, and $\text{-}SO_2OH$ on the other. All these dyes have the same chromophore, but different auxochromes. Furthermore, in aqueous solution they change color depending on the pH (they have two forms depending on the pH), and so are used as indicators. Aniline is the starting point for the synthesis of many dyes because of the general coupling reaction that introduces a chromophore.

While we are talking about dyes, it may be interesting to consider a very old dye that is still used, the blue dye indigo, familiar from blue jeans. It was prepared by oxidation of the substance *indican*, a glucoside from the *Indigofera tinctoria* and related plants, which are legumes. At the present time indigo is prepared synthetically. The chromophore is the O=C-C=C-C=O chain in the *keto* form of the molecule. This insoluble compound is rendered soluble by reduction with $NaHSO_3$, which alters it to the colorless but soluble *enol* form. After the cloth is dyed, exposure to the air restores the blue form by oxidation. This procedure is typical of a *vat* dye, of which indigo is an example. Another ancient dye was red *madder*, from the roots of *Rubia tinctorum*, of which a close modern relative is alizarin, an anthraquinone dye. These dyes are based on a nucleus of two benzene rings joined by two C=O ketone bridges. Indigo and madder are good dyes, but monotony of color was the rule until artificial dyes were introduced. The first synthetic dye was yellow picric acid, discovered in 1771. Coal-tar dyes (those based on benzene rings) were discovered in 1856 by Perkin.

A dye must be insoluble, or else bond strongly with the fabric, or it will be washed out. On the other hand, it must be soluble to be distributed over the fabric. These conflicting requirements may be met as described above for vat dyes, which have two suitable forms. Some dyes are so insoluble that they must be made "in place" on the fabric. These are called *developed* dyes. A good example is the azo dye Para Red, which is brilliant red, whose structure is shown at the right. It is made by the coupling reaction of para-nitrodiazobenzene (hence the name Para) and â-naphthol, a phenol-like derivative of naphthalene. The fabric is first soaked in a solution of the sodium salt of â-naphthol and coated with the $BzBzO^-$ ion. Then it is passed through a solution of nitrobenzenediazonium chloride, which forms Para Red in intimate contact with the fibres. Para Red can be prepared in powder form for use in coloring smokes or for dispersion in plastics.

A bright yellow dye, auramine, is made as shown at the left. Without the chlorine, the compound is colorless, but the addition of chlorine induces the structure shown, which has numerous alternating double bonds. Auramine is an example of a *ketoimine* dye. It is not very fast, but is an excellent yellow that is used to color smoke. With indigo, it makes a green smoke by additive color mixing. The chromophore in this case seeems to be the entire upper ring system. The $-NH_2$ and $-N(CH_3)_2$ groups are auxochromes.

Methylene blue, whose structure is shown at the right, is an important biological stain. Tissues are almost transparent under the microscope, but stains tint tissues selectively, allowing them to be distinguished. This was first reported in 1838. Methylene blue stains cell nuclei and bacteria. It is an example of a *thyazine* dye. The important dyes indigo, para red, auramine and methylene blue have now been introduced. There are still many other kinds of dyes, but these examples should show how organic compounds can exhibit infinite variety.

Sulphur Compounds

Although á- and â-naphthol occur in coal tar, the amounts available from this source are too small to support the dye industry. They can, however, be synthesized from the more abundant naphthalene with the aid of sulphuric acid. Before discussing this, let's look at some important organic compounds containing sulphur. Sulphur with valence -2 can replace oxygen in many compounds, which are similar to the oxygen analogues. Sulphur also has a great affinity for electrons, like oxygen, but its unbonded pairs are not as tightly held, and do not form hydrogen bonds of the same strength. Sulphur exhibits positive valence states of +2, +4 and +6, notably in compounds with oxygen, and can be a reducing agent as well as an oxidizing agent.

Two series of compounds can be derived from hydrogen sulphide, H_2S, the analogue of water. Unlike water, hydrogen sulphide melts at -83.9°C and boils at -59.6°C, because of the lack of hydrogen bonding. It is a weak acid in aqueous solution, giving H^+ and SH^- ions, and a little S^{--} by further ionization. It is a dangerous poison, though the effects of a little wear off quickly in fresh air. It smells, as is well known, like rotten eggs.

If one hydrogen is replaced by an organic radical R, a *thioalcohol* or *mercaptan* is formed. MeSH is methyl mercaptan or methanethiol, boiling at 6°C. EtSH is ethyl mercaptan, boiling at 35.1°C. Propyl mercaptan can also be described as 1-propanethiol, and isopropyl mercaptan as 2-propanethiol. The alkyl mercaptans have foul smells, and are added in small amounts to natural gas to give it a detectable odor. Phenyl mercaptan, BzSH, is better known as thiophenol. It is a liquid over the wide range -15° to 170°C. Its odor must be peculiar.

If both hydrogens are replaced, a *thioether* is formed. Dimethyl sulphide, $(Me)_2S$, boils at 37.3°C, while dimethyl ether boils at -23.7°C. This shows the attraction between the sulphur and the methyl group is greater than the attraction between the sulphur and the hydrogens in hydrogen sulphide, and also stronger than the attraction between oxygen and a methyl group.

Sulphur burns in air or oxygen to form sulphur dioxide, which dissolves slightly in water to form sulphurous acid. The first ionization of sulphurous acid gives the bisulphite ion, which appears in several useful inorganic salts. Sulphur dioxide oxidizes slowly in oxygen to form the trioxide. Processes that speed up the oxidation by catalysis are those that make sulphuric acid, the most useful industrial chemical. Sulphur dioxide dissolves readily in water to form sulphuric acid, which is only partly ionized. 100% sulphuric acid can even dissolve more SO_3, becoming *fuming sulphuric acid*, or *oleum*. The bisulfate ion is analogous to the bisulfite ion, forming acid sulphate salts. Of course, both sulphite and sulfate ions are also found, resulting from complete ionization of the acids.

The SO_3 in fuming sulphuric acid is a very strong electrophile, like the NO_2^+ ion, and can likewise attack the benzene ring electrons. The result is replacement of a hydrogen by the *sulphone* radical, producing benzenesulphonic acid. Note that the ring carbon is bound directly to a sulphur, so this is not a sulphate ester. There is a similar sulphine group, but we are not concerned with it here. Sulphonic acids are reasonably strong, as may be expected. There is an homologous series of alkyl sulphonic acids beginning with methanesulphonic acid, $HMeSO_3$. Note that these are not sulphites, but have a different structure. They can be produced by reaction with sodium sulfite, however: $RCl + Na_2SO_3 \rightarrow RSO_2OH + NaCl$. This way of writing the sulphone distinguishes it from a sulphite. The other hydrogen can also be replaced, giving sulphones like $Ar\text{-}SO_2\text{-}Ar$, where Ar is an aromatic radical.

The great advantage of the sulphonic acids is that the defenses of the benzene ring have been broken down, and further reactions are possible. Among the many possibilities, we are interested in *alkali fusion*, which has the effect of eliminating the bracketed atoms in $Bz[SO_2ONa + H]ONa$, producing BzONa which hydrolyzes to BzOH, or to the BzO^- ion. This is the way to make phenol from benzene. Phenol can be triply sulphonated, from which the trinitrate, picric acid, can be made.

Naphthalene, as we have seen, consists of two fused benzene rings. It can be sulphonated in exactly the same way as benzene. From 80° to 100°C, &alpha-naphthol is produced; at 160°C the product is &beta-naphthol. We actually make the negative ions, but that is just what is desired to carry out the coupling reactions of dye synthesis.

7

Chemical Kinetics

Chemical kinetics is the study of chemical reactions and how they change based on varying conditions. The primary determination of a chemical reaction's effect is mostly outside the substance's actual makeup. Chemical kinetics studies these conditions to determine how and why a reaction occurs as it does.

The primary applied use of the science is creating efficient, non-destructive and non-poisoning reactions for use in manufacturing, materials processing and the pharmaceutical industries. Even so, the majority of this field is pure science and research.

The base methods and responses during a chemical reaction are determined by the chemical itself. No matter what conditions are present, some materials will not react with other chemicals or with environmental factors. This forms the baseline used by chemical kinetics. Once a reaction is understood in a controlled environment, changes to the reaction can be directly attributed to changes in the conditions of the experiment.

Apart from what the initial substance actually is, the state and the concentration of the substance will play an important factor in chemical kinetics. These two factors are directly related to the condition of the initial material, rather than environment. The state of the material refers to whether it is a solid, liquid or gas. The concentration is the amount of reactant when compared to another substance or volume. This may be expressed as a 'parts per 1,000 of X chemical' or as a percentage of space used in the experimental area.

The concentration of material is of great importance to chemical kinetics for two reasons. First, the larger the amount of reactants, the faster the reaction will occur. This was one of the first major breakthroughs in this field and is often considered the birth point of the discipline. The second major effect is in regards to chemical interaction. If the concentration of two reactants is very low within a third non-reactive substance, then it will take a noticeable amount of time for the two reactants to actually encounter one another.

In addition to the physical properties of the material, the environment is also a big part of chemical kinetics. Environmental factors generally come down to temperature and pressure. As the temperature increases, the reactants absorb thermal energy and move faster. This allows them to interact with each other more frequently, which speeds up the reaction. Likewise, higher pressure makes more activities happen in a smaller space, increasing the likelihood that the reactants encounter one another.

The last major part of chemical kinetics is the use of catalysts. These 'third-party' chemicals change the way in which the reaction occurs without changing the end result of the reaction. A catalyst will interact with one or more reactants and change the way they behave. This typically means they increase in energy, move faster, interact more and increase the overall reaction speed. In order to be a catalyst and not a reactant, the catalysing material must remain unchanged during the reaction.

Chemical kinetics is the study and discussion of chemical reactions with respect to *reaction rates, the effect of various variables, re-arrangement of atoms, formation of intermediates etc*. There are many topics to be discussed, and each of these topics is a tool for the study of chemical reactions. By the way, the study of motion is called kinetics, from Greek *Kinesis*, meaning movement.

At the macroscopic level, we are interested in amounts reacted, formed, and the rates of their formation. At the molecular or microscopic level, the following considerations must also be made in the discusion of chemical reaction mechanism.

- Molecules or atoms of reactants must collide with each other in chemical reactions.
- The molecules must have sufficient energy (discussed in terms of activation energy) to initiate the reaction.
- In some cases, the orientation of the molecules during the collision must also be considered.

Reaction Rates

Chemical reaction rates are the rates of change in concentrations or amounts of either reactants or products. For changes in amounts, the units can be one of mol/s, g/s, lb/s, kg/day etc. For changes in concentrations, the units can be one of mol/(L s), g/(L s), %/s etc.

With respect to reaction rates, we may deal with *average rates, instantaneous rates, or initial rates* depending on the experimental conditions.

Thermodynamics and kinetics are two factors that affect reaction rates. The study of energy gained or released in chemical reactions is called thermodynamics, and such energy data are called thermodynamic data. However, thermodynamic data have no direct correlation with reaction rates, for which the kinetic factor is perhaps more important. For example, at room temperature (a wide range of temperatures), thermodynamic data indicates that diamond shall convert to graphite, but in reality, the conversion rate is so slow that most people think that *diamond is forever*.

Different Ways of Expressing the Rate of Reaction

There is usually more than one way to measure the rate of a reaction. We can study the decomposition of hydrogen iodide, for example, by measuring the rate at which either H_2 or I_2 is formed in the following reaction or the rate at which HI is consumed.

$$2\,HI(g) \rightleftharpoons H_2(g) + I_2(g)$$

Experimentally we find that the rate at which I_2 is formed is proportional to the square of the HI concentration at any moment in time.

$$\frac{d(I_2)}{dt} = k(HI)^2$$

What would happen if we studied the rate at which H_2 is formed? The balanced equation suggests that H_2 and I_2 must be formed at exactly the same rate.

$$\frac{d(H_2)}{dt} = \frac{d(I_2)}{dt}$$

What would happen, however, if we studied the rate at which HI is consumed in this reaction? Because HI is consumed, the change in its concentration must be a negative number. By convention, the rate of a reaction is always reported as a positive number. We therefore have to change the sign before reporting the rate of reaction for a reactant that is consumed in the reaction.

$$\frac{-d(HI)}{dt} = k'(HI)^2$$

The negative signs does two things. Mathematically, it converts a negative change in the concentration of HI into a positive rate. Physically, it reminds us that the concentration of the reactant decreases with time.

What is the relationship between the rate of reaction obtained by monitoring the formation of H_2 or I_2 and the rate obtained by watching HI disappear? The stoichiometry of the reaction says that two HI molecules are consumed for every molecule of H_2 or I_2produced. This means that the rate of decomposition of HI is twice as fast as the rate at which H_2 and I_2 are formed. We can translate this relationship into a mathematical equation as follows.

$$-\frac{d(HI)}{dt} = 2\left[\frac{d(H_2)}{dt}\right] = 2\left[\frac{d(I_2)}{dt}\right]$$

As a result, the rate constant obtained from studying the rate at which H_2 and I_2 are formed in this reaction (*k*) is not the same as the rate constant obtained by monitoring the rate at which HI is consumed (*k'*).

TRANSITION STATES AND ACTIVATION ENERGIES

Transition State Theory

Transition state theory describes a hypothetical transition state that exists between reactants and products during a chemical reaction. The species formed in this hypothetical transition state is called the activated complex. This theory is used to explain how chemical reactions take place.

If the rate constant has been experimentally determined, the theory can also be used to determine the standard Gibbs free energy, enthalpy, and entropy of the reaction. It is closely related tocollision theory. Transition state theory is sometimes abbreviated TST, and alternate names for include activated-complex theory and absolute-rate theory.

History

Before the transition state theory was formalized, the Arrhenius equation of 1889 was the primary equation used to describe the rate of a chemical reaction. The Arrhenius equation is represented mathematically as,

k=Ae–EaRT

where k is the chemical reaction rate, A is the pre-exponential factor, E_a is the activation energy, R is the gas constant, and T is the temperature. However, this equation was determined empirically and the mechanical basis for the pre-exponential factor and activation energy was not understood.

Research to determine such a mechanical basis led to transition state theory and the Eyring equation.

The development of transition state theory is primarily credited to Henry Eyring of Princeton University. There may also have been a simultaneous development of the theory by Meredith Gwynne Evans and Michael Polanyi of the University of Manchester, but not all sources cite them as contributors. Proposed in 1935, the theory led to the development of the Eyring equation, which explains the mechanical basis behind the pre-exponential factor and the activation energy. The theory has some limitations, and does not work as well for reactions with small activations energies or high temperatures. As a result, some alternatives have been proposed including microcanonical variational TST, canonical variational TST, and improved canonical variational TST.

The Theory

According to TST, between the state where molecules are reactants and the state where molecules are products, there is a state known as the transition state. In the transition state, the reactants are combined in a species called the activated complex. The theory suggests that there are three major factors that determine whether a reaction will occur:

1. The concentration of the activated complex
2. The rate at which the activated complex breaks apart
3. The way in which the activated complex breaks apart: whether it breaks apart to reform the reactants or whether it breaks apart to form a new complex, the products.

Collision theory proposes that not all reactants that combine undergo a reaction. However, assuming the stipulations of the collision theory are met and a successful collision occurs between the molecules, transition state theory allows one of two outcomes: a return to the reactants, or a rearranging of bonds to form the products.

Applications

The main application of the transition state theory is in reactions catalyzed by enzymes. The introduction of an enzyme catalyst into a reaction lowers the activation energy of that reaction. Research detailing enzymes' specific interactions with molecules, including those in the transition state, has shown that the enzymes actually increase the stability of the activated complex in the transition state.

This is important in terms of enzyme activity such as the induced fit model and enzymes used in inhibitors. In more general terms, however, the transition state theory is useful in determining a reaction will proceed. By knowing which transition states will form, and what differing activation energies are, it is possible to map out the course of a reaction, and calculate quantities such as the reaction rate and the rate constant.

Activation Energies

All molecules possess a certain minimum amount of energy. The energy can be in the form of kinetic energy or potential energy.

Fig.: In Greek mythology Sisyphus was punished by being forced roll an immense boulder up a hill, only to watch it roll back down, and to repeat this action forever. If this were a chemical reaction, then it would never be observed, since the reactants must overcome the energy barrier to get to the other side (products).

When molecules collide, the kinetic energy of the molecules can be used to stretch, bend, and ultimately break bonds, leading to chemical reactions. If molecules move too slowly with little kinetic energy, or collide with improper orientation, they do not react and simply bounce off each other. However, if the molecules are moving fast enough with a proper collision orientation, such that the kinetic energy upon collision is greater than the minimum energy barrier, then a reaction occurs. The minimum energy requirement that must be met for a chemical reaction to occur is called the activation energy, Ea.

The reaction pathway is similar to what happens. To get to the other end of the road, an object must roll with enough speed to completely roll over the hill of a certain height. The faster the object moves, the more kinetic energy it has. If the object moves too slowly, it does not have enough kinetic energy necessary to overcome the barrier; as a result, it eventually rolls back down. In the same way, there is a minimum amount of energy needed in order for molecules to break existing bonds during a chemical reaction. If the kinetic energy of the molecules upon collision is greater than this minimum energy, then bond breaking and forming occur, forming a new product (provided that the molecules collide with the proper orientation).

The activation energy (Ea), labeled $\Delta G‡$ is the energy difference between the reactants and the activated complex, also known as transition state. In a chemical reaction, the transition state is defined as the highest-energy state of the system. If the molecules in the reactants collide with enough kinetic energy and this energy is higher than the transition state energy, then the reaction occurs and products form. In other words, the higher the activation energy, the harder it is for a reaction to occur and vice versa.

The activation energy (Ea), labeled ΔG‡ is the energy difference between the reactants and the activated complex, also known as transition state. In a chemical reaction, the transition state is defined as the highest-energy state of the system. If the molecules in the reactants collide with enough kinetic energy and this energy is higher than the transition state energy, then the reaction occurs and products form. In other words, the higher the activation energy, the harder it is for a reaction to occur and vice versa.

Effects of Enzymes on Activation Energy

However, if a catalyst is added to the reaction, the activation energy is lowered because a lower-energy transition state is formed. Enzymes can be thought of as biological catalysts that lower activation energy. Enzymes are proteins or RNA molecules that provide alternate reaction pathways with lower activation energies than the original pathways. Enzymes affect the rate of the reaction in both the forward and reverse directions; the reaction proceeds faster because less energy is required for molecules to react when they collide. Thus, the rate constant (k) increases.

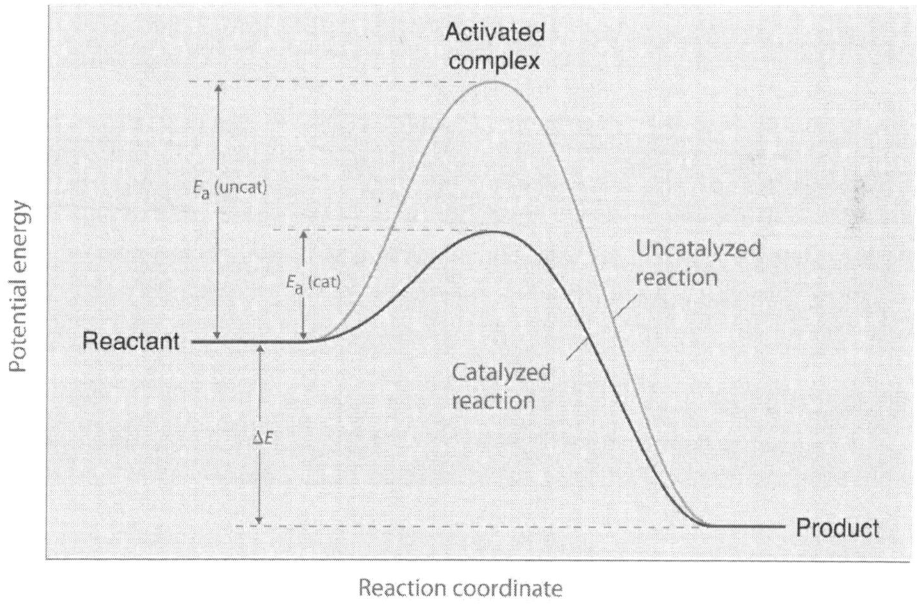

Fig. : Lowering the Activation Energy of a Reaction by a Catalyst. This graph compares potential energy diagrams for a single-step reaction in the presence and absence of a catalyst. The only effect of the catalyst is to lower the activation energy of the reaction. The catalyst does not affect the energy of the reactants or products (and thus does not affect ΔG).

A catalyst helps lower the activation energy barrier, increasing the reaction rate. In the case of a biological reaction, when an enzyme (a form of catalyst) binds to a substrate, the activation energy necessary to overcome the barrier is lowered, increasing the rate of the reaction for both the forward and reverse reaction.

Temperature independence and the relation to the Arrhenius equation

The Arrhenius equation gives the quantitative basis of the relationship between the activation energy and the rate at which a reaction proceeds. From the Arrhenius equation, the activation energy can be found through the relation

$$k = Ae^{-E_a/RT}$$

where A is the frequency factor for the reaction, R is the universal gas constant, T is the temperature (in kelvin), and k is the reaction rate coefficient. E_a can be evaluated from the variation in reaction rate coefficients as a function of temperature (within the validity of the Arrhenius equation).

Negative activation energy

In some cases, rates of reaction *decrease* with increasing temperature. When following an approximately exponential relationship so the rate constant can still be fit to an Arrhenius expression, this results in a negative value of E_a.

Elementary reactions exhibiting these negative activation energies are typically barrierless reactions, in which the reaction proceeding relies on the capture of the molecules in a potential well.

Increasing the temperature leads to a reduced probability of the colliding molecules capturing one another (with more glancing collisions not leading to reaction as the higher momentum carries the colliding particles out of the potential well), expressed as a reaction cross section that decreases with increasing temperature.

Such a situation no longer leads itself to direct interpretations as the height of a potential spot.

Catalysis

The relationship between activation energy (Ea) andenthalpy of formation (ΔH) with and without a catalyst, plotted against the reaction coordinate.

The highest energy position (peak position) represents the transition state. With the catalyst, the energy required to enter transition state decreases, thereby decreasing the energy required to initiate the reaction.

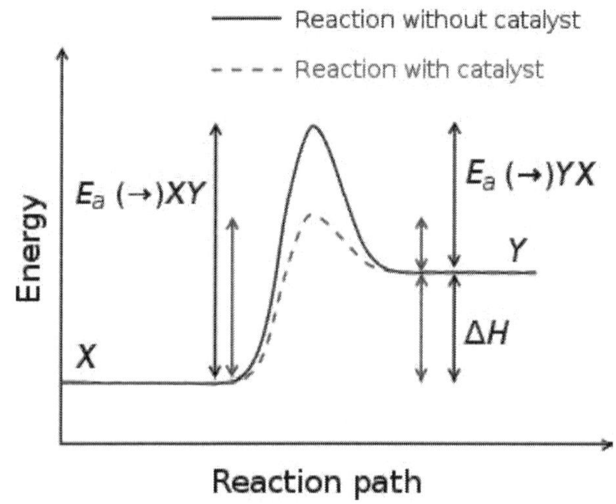

A substance that modifies the transition state to lower the activation energy is termed a catalyst; a biologicalcatalyst is termed an enzyme. It is important to note that a catalyst increases the rate of reaction without being consumed by it. In addition, while the catalyst lowers the activation energy, it does not change the energies of the original reactants or products. Rather, the reactant energy and the product energy remain the same and only the*activation energy* is altered (lowered).

Relationship with Gibbs free energy

In the Arrhenius equation, the term activation energy (E_a) is used to describe the energy required to reach thetransition state. Likewise, the Eyring equation is a similar equation that also describes the rate of a reaction. Instead of also using E_a, however, the Eyring equation uses the concept of Gibbs free energy and the symbol * $\Delta G^{\ddagger}$ to denote the energy of the transition state.

CHEMICAL KINETICS, A CLOCK REACTION

Chemical kinetics encompasses the study of reaction rates, how these rates change due to conditions, and the molecular level activity that occurs in a reaction. The four common variables that influence reaction rate are the concentration of the reactant, temperature, catalyst, and surface area. For a reaction to occur, the molecules must collide and more collisions occur with increased thermal energy to greater number of molecules present.

To further the understanding of chemical kinetics and the reaction rates dependence on concentration, temperature, and the presence of a catalyst, this experiment focused on the primary reaction between iodide, bromate, and hydrogen ions and determining the reaction's rate law:

$$6I^-(aq) + BrO_3^-(aq) + 6H^+(aq) \rightarrow 3I_2(aq) + Br^-(aq) + 3H_2O(1)$$

$$\text{rate} = k[I^-]^x[BrO_3^-]^y[H^+]^z$$

In this reaction, there are three reactants and different concentrations of each reactant were used in the five different mixtures to obtain the orders, x, y and z. Hence, the rate constant k can then be calculated. It is expected that the reaction occurs more quickly in the presence of greater concentration of reactants.

In order to make sure that the same small amount of I_2 product formed for each mixture reaction, sodium thiosulfate was used to create a clock reaction that occurred faster than the primary reaction:

$$I_2(aq) + 2S_2O_3^{2-}(aq) \rightarrow 2I^-(aq) + S_4O_6^{2-}(aq)$$

The addition of a set amount of sodium thiosulfate consumed a set amount of I_2. Therefore, the blue color, which is created by the interaction between I_2 and starch, formed once the thiosulate was fully consumed. The relationship between bromate and thiosulfate was formed:

$$\frac{3 \text{ mol } I_2}{1 \text{ mol } BrO_3^-} \times \frac{2 \text{ mol } S_2O_3^{2-}}{1 \text{ mol } I_2} \text{ accounts for } \frac{\Delta [BrO_3^-]}{\Delta t} = \frac{1}{6}\frac{\Delta [S_2O_3^{2-}]}{\Delta t}$$

The four different temperatures settings were used to show the relationship between temperature and the reaction rate. Using the Arrhenius equation:

$$\ln k = \frac{-E_a}{R}\left(\frac{1}{T}\right) + \ln A \text{ ; A is a constant; R = 8.314 J/molK}$$

the activation energy Ea can be calculated and it is expected that reactions occurring at a higher temperature will have an increased average kinetic energy of the molecules, allowing more molecules to overcome the activation energy barrier.

Hence, the increase in temperature speeds up the reaction rate. In addition, a decrease in temperature slows down the reaction. Lastly, the use of ammonium molybdate, which is a catalyst to the reaction, will lower the activation energy and reaction occurs in a shorter time span.

Experimental Reaction

The contents in reaction flask 2 were poured into the reaction flask and the time was taken to see how long it would take for the solution to turn blue. The mixture was continuously swirled until it turned blue. Although it was recommended to use three drops of starch, six drops of starch was used for each trial. The final temperature was also recorded for each trial.

Table. Volume of Reagents for Mixtures 1 to 5

	Reaction Flask 1(250 mL)		
Mix	***0.010 M KI***	***0.0010 M $Na_2S_2O_3$***	***H_2O***
1	10 mL	10 mL	10 mL
2	20 mL	10 mL	0 mL
3	10 mL	10 mL	0 mL
4	10 mL	10 mL	0 mL
5	8 mL	10 mL	12 mL
	Reaction Flask 2 (125mL)		
	0.040 M KBrO3	***0.10 M HC1***	***Starch***
1.	10 mL	10 mL	3 drops
2.	10 mL	10 mL	3 drops
3.	20 mL	10 mL	3 drops
4.	10 mL	20 mL	3 drops
5.	5 mL	15 mL	3 drops

For the second part, mixture 1 reaction was completed in the four different temperature settings, 40, 20, 10 and 0 C. To ensure constant temperature from the beginning to end of the reaction, the flasks were kept in the necessary temperature water or ice baths. Time was also taken to see how long it would take for the solution to turn blue.

For the third part, mixture 1 was used and the addition of ammonium molybdate, the catalyst. The catalyst's function is to lower the activation energy and create new elementary steps to the reaction and transition states. Overall, it speeds up the reaction. One drop of 0.5 M $(NH_4)_2MoO_4$ was added to the reagents in reaction flask 2, which was later mixed in with reaction flask 1. The reaction times for with and without the catalyst were both recorded.

Reaction Time

The reaction time varies with the reactant concentrations of iodide, bromate, and hydrogen ions for the different mixtures. As the iodide ion concentration doubles in mix 2, the time of the reaction halves, when compared to mix 1.

As the bromate ion concentration doubles in mix 3, the time of the reaction decreases, when compared to mix 1. As the hydrogen ion concentration doubles in mix 4, there is a three fold decrease in reaction time, when compared to mix 1. In mix 5, the reaction has the least reactant concentration and it took the longest for the solution to turn blue.

Table. Reaction time and rates for Mixtures 1 to 5

Mix	Time (s)	Rate $-\Delta[BrO_3^-]/\Delta t$ = 3.33 x 10^{-5} (mol/L)/Δt	Reactant concentration (mol/L) $[I^-]$	$[BrO_3^-]$	$[H^+]$	Temp (°C)
1	160	2.083E-7	0.0020	0.008	0.002	20.8-21
2	82	4.065E-7	0.0040	0.008	0.002	20.8-21
3	99	3.367E-7	0.0020	0.016	0.002	20.8-21
4	46	7.246E-7	0.0020	0.008	0.004	20.8-21
5	210	1.587E-7	0.0016	0.004	0.003	20.8-21

From chemical kinetics, a higher reactant concentration results in more molecules likely to collide and interact with each other and allowing the reaction to occur more quickly.

Therefore, mixtures 2, 3, and 4 have greater number of collisions between the sodium thiosulfate and iodine and allowing the clock reaction to occur quickly and allowing the iodine to react with the starch to turn the solution blue. When the reactants for mix 1 were heated to 40C and later mixed, it took 60 seconds for the reaction to occur. At higher temperatures, the increased thermal energy allows the molecules to collide more often and react. In contrast, the colder temperatures of 10C and 1.8C resulted in longer reaction times, 406 and 660 seconds, respectively.

Hence, the trend shows that the decrease in temperature results in a longer reaction time and smaller rate value. According to the lecture notes, a 10 Celsius increases correlates with a doubling or tripling of the reaction rate.

When comparing the reaction rates for 10 and 1.8 C, there is a 1.6 fold difference and when comparing 10C to 20C, there is a 2.5 fold change in the rate. By comparing these results to a theoretical concept, there is variability in the change of rate as the temperature increases in 10 C increments.

Table. Reaction and rates for Mix 1 at 40, 20, 10, 1.8 C

Mixture	Time (s)	Rate = $-\Delta[BrO_3^-]/\Delta t$ (mol/L-s)	Temp (°C)	Calculated k ($1/M^3s$)
1A	60	5.56E-7	40	8680.56
1B	160	2.08E-7	20.8	3255.21
1C	406	8.21E-8	10	1282.84
1D	660	5.05E-8	1.8	789.141

The trend line for the ln k vs 1/T graph shows that the slope is -5526 K and the activation energy derived from this trend line is 46 kJ/mol. The calculated slope for these points is -5446 K and the activation energy Ea is 45 kJ/mol.

Since the rate constant k increases with temperature, the rate of reaction will increase at any give reactant concentration. This clock reaction experiment shows an Arreneius behavior and the high Ea indicates a strong temperature dependence of the rate constant.

When comparing the calculated slope and Ea to the trend line slope and derived Ea, the values are pretty close. From online literature sources, the Ea for an iodine clock reaction is 53kJ/mol, which is higher than what was calculated in the experiment.

Since only four temperature settings were used, a more accurate Ea could be derived by conducting the experiment with a greater range of temperature settings.

When introducing the homogenous catalyst ammonium molybdate into the reaction mix 1, the reaction takes 15 seconds. The activation energy of the catalyzed reaction is smaller than the Ea of an uncatalyzed reaction. Since the function of the catalyst is to lower the activation energy, the reactions moves forward a lot quicker, in comparison to the 174 seconds for an uncatalyzed reaction to occur. Although the catalyst doesn't get consumed in the reaction, it creates new transition states and elementary steps to allow the reaction to precede a lot faster. Hence, the catalyst lowers the Ea for the sodium thiosulfate and iodine reaction and this experiment demonstrated the function of a catalyst in chemical kinetics.

8

Crystals and Lattices

INTRODUCTION

The word "crystal" is from the Greek krustallos, "ice," and was first applied to quartz, which seemed to be a kind of permanent ice. After the late middle ages, it came to mean any substance, usually a mineral, showing plane faces in symmetrical relations. Until X-rays allowed us to examine these bodies in microscopic (actually, sub-microscopic) detail after 1912, the faces were the only obvious clue to internal structure. Crystal faces, produced naturally, vary widely in shapes and sizes, even in the same crystal. Niels Stensen (Nicolaus Steno, 1638-1686) recognized in 1669 that the angles between the normals to faces were more fundamental than any accidents of shape, and were the same in all crystals of a given substance. This allowed the classification of the symmetry of crystals, and established *goniometry* as the basis for mathematical crystallography. Many crystalline substances do not occur as crystals with well-defined faces (as *euhedral* crystals), and the individual crystals may be tiny, so their natures remained obscure. All metals, for example, are crystalline. When we say "microscopic," we generally mean "on an atomic scale," not literally microscopic. "Macroscopic" is used when the atomic constitution is not apparent.

Crystalline substances have certain distinguishing characteristics aside from the existence of faces. First, they have definite chemical compositions; second, they melt sharply, unlike glasses which soften and melt over a range of temperature; third, they may exhibit *cleavage*. Calcite is well-known to be easily cleavable into cleavange rhombs, all with the same angles between faces. Some crystals have only one cleavage direction, and many have none. Some transparent crystals (those of low enough symmetry) show optical properties that vary with direction. Again, the *double refraction* in calcite is famous, and quartz is also optically anisotropic. These properties are all evidence of some structural regularity in crystals.

The only properties that can be measured macroscopically are averages over volumes that contain many fundamental units, $\langle \grave{U} \rangle = (1/\Delta V)+''\grave{U}(r)d^3r$, where $\grave{U}$ is a typical property. In a *homogeneous* substance, these properties are invariant under translation, $\grave{U}(r + a) = \grave{U}(r)$, for any translation a. As a typical number, properties averaged over 10 atoms or molecules can be considered macroscopic. In an *isotropic* substance, the properties are invariant under rotation.

Crystals are, in general, anisotropic, but cubic crystals are isotropic. Properties that vary with rotation can be classified by their *tensor* nature, as scalar, vector and so on. Scalars are naturally invariant under rotation. Vectors, and other tensors, transform in definite and particular ways under rotation. The existence of tensor properties in crystals is very important, providing evidence of their internal structure. The optical properties of crystals are macroscopic ones, since the wavelengths of 500 nm or so average over many lattice points, and depend on indices of refraction, which are macroscopic parameters. Crystal symmetries are often reflected in macroscopic properties, of course.

In 1784, René Haüy (1743-1822) made the first step in connecting internal structure with external form by showing that the observed faces of calcite crystals could be produced by stacking cleavage rhombs. If these elementary rhombs were small enough, the faces would appear macroscopically smooth, though stepped microscopically. Robert Hooke (1635-1703) had proposed similar ideas in 1665, as did Christiaan Huygens about the same time in connection with calcite. The rise of the atomic theory after 1800 suggested that the elementary units were atoms or molecules arranged in regular space *lattices*. In 1848, Auguste Bravais (1811-1863) made these suggestions concrete by showing that there were 14 possible space lattices belonging to the 7 systems of crystal symmetry. This model confirmed the empirical Law of Rational Indices established by goniometry, and provided strong evidence for the atomic theory of matter.

Two atoms of the same kind are absolutely identical. This means that crystal lattices are perfect, far more exact than is ever possible in the macroscopic world of peas in a pod. This precision is seen in the beauty and regularity of crystal faces, which are far more exact than in any artificially cut gem. The faces of a cut gem have no connection with the internal structure, though cleavage is often used to rough out the shape of a gem. The perfection of a lattice is disturbed by lattice vibrations (phonons), which have observable effects on microscopic properties, such as X-ray diffraction, as well as by impurities and lattice defects such as dislocations.

In this article, the broad and important subject of crystal symmetry will not be treated in any detail, and details of X-ray scattering, beyond the existence of diffraction maxima, will also not be considered. For these matters, the reader should consult the References. This article deals principally with the utility of the reciprocal lattice, a fundamental concept in the study of the crystalline state, and one with many important applications.

THE DIRECT LATTICE

The seven crystal systems are: triclinic (no symmetry axes), monoclinic (one 2-fold axis), orthorhombic (3 2-fold axes), tetragonal (one 4-fold axis), trigonal (one 3-fold axis), hexagonal (one 6-fold axis) and cubic (four 3-fold axes and three 4-fold axes). Axes of other multiplicity, such as 5 or 7, are not found in crystals. Each class includes crystals of the full symmetry, with all other symmetry elements consistent with the class (planes of symmetry, 2-fold axes, centres of symmetry, etc.), as well as those of lesser symmetry consistent with the crystal class.

The three Bravais lattices belonging to the cubic system are shown at the right. These *unit cells* are to be imagined as repeated to fill space. If the "molecules" are spherically symmetric, then each lattice will have the full symmetry of a cube, and crystals with these lattices are called *holohedral*, since all crystal faces are possible. The simple cubic lattice has one lattice point per unit cell, or one lattice point per volume of a^3, where a is the side of the unit cell. Note that there are 8 corners, and each corner is shared with 8 unit cells, so it contributes 1/8 of a lattice point to the unit cell. If a is known, then the theoretical density of the crystal can be calculated. This calculation can be performed in reverse to obtain the value of a. It is found that a is on the order of 10^{-10} m, or an Ångstrom unit, more than a thousandth of the wavelength of visible light.

The simple cubic lattice can be defined by the three basis vectors a_1, a_2 and a_3. In this case, they are of equal length and directed along the x,y and z axes. The volume of the unit cell is given by $V = a_1 \cdot a_2 x a_3$, the triple scalar product of the three basis vectors, which in this case is a^3. Sometimes we may write this volume as $(a_1a_2a_3)$, to make clear which basis vectors are involved. The simple cubic lattice is far too simple and special for deriving general results, but offers clear illustrations. In general, however, we can define any unit cell by three basis vectors, and its volume is given by their triple product. In general, however, the basis vectors will not be the same length and will not be at right angles.

The body-centered cubic lattice has an additional lattice point at the center of the unit cell, so the unit cell contains 2 lattice points. Each lattice point then occupies a volume of $a^3/2$. The face-centered cubic lattice has an additional lattice point at the center of each of the six faces, which is shared with the adjoining unit cell, so that a total of 1 + 3 = 4 lattice points are contained in each unit cell, each occupying a volume of $a^3/4$. A unit cell that contains only one lattice point is called a *primitive* unit cell, and for some purposes it is essential to work with primitive unit cells. The simple cubic unit cell is already primitive, and it is possible to find primitive unit cells for the body-centered and face-centered lattices as well.

One way of doing this for the body-centered lattice is shown at the left. A corner point is joined with three nearest body points to give the basis vectors for a rhombohedral primitive unit cell. If repeated, it fills space just as the body-centered unit cell does, and gives exactly the same lattice. These basis vectors are equal in length, but are clearly not at right angles, and the rhomb-shaped unit cell gives no evident hint of the cubic symmetry. This is the reason for the use of the non-primitive unit cells. Simple cubic crystals are not uncommon (CsCl is the usual example), but elements seem to avoid this structure, since it is not energy-favored. Body- and face-centered cubic lattices are very common and important (most elements and metals crystallize in these lattices). The reader may check that the primitive body-centered unit cell is indeed of half the volume of the cube by finding the triple scalar product of the basis vectors given. Spheres may close-pack in either the face-centered cubic (fcc) or the hexagonal close-packed (hcp) structures, and ideally occupy 74% of the volume.

To specify any position in the lattice, we could choose any lattice point as origin and define three orthonormal unit vectors i,j,k or e_1,e_2,e_3 in arbitrarily chosen x,y and z or x_1,x_2,x_3 directions. Note the different ways the three directions might be distinguished. This would be especially appropriate for simple cubic crystals, where the axes could be chosen along the sides of the unit cell. Because the unit vectors satisfy the orthonormality relation $e_i \cdot e_j = \ddot{a}_{ij}$, it is easy to express any vector in terms of rectangular components: $x = x_i e_i$ (summation convention: sum over i from 1 to 3!) or x = xi + yj + zk. The scalar product of two vectors is then simply $x \cdot y = x_i y_i$, the sum of the products of corresponding components. It is convenient to use unit vectors to specify directions as well. This system is so convenient that we adopt it wherever it is applicable.

For crystals, however, there is a problem. The coordinates are not obviously related to the lattice points or unit cells when we use orthonormal unit vectors. For cubic crystals, we can get around this by choosing the unit of distance as a = 1, but this cannot be done in general, since the lengths of basis vectors may not be equal, and they may not be at right angles. We will not be able to make any deductions until our coordinate system is adapted to the crystal lattice, and in that case we must give up many of the conveniences of an orthonormal basis.

Therefore, we use the basis vectors of a unit cell as the basis vectors for our coordinates, and write a general position $r = m_i a_i$. Integral values of the m_i correspond to the corner of some unit cell in the lattice. Positions differing by integral values of the m_i are equivalent in the lattice, since all properties have the periodicity of the lattice. The range 0 d" m_i d" 1 covers the unit cell. This is the *direct lattice* in ordinary space. If we have a periodic function in one dimension, $f(x + nL) = f(x)$, we know that we can expand the function in a Fourier series of sinusoids of wavelengths L, L/2, L/3,... knowing only f(x) in the interval x = 0 to x = 1, and that this expansion will be valid everywhere. Crystal properties can be expanded in exactly the same way knowing only values within the unit cell. This is one immediate and huge benefit of the new coordinate system, but there are many others.

THE RECIPROCAL LATTICE

If we expressed r in terms of an orthonormal basis, it would be easy to find, say, the 1-component by scalar multiplication with e_1: $x_1 = e_1 \cdot r$. It is not so simple if we expand in terms of the basis vectors of a unit cell. In this case, we require a vector b_1 such that $b_1 \cdot r = m_1$. That is, b_1 must be orthogonal to a_2 and a_3, and its scalar product with a_1 must be unity. It is not difficult to find such a vector. It must be proportional to a_2xa_3, so the required vector is $b_1 = [a_2xa_3]/(a_1a_2a_3)$. Its two companions b_2 and b_3 are given by similar expressions obtained by cyclically permuting the indices 1,2,3. Now we have three noncoplanar vectors for finding the direct lattice components m_i

By direct calculation, we can show that $(b_1b_2b_3) = 1/(a_1a_2a_3)$, and that $a_1 = [b_2xb_3]/(b_1b_2b_3)$, with the other two basis vectors found by cyclic permutation. The triplets {a} and {b} are, therefore, mutually reciprocal, and the unit cells defined by them fill space. The vectors $r = m_i a_i$ for integral values of m_i define the *direct lattice,* as we have seen, and the vectors $B = l_i b_i$ for integral values of l_i in the same way define the *reciprocal lattice*. The two lattices have a fixed relation in space, so that if the crystal is rotated, both lattices rotate at the same time by the same amount. They are, however, reciprocally related in size. As direct lattice spacing increases, the reciprocal lattice shrinks, and vice-versa.

Any vector B can be expressed as three numbers in parentheses: $(h_1h_2h_3)$. If the h's are integers, then these are the reciprocal lattice points. The vector b_1 or (100) is normal to the plane of lattice points defined by a_2 and a_3, and similar statements can be made about the other two reciprocal lattice basis vectors, written (010) and (001). We can now show that any such vectors with integral h's correspond to planes of lattice points in the direct lattice. Any plane that cuts the three direct basis vectors of the unit cell at some fractions 1/h, 1/k, 1/l of their lengths, where h,k,l are integers will sooner or later pass through lattice points, and the plane will contain an infinite number of them in an infinite crystal. Be sure you understand why this is so. The same is true for any multiple of these fractions. If, however, the fractions are irrational, the plane will pass through *no* lattice points at all. If a face does not intersect an axis, the corresponding index is 0.

The plane will intersect the sides of the unit cell in three lines. Any two of these intersections, considered as vectors, will define the plane and their cross product will be parallel to the normal to the plane. Two such vectors are $a_2/k - a_1/h$ and $a_3/l - a_1/h$. Their cross product can be written in terms of the b's as $(V/hkl)[hb_1 + kb_2 + lb_3]$. The normal to this plane is, then, the reciprocal lattice vector (hkl). Normally, no commas appear and minus signs are written over the index. Every lattice point in the reciprocal lattice corresponds to a plane in the direct lattice that passes through lattice points. By goniometry we measure the angles between face normals, and so can check this prediction of the lattice hypothesis. The agreement is, in fact, precise, and is called the Law of Rational Indices. This is a demonstration of the existence of atoms by using only macroscopic measurements, a remarkable thing (there are, of course, many such demonstrations).

The values of (hkl) for a given face depend on the choice of the unit cell. It is important that there always exists some choice that gives small integers for (hkl). The choice of a reference plane (111) defines the lengths of the basis vectors; any plane can be assigned to be (111), but some choices are much better than others. A particularly bad choice may give inconvenient numbers, but the numbers will always be found to be rational, if sufficiently precise measurements can be made. The numbers (hkl) are called the Miller indices of a face. It is a good idea to practice with a simple cubic lattice if you are not familiar with the relation between faces and Miller indices. The (111) plane is taken as the plane through the ends of the basis vectors.

Another remarkable result is that the reciprocal of the length of B is the distance d between the plane and a parallel plane through the origin, or $d = 1/|B|$. The scalar product of the vector a_1/h, whose length is the distance along the 1-axis cut by the two parallel planes, and the vector B in the direction of the normal, is equal to unity, since the 1-component of B is h, and $h/h = 1$. It is also equal to the length of B times the projection of a_1/h on the normal, which is just the distance d. Therefore, $1 = |B|d$, or $d = 1/|B|$, as was to be proved. The planes (222) are twice as closely spaced as are (111) planes, (333) planes three times, and so on.

The scalar product of two vectors, one referred to the a's and one referred to the b's, is simply the sum of the products of the components, just as in the case of the orthonormal basis. In other connections, these components are called *contravariant* and *covariant*, and it is similarly easy to form the scalar product. Of course, it is possible to form the scalar product of two vectors in the direct lattice or two vectors in the reciprocal lattice, but then it is not so easy, and the scalar products of the basis vectors are involved. Any vector can be expanded in terms of either set of basis vectors, but the components will not, of course, be the same.

We have found that the vector product of two direct lattice vectors can be expressed as a reciprocal lattice vector. Conversely, the vector product of two face normals (hkl) and (h'k'l') can be expressed as a direct lattice vector that is in the direction of the line of intersection of the two faces, or a crystal edge. The result is $(hk' - kh')a_1 + (lh' - hl')a_2 + (kl' - lk')a_3$ times 1/V, an unimportant factor. The coefficients can be written as 2 x 2 matrices. Therefore, if h,k,l and h',k',l' are integers, then so are the coefficients. We can remove any common factors without changing the direction of the edge vector. The vector can be written [pqr] in square brackets, where p = hk' - kh', and so on.

A set of faces whose intersections are parallel lines is called a *zone*. The zone direction is perpendicular to any normal to the faces of a zone. Therefore, the condition that a face (hkl) belong to zone [pqr] is that their scalar product vanish. Since the vectors are in reciprocal spaces, this condition is hp + kq + lr = 0. We note that zone axes also obey the Law of Rational Indices, and are given by [pqr] with p,q,r (usually) small integers. It is easy to see that the condition that three faces (hkl), (h'k'l') and (h",k",l") belong to the same zone is that the 3 x 3 determinant with these indices as rows (or columns) vanish. Summarizing, (hkl) is a direction in the reciprocal lattice, while [pqr] is a direction in the direct lattice.

A set of faces described by three numbers h,k,l in any order and including negative values is called a *form* and denoted {hkl}. For a cubic unit cell, the form {100} consists of the six faces of a cube: (100), (010), (001), (-100), (0-10), (00-1). The minus signs are not written in the proper places because this is hard to do in HTML. Similarly, the form {111} is an octahedron. Here we distribute 0,1,2 and 3 minus signs in all possible different ways. Phillips shows how to draw forms on clinometric axes, a delightful skill.

Physicists confuse things considerably by multiplying the reciprocal lattice basis vectors b by 2ð (as in Kittel). This avoids having to write this factor explicitly in several applications (notably to the Fourier transform), but destroys the mutual reciprocity of the direct and reciprocal lattices. It is not hard to allow for this, but the reader should be alert to which definition is used. The method used here to derive the reciprocal lattice is somewhat different than is normally used by either crystallographers or solid-state physicists, and rests more on the general mathematical properties of dual or reciprocal spaces, as the mention of contravariant and covariant components indicates.

It is instructive to admire the importance of the reciprocal lattice when dealing with crystals (or any periodic structure). We can expand vectors in direct space in terms of the basis vectors of the unit cell, whatever its shape, and the coefficients will be integers. Vectors can also be expanded in reciprocal space in terms of the reciprocal basis vectors. Integral coefficients then correspond to planes containing lattice points in direct space. The scalar product of two such vectors, one of each type, will then be integral (whatever the lengths and angles of the unit cell), and from this flow many remarkable results.

X-Ray Diffraction

Crystals may be probed with anything with a wavelength comparable to lattice spacings. The usual probes are X-rays, neutrons and electrons. Electrons interact strongly with matter because they are charged, and so are useful only for surface investigations. Neutrons require a strong neutron source and BF_3 detectors, so the experimental setup is expensive and complex. They interact with nuclei, and with the magnetic moments of electrons. X-rays, interacting with the electron density, are by far the most convenient probe, and can easily be used in any laboratory. X-rays can be detected by photographic emulsions, as well as by ionization chambers. The usual energies are 10-50 keV (the wavelength is 1.24/E nm, where E is in keV). The usual methods are Laue diffraction, rotating-crystal and powder camera, the last being the most popular and easiest to use. The powder camera was introduced by Debye and Scherrer, and by Hull, in 1916. The theory of von Laue, and the experiments of Friedrich and Knipping on ZnS, published on 8 June 1912, were the effective beginning of solid-state physics. W. L. Bragg reported the first crystal structure determination, that of KCl, in 1913, using a crystal spectrometer and ionization-chamber detectors. These were events of the first order in Physics, connecting us directly with the microscopic world of atoms and molecules.

Suppose a crystal is irradiated by an X-ray beam of wave vector k. The magnitude of this vector is k = 2ð/ë. The amplitude of the incident wave at any point r is $Ae^{i(k\cdot r\ -\ iùt)}$, where some point O has been chosen as origin. In general, we shall drop the time factor, which is the same for all quantities to be considered. The conventions are those of physicists, who use k and the angular frequency ù instead of 1/ë and f, and the time factor with a minus sign. We observe the radiation scattered by the crystal at some point P at R, which is taken as very distant to avoid having to consider the inconsequential details of a finite distance from the crystal to P, just as in optical diffraction theory. The amplitude at P is the sum of the amplitudes scattered by each volume element of the crystal, and the observed intensity is the absolute value squared of this. Consider the scattering associated with some lattice point Q at position ñ in the direct lattice. The amplitude of the spherical scattered wave will depend on e^{ikr}/r and the integral of the electron density at that point. We shall assume each lattice point contributes the same amount, but exactly what that amount is will be ignored, and we shall consider only the r-dependence. The amplitude at P is, then, proportional to $(e^{ik\cdot ñ})(^{ikr}/r)$. If R >> ñ then r is approximately R - ñ cos ö (to see this, expand r as found from the Law of Cosines in powers of ñ/R). Collecting all factors that do not depend strongly on ñ and considering them to be a constant, the amplitude at P is $(Ae^{ikR}/R)e^{i(k\cdot ñ - kñ \cos ö)}$. If now we introduce k′ = k(R/R), the exponential factor can be written $e^{i\Delta k\cdot ñ}$ in terms of Δk = k′ - k, the change in wave vector in the scattering observed at P.

This factor is easily interpreted in terms of the reciprocal lattice. In the exponent, we have the scalar product of two vectors. One, ñ, is a vector [qrs] in direct space, and the components are integers. If, then, Δk/2ð should be a vector (hkl) in reciprocal space, their scalar product is simply hq + kr + ls. If h,k,l are integers, then so is the scalar product, and $e^{i\Delta k\cdot ñ} = e^{2ðni} = 1$. This means that the contribution from every direct lattice point is the same, so that the total amplitude at P will be NA, if A is the contribution from one lattice point, and N is the number of lattice points in the crystal. That is, all the contributions add in phase, and the intensity will be $N^2|A|^2$, enormously greater than the intensity due to a single lattice point. This coherent superposition is like that which produces a spectral line from a grating, except that it is in three dimensions, and N is very much larger. Note how easily the reciprocal lattice, and the Law of Rational Indices, give this result!

Therefore, every reciprocal lattice point corresponds to a possible diffraction maximum. A maximum will be observed only if there is a nonzero contribution from each lattice point. The intensity of each maximum depends on the details of the scattering from the electron density around each direct lattice point. The strength and angles of these maxima are measured, and from them the structure of the crystal can be deduced. The Ewald Construction shows clearly the conditions under which a diffracted beam can be observed. If the wave vector k is used, the reciprocal lattice is the physicist's, expanded by a factor 2ð. The construction is to draw k ending at any lattice point, and the sphere partly shown with center at the beginning. Then, a maximum is possible if the sphere passes through a reciprocal lattice point. This shows just how difficult it is to satisfy the conditions for a diffraction maximum. In terms of the reciprocal lattice, let n be a unit vector in the direction of the incident radiation, and n′ a unit vector in the direction of the diffracted beam. A diffracted beam is observed if (n′ - n)/ë is some reciprocal lattice vector B with integral components. This assumes elastic scattering of the X-rays, which does not change the wavelength ë. Incidentally, the vector p = (h/ë)n, where h is Planck's constant, is the momentum of the X-ray photon. This scattering condition implies that the change of momentum is h times a reciprocal lattice vector. This momentum is absorbed by the whole crystal, which does not recoil because of its large mass, and so the scattering is elastic. Interactions with *phonons*, which are unimportant with X-rays, lead to inelastic scattering.

The most familiar description of X-ray scattering by crystals is by Bragg's Law. An X-ray beam is shown "reflected" from two crystal planes at a glancing angle è. The path difference ab is seen to be 2d sin è, and if this is equal to a wavelength the waves from these two planes will interfere constructively, and so on for any number of planes.

The integer n is the "order" of the diffraction. Though always presented in elementary discussions, it is certainly not a satisfying derivation of the diffraction condition, since it depends on arbitrary and unlikely assumptions. No "reflection" actually occurs in any sense. We see that the beam is scattered through an angle of 2è. The Ewald construction gives 2(1/ë)sin è = |B|, or ë = 2d sin è, which is just the Bragg condition. For a given spacing d, the wavelength and angle must be connected by this relation. If è is fixed (but perhaps different for different planes), as in a Laue experiment, then an X-ray beam containing a continuum of wavelengths will search out those spacings d for which the equation is satisfied, producing scattered beams only at certain angles. If the X-ray beam is monochromatic and the crystal is rotated, then a diffracted beam will be observed for a given d when the angle is correct. These beams are very sharp, because they result from the interference of a large number of components. Consequently, the measurements can be very precise. Computer processing has reduced the great tedium of analyzing the results.

The integral for the diffraction amplitude looks very much like a three-dimensional Fourier transform of the electron density from the direct space to the reciprocal space. If we knew the amplitudes, the transform could be inverted to give the electron density. What we know, however are the intensities, whose square roots only give the amplitudes up to a phase. This makes the inversion difficult, but progress can be made nevertheless. Since the transform is discrete and not continuous, the inversion is essentially a summation of plane waves, analogous to a Fourier series in one dimension.

These results apply not only to X-ray diffraction in crystals, but to the general problem of diffraction by a three-dimensional lattice. We note, in particular, the property of such diffracting systems of selecting wavelengths. A two-dimensional grating will make diffraction maxima for any incident wavelength, but a three-dimensional grating will not do so, selecting a particular wavelength from a white incident beam, as in white-light holograms or Laue photographs. The concept of the reciprocal lattice makes the explanation of these effects simple and straightforward, as we have seen.

Examples

Let's consider first a primitive orthorhombic lattice, in which the direct basis vectors are ai, bj, ck, in terms of the usual orthogonal unit vectors. The volume of the unit cell is V = abc. It is easy to see that the reciprocal basis vectors are (1/a)i, (1/b)j, (1/c)k. The name "reciprocal" is clearly well-chosen. The reciprocal lattice is also orthorhombic, and the volume of its unit cell is 1/abc. the vector (hkl) is B = (h/a)i + (k/b)j + (l/c)k. The length of this vector is B = "$[(h/a)^2 + (k/b)^2 + (l/c)^2]$. Therefore, the spacing of the (hkl) planes is d = 1/B. These results may be specialized for a primitive tetragonal lattice, a = b `″ c, or for a cubic lattice, a = b = c. The reciprocal lattice of a primitive hexagonal lattice is also a hexagonal lattice, but with a rotation. The hexagonal unit cell is a prism with angles 120° and 60° between the sides.

Kittel shows that the lattice reciprocal to the body-centered cubic is face-centered cubic, and vice-versa. The first *Brillouin zone* is a specially-chosen reciprocal unit cell. From the origin, vectors are drawn to the nearest lattice points in the reciprocal lattice, and planes drawn perpendicular to these vectors at their midpoints. The smallest volume enclosed by these planes is the Brillouin zone. It is a unit cell, and fills space when it is repeated. Brillouin zones are useful in studying wave motion in periodic structures, especially electron waves. The only allowed waves are those with wave vectors that fall in the Brillouin zone. The first Brillouin zone of a body-centered cubic lattice is a regular rhombic dodecahedron. That of a face-centered cubic lattice is a truncated octahedron.

If the direct basis vectors are given the dimension of length, then the reciprocal basis vectors will have the dimension of $(\text{length})^{-1}$. This suggests that it may be useful to consider the direct and reciprocal spaces as different in nature. In this case, direct vectors represent distances, while reciprocal vectors represent *spatial frequencies*. Exponents of the form B·r will then be dimensionless, and suitable for the exponential factors in Fourier transforms. Indeed, we have already made use of this in X-ray diffraction. In quantum mechanics, momentum is related to wavelength by p = h/ë = (h/2ð)k, so with proper normalization the reciprocal space turns out to be momentum space. This was suggested in connection with the Ewald construction, which follows from momentum conservation.

If we consider the first Brillouin zone as a region in momentum space, then any point within it corresponds to the wave vector of a certain plane wave whose frequency is a function of position. That is, we can specify the *dispersion relation* f = f(n/ë) or ù = ù(k) for wave vectors in this zone. [Spectroscopists write 1/ë = ó, and call it a *wave number*. Physicists generally multiply things by 2ð for some reason, and also write í instead of f for frequency.] Only wave vectors in this zone are necessary to specify all possible plane waves. As the discrete structure is imagined to become continuous by a decrease in the lattice spacing, the Brillouin zone expands to fill all space, and a wave may have any wave vector. This formalism can also be used to describe electron states, and in expressing the energy-momentum relation E = E(p). The first Brillouin zone should not be confused with the Fermi surface in this application. The Fermi surface is also in reciprocal space, but gives those momenta for which E = E_F, the Fermi energy of the electron gas. The Wigner-Seitz zone is constructed like the Brillouin zone, but in direct space, and is an alternative unit cell.

The internal energy of an insulating crystal is in the form of lattice vibrations, which can be described by wave vectors in reciprocal space. Physicists usually speak of wave vectors k = (2ð/ë)n in a reciprocal space expanded by a factor 2ð. All possible modes have wave vectors in the first Brillouin zone. In the case of X-rays, the wave vectors were large, much greater than the reciprocal lattice spacing. Here, the wave vectors are small. Wave vectors close to the origin represent ordinary sonic and ultrasonic waves in the crystal. These vibrations are, of course, quantized. Quantum effects are not evident for the small wave vectors, but become more prominent as the wave vectors approach the boundary of the Brillouin zone. At a temperature T, the oscillators representing the vibrational modes are excited according to Bose-Einstein statistics. In the familiar Debye approximation, the modes are assumed to be those of a continuum, extending to a maximum frequency f_D usually specified by the Debye temperature È, where hf_D = kÈ.

We can think of the lattice energy as resident in *phonons* of frequency f and wave vector k. Curiously, phonons of non-zero k do not carry actual momentum, though k is conserved in their interactions as if proportional to momentum in the usual way: p = (h/2ð)k. The zero-frequency mode is the only one carrying real momentum, and this is momentum of the lattice as a whole. If the lattice oscillators are perfectly harmonic, then phonons do not interact with one another. If this were true in a real crystal, the lattice could never come to thermal equilibrium. Energy put into phonons at one location would simply move to another location without resistance, and thermal conductivity could not be expressed as dependent on a temperature gradient; it would, in effect, be infinite. We actually see this in the case of ordinary sound waves, which certainly do not diffuse like heat.

Since heat, which after all is just lattice waves, does come into thermal equilibrium, and crystals show normal heat conduction proportional to a temperature gradient, there must be some mechanism for a system of high-frequency phonons to approach thermal equilibrium. If the lattice oscillators are anharmonic (their potential energy containing terms like $ex^3 + fx^4$, for example), we know that if vibrations of frequency f_1 and f_2 are simultaneously applied, the resulting motion will contain vibrations of frequency $f_3 = f_1 \pm f_2$. This implies that for phonons, we may observe processes like $k_1 + k_2 \rightarrow k_3$, and that these processes will conserve energy ($f_3 = f_1 + f_2$) as well as wave vector. Such phonon "collisions" may be a way to approach thermal equilibrium. A closer consideration of these "N" processes, however, shows that they cannot by themselves result in thermal equilibrium.

To see why, consider the case of translational energy in a gas. This energy equilibrates rapidly; any molecule of larger than normal velocity is quite rapidly slowed down by losing energy in collisions, and the direction of its momentum is quickly randomized. The thermal conductivity K, defined by $Q = K(dT/dx)$, is approximately $Cvs/3$, where C is the translational specific heat, v the average velocity, and s the mean free path between collisions. In an N process, the wave vector after the collision is in the same direction as the wave vectors before the collision. The hard collisions that produced equilibrium in the case of translation are not available.

However, suppose that the initial wave vectors are large enough that k_3 lies outside the Brillouin zone. To bring it back within the zone, it is necessary to add a lattice vector B. As in Bragg diffraction, the momentum difference is absorbed by the lattice as a whole while carrying away a negligible amount of energy, since the lattice is massive. The possible vectors B are the smallest reciprocal lattice vectors. The process $k_1 + k_2 \rightarrow k_3 + B$ is called an *umklapp* or "U" process. It is easily seen in a vector diagram that k_3 may be reversed in direction relative to k_1 or k_2. This supplies the role of the necessary momentum-reversing collisions. The mean free path s in the expression for thermal conductivity is the mean free path between U processes.

The initial wave vectors in a U-process must be large enough that their sum will go outside the Brillouin zone, so U processes will be important only at high enough temperatures for such wave vectors to be available. At low temperatures, s may increase to such an extent that only collisions with the boundaries of the crystal will be effective (these, too, can be "hard" and reverse momenta). This "shape effect" has been observed. The wave vectors of sound waves are much too small for U processes, so they do not equilibrate. These matters were brilliantly explained by R. Peierls, and are another example of the power of the reciprocal lattice.

The structures of face-centered cubic KCl (a = 0.629 nm) and NaCl (a = 0.563 nm) were those first deciphered by W. L. Bragg. He showed conclusively that the crystal was composed of alternating positive and negative ions, not of KCl molecules. The (100) planes are a checkerboard of positive and negative ions, and all these planes scatter equally. The planes are effectively spaced at half the lattice constant. Using the $K_{á1}$ line of Cu (0.1541 nm), the Bragg Law gives 2(0.563/2)sin è = (0.1541), or è = 15.89°. This is actually a (200) reflection. The (111) planes are of two types, planes of K^+ ions halfway between planes of Cl^- ions. Scattering from the two planes is opposite in phase, and of nearly equal intensity, so the (111) maxima are very weak (but are there). The (222) maxima are strong, as can be expected. Incidentally, the Mo $K_{á1}$ line at 0.0709 nm is also useful in crystal studies.

CRYSTALLOGRAPHY

Crystal Structure

In mineralogy and crystallography, a crystal structure is a unique arrangement of atoms in a crystal. A crystal structure is composed of a motif, a set of atoms arranged in a particular way, and a lattice. Motifs are located upon the points of a lattice, which is an array of points repeating periodically in three dimensions. The points can be thought of as forming identical tiny boxes, called unit cells, that fill the space of the lattice. The lengths of the edges of a unit cell and the angles between them are called the lattice parameters. The symmetry properties of the crystal are embodied in its space group. A crystal's structure and symmetry play a role in determining many of its properties, such as cleavage, electronic band structure, and optical properties.

Solids

Amorphous solids are homogeneous and isotropic because there is no long range order or periodicity in their internal atomic arrangement. By contrast, the crystalline state is characterised by a regular arrangement of atoms over large distances. Crystals are therefore anisotropic – their properties vary with direction. For example, the interatomic spacing varies with orientation within the crystal, as does the elastic response to an applied stress. Engineering materials are usually aggregates of many crystals of varying sizes and shapes; these polycrystalline materials have properties which depend on the nature of the individual crystals, but also on aggregate properties such as the size and shape distributions of the crystals, and the orientation relationships between the individual crystals. The randomness in the orientation of the crystals is a measure of texture, which has to be controlled in the manufacture of transformer steels, uranium fuel rods and beverage cans. The crystallography of interfaces connecting adjacent crystals can determine the deformation behaviour of the polycrystalline aggregate; it can also influence the toughness through its effect on the degree of segregation of impurities to such interfaces.

Metals and ceramics are the basic materials of nuclear reactors. The regular arrangement of the atoms in such solids is termed a crystal lattice. Pure solids (whether elemental or binary) need not retain the same crystal structure from low temperature to the melting point; iron and uranium exhibit three crystal structures, each confined to a definite temperature interval, but uranium dioxide has only one. The change from one crystal structure to another is called a phase transformation. Such changes are the solid-solid equivalents of melting and vaporization.

The crystal structure can exert a profound effect on material's behaviour in the environment of a nuclear reactor, as seen from the following examples:

- Void swelling can cause unacceptable dimensional changes in structures of fast reactors or fusion reactors (but not generally in light water reactors, except at higher doses and intermediate temperatures in austenitic stainless steels). The crystal structure of the austenitic form of steel is susceptible to this radiation effect but the different crystal structure of the ferritic form is immune until very high doses (>H"50 displacements per atom, dpa).
- Under fast-neutron irradiation, Zircaloy cladding of LWRs undergoes growth in the axial direction. This effect is due to the anisotropy of the crystal structure of zirconium.
- The relation between crystal anisotropy and the directional dependence of macroscopic properties in zirconium was covered in Sect I.2.
- The utility of uranium metal as a nuclear fuel is diminished because of the volume change accompanying a solid phase transformation that occurs at relatively low temperature.Imperfections in the crystal lattice are even more important than the details of the atomic structure.
- Missing atoms in the atomic lattice called vacancies, or extra atoms in nonregular positions called interstitials, are responsible for the mobility of atoms in the solid.
- Many of the mechanical properties of metals are governed by a linear defect in the atomic structure called a dislocation.
- All structural alloys and ceramic fuels consist of a large number of small crystals, or grains, joined at their peripheries. The discontinuities in the crystal structure at these internal surfaces are called grain boundaries. Their presence influences a variety of mechanical and transport properties, including cracking in steel and fission gas movement in fuel.

For elemental solids, only 14 distinct structures, or spatial arrangements of atoms, are possible. Each crystal structure is characterized by a unit cell, which is a small group of atoms that contains the unique features of the particular lattice type. A macroscopic crystal is composed of large numbers of unit cells stacked together.

The elemental and binary solids important in LWRs are restricted to only a few of the 14 possible lattice types, mainly those with the highest degrees of symmetry and the tightest packing of atoms. With one exception, these unit cells are parallelepipeds (all angles 90o) with side lengths denoted by a, b, and c.

The exception is a structure whose unit cell is a hexagonal prism with only two characteristic dimensions. Only the parallelepiped with all sides of equal length (*i.e.*, a cube) is isotropic. All the others are anisotropic, meaning that properties differ in the principal coordinate directions.

The Lattice

Crystals have translational symmetry: it is possible to identify a regular set of points, known as the lattice points, each of which has an identical environment. The set of these lattice points constitutes a three dimensional lattice. A unit cell may be defined within this lattice as a space–filling parallelepiped with origin at a lattice point, and with its edges defined by three non-coplanar basis vectors a1, a2 and a3, each of which represents translations between two lattice points. The entire lattice can then be generated by stacking unit cells in three dimensions. Any vector representing a translation between lattice points is called a lattice vector. The unit cell defined above has lattice points located at its corners. Since these are shared with seven other unit cells, and since each cell has eight corners, there is only one lattice point per unit cell. Such a unit cell is primitive and has the lattice symbol P. Non–primitive unit cells can have two or more lattice points, in which case, the additional lattice points will be located at positions other than the corners of the cell. A cell with lattice points located at the centres of all its faces has the lattice symbol F; such a cell would contain four lattice points. Not all the faces of the cell need to have face–centering lattice points; when a cell containing two lattice points has the additional lattice point located at the centre of the face defined by a2 and a3, the lattice symbol is A and the cell is said to be A-centred. B-centred and C-centred cells have the additional lattice point located on the face defined by a3 & a1 or a1 & a2 respectively.

A unit cell with two lattice points can alternatively have the additional lattice point at the body-centre of the cell, in which case the lattice symbol is I. The lattice symbol R is for a trigonal cell; the cell is usually defined such that it contains three lattice points. The basis vectors a1, a2 and a3 define the the unit cell; their magnitudes a1, a2 and a3 respectively, are the lattice parameters of the unit cell. The angles a1^a2, a2^a3 and a3 ^a1 are conventionally labelled g,aand b respectively. Note that our initial choice of the basis vectors was arbitrary since there are an infinite number of lattice vectors which could have been used in defining the unit cell. The preferred choice includes small basis vectors which are as equal as possible, provided the shape of the cell reflects the essential symmetry of the lattice.

The Bravais Lattices

The number of ways in which points can be arranged regularly in three dimensions, such that the stacking of unit cells fills space, is not limitless; Bravais showed in 1848 that all possible arrangements can be represented by just fourteen lattices. The fourteen Bravais lattices can be categorised into seven crystal systems (cubic, tetragonal, orthorhombic, trigonal, hexagonal, monoclinic and triclinic); the cubic system contains for example, the cubic-P, cubic-F and cubic-I lattices. Each crystal system can be characterised uniquely by a set of defining symmetry elements, which any crystal within that system must possess as a minimum requirement.

The Bravais lattices are each as a projection along the a_3 axis. Projections like these are useful as simple representations of three–dimensional objects. The coordinate of any point with respect to the a_3 axis is represented as a fraction of a_3 along the point of interest; points located at $0a3$ are unlabelled; translational symmetry requires that for each lattice point located at $0a_3$, there must exist another at $1a_3$.

Directions

Any vector u can be represented as a linear combination of the basis vectors ai of the unit cell (i = 1, 2, 3):

$$u = u_1a_1 + u_2a_2 + u_3a_3$$

and the scalar quantities u_1, u_2 and u_3 are the components of the vector u with respect to the basis vectors a_1, a_2 and a_3. Once the unit cell is defined, any direction u within the lattice can be identified uniquely by its components [u1 u2 u3], and the components are called the Miller indices of that direction and are by convention enclosed in square brackets.

Planes

If a plane intersects the a1, a2 and a3 axes at distances x1, x2 and x3 respectively, relative to the origin, then the Miller indices of that plane are given by (h1 h2 h3) where:

$$h_1 = \phi\frac{a_1}{x_1},\quad h_2 = \phi\frac{a_2}{x_2},\quad h_3 = \phi\frac{a_3}{x_3},$$

ϕ is a scalar which clears the numbers *hi* off fractions or common factors. Note that *xi* are negative when measured in the "*ai* directions. The intercept of the plane with an axis may occur at 1, in which case the plane is parallel to that axis and the corresponding Miller index will be zero. Miller indices for planes are by convention written using round brackets: (h1 h2 h3) with braces being used to indicate planes of the same form: {h1 h2 h3}.

The Reciprocal Lattice

The reciprocal lattice is a special co–ordinate system. For a lattice represented by basis vectors a1, a2 and a3, the corresponding reciprocal basis vectors are written a_1^*, a_2^* and a_3^*, such that:

$$a_1^* = \frac{(a_2 \wedge a_3)}{(a_1.a_2 \wedge a_3)}$$

$$a_2^* = \frac{(a_3 \wedge a_1)}{(a_1.a_2 \wedge a_3)}$$

$$a_3^* = \frac{(a_1 \wedge a_2)}{(a_1.a_2 \wedge a_3)}$$

In equation 2a, the term $(a_1.a_2 \wedge a_3)$ represents the volume of the unit cell formed by ai, while the magnitude of the vector $(a_2 \wedge$ a3) represents the area of the (1 0 0)A plane. Since $(a_2 \wedge a_3)$ points along the normal to the (1 0 0)A plane, it follows that a_1^* also points along the normal to (1 0 0)A and that its magnitude | | is the reciprocal of the spacing of the (1 0 0)A planes. The components of any vector referred to the reciprocal basis represent the Miller indices of a plane whose normal is along that vector, with the spacing of the plane given by the inverse of the magnitude of that vector. For example, the reciprocal lattice vector u* = (1 2 3) is normal to planes with Miller indices (1 2 3) and interplanar spacing 1/|u*|.

$$a_i \cdot a_j^* = 1 \quad \text{when } i = j, \quad \text{and } ai \cdot a_j^* = 0 \quad \text{when } i \neq j$$

or in other words, $a_i \cdot a_j^* = \delta_{ij}$.

δ_{ij} is the Kronecker delta, which has a value of unity when i = j and is zero when i $\neq$ j

Electrons in Metals

Metals are electrical conductors because some of the electrons are able to move freely, even though they move in a periodic array of positive metal ions. Electrons are waves, characterised by a wave number *k*,

$$k = \pm\frac{2\pi}{\lambda}$$

where λ is the wavelength. The lattice does not affect the motion of these electrons except at critical values of k, where the lattice planes reflect the electrons†. For a square lattice, these critical values of *k* are given by,

$$k = \frac{n\pi}{a\sin\theta}$$

where a is the lattice parameter and μ is the direction of motion. The component of k along the *x* axis is $kx = k \sin \mu$ and since $\mu = 0$, it follows that reflection occurs when

$$kx = \pm\frac{1/4}{a}$$

and similarly when,

$$ky = \pm\frac{1/4}{a},$$

This can be represented in *k*–space, which is reciprocal space with a reciprocal lattice parameter of magnitude 2p/a. Electrons are reflected in the lattice whenever k falls on any point on the square ABCD. This square is known as the first Brillouin zone boundary. Electron energy contours are frequently plotted in *k*–space. Inside a Brillouin zone, the energy of electrons can increase 'smoothly' with *k*; there is then a discontinuity (an energy gap) at the zone boundary.

Unit Cell

The crystal structure of a material or the arrangement of atoms in a crystal structure can be described in terms of its unit cell. The unit cell is a tiny box containing one or more motifs, a spatial arrangement of atoms. The units cells stacked in three-dimensional space describes the bulk arrangement of atoms of the crystal. The unit cell is given by its lattice parameters, the length of the cell edges and the angles between them, while the positions of the atoms inside the unit cell are described by the set of atomic positions (*xi*, *yi*, *zi*) measured from a lattice point.

Although there are an infinite number of ways to specify a unit cell, for each crystal structure there is a conventional unit cell, which is chosen to display the full symmetry of the crystal. However, the conventional unit cell is not always the smallest possible choice. A primitive unit cell of a particular crystal structure is the smallest possible volume one can construct with the arrangement of atoms in the crystal such that, when stacked, completely fills the space. This primitive unit cell will not always display all the symmetries inherent in the crystal. A Wigner-Seitz cell is a particular kind of primitive cell which has the same symmetry as the lattice. In a unit cell each atom has an identical environment when stacked in 3 dimensional space. In a primitive cell, each atom may not have the same environment.

Symmetry

Although the properties of a crystal can be anisotropic, there may be different directions along which they are identical. These directions are said to be equivalent and the crystal is said to possess symmetry. That a particular edge of a cube cannot be distinguished from any other is a measure of its symmetry; an orthorhombic parallelepiped has lower symmetry, since its edges can be distinguished by length. Some symmetry operations are illustrated in Fig. 6; in essence, they transform a spatial arrangement into another which is indistinguishable from the original. The rotation of a cubic lattice through 90° about an axis along the edge of the unit cell is an example of a symmetry operation, since the lattice points of the final and original lattice coincide in space and cannot consequently be distinguished. We have already encountered translational symmetry when defining the lattice; since the environment of each lattice point is identical, translation between lattice points has the effect of shifting the origin.

Symmetry Operations

An object possesses an n-fold axis of rotational symmetry if it coincides with itself upon rotation about the axis through an angle $360°\pm/n$. The possible angles of rotation, which are consistent with the translational symmetry of the lattice, are 360°, 180°, 120°, 90°and 60° for values of n equal to 1, 2, 3, 4 and 6 respectively. A five–fold axis of rotation does not preserve the translational symmetry of the lattice and is forbidden. A one-fold axis of rotation is called a monad and the terms diad, triad, tetrad and hexad correspond to n = 2, 3, 4 and 6 respectively.

All of the Bravais lattices have a centre of symmetry. An observer at the centre of symmetry sees no difference in arrangement between the directions $[u_1\ u_2\ u_3]$ and $[-u_1\ -u_2\ -u_3]$. The centre of symmetry is such that inversion through that point produces an identical arrangement but in the opposite sense. A rotoinversion axis of symmetry rotates a point through a specified angle and then inverts it through the centre of symmetry such that the arrangements before and after this combined operation are in coincidence. For example, a three-fold inversion axis involves a rotation through 120° combined with an inversion, the axis being labelled $\bar{3}$. A rotation operation can also be combined with a translation parallel to that axis to generate a screw axis of symmetry. The magnitude of the translation is a fraction of the lattice repeat distance along the axis concerned. A 31 screw axis would rotate a point through 120° and translate it through a distance t/3, where t is the magnitude of the shortest lattice vector along the axis. A 32 operation involves a rotation through 120° followed by a translation through 2t/3 along the axis. For a right–handed screw axis, the sense of rotation is anticlockwise when the translation is along the positive direction of the axis. A plane of mirror symmetry implies arrangements which are mirror images. Our left and right hands are mirror images. The operation of a 2 axis produces a result which is equivalent to a reflection through a mirror plane normal to that axis. The operation of a glide plane combines a reflection with a translation parallel to the plane, through a distance which is half the lattice repeat in the direction concerned. The translation may be parallel to a unit cell edge, in which case the glide is axial; the term diagonal glide refers to translation along a face or body diagonal of the unit cell. In the latter case, the translation is through a distance which is half the length of the diagonal concerned, except for diamond glide, where it is a quarter of the diagonal length.

Classification of Crystals by Symmetry

The defining property of a crystal is its inherent symmetry, by which we mean that under certain operations the crystal remains unchanged. For example, rotating the crystal 180 degrees about a certain axis may result in an atomic configuration which is identical to the original configuration. The crystal is then said to have a twofold rotational symmetry about this axis. In addition to rotational symmetries like this, a crystal may have symmetries in the form of mirror planes and translational symmetries, and also the so-called compound symmetries which are a combination of translation and rotation/ mirror symmetries. A full classification of a crystal is achieved when all of these inherent symmetries of the crystal are identified.

9

Equilibrium Chemistry

In a chemical reaction, chemical equilibrium is the state in which both reactants and products are present at concentrations which have no further tendency to change with time. Usually, this state results when the forward reaction proceeds at the same rate as the reverse reaction. The reaction ratesof the forward and backward reactions are generally not zero, but equal. Thus, there are no net changes in the concentrations of the reactant(s) and product(s). Such a state is known as dynamic equilibrium.

HISTORICAL INTRODUCTION

The concept of chemical equilibrium was developed after Berthollet (1803) found that some chemical reactions are reversible. For any reaction mixture to exist at equilibrium, the rates of the forward and backward (reverse) reactions are equal.

By convention the products form the numerator. However, the law of mass action is valid only for concerted one-step reactions that proceed through a single transition state and is not valid in general because rate equations do not, in general, follow thestoichiometry of the reaction as Guldberg and Waage had proposed (see, for example, nucleophilic aliphatic substitution by S_N1 or reaction of hydrogen and bromine to form hydrogen bromide). Equality of forward and backward reaction rates, however, is anecessary condition for chemical equilibrium, though it is not sufficient to explain why equilibrium occurs.

Despite the failure of this derivation, the equilibrium constant for a reaction is indeed a constant, independent of the activities of the various species involved, though it does depend on temperature as observed by the van 't Hoff equation. Adding a catalyst will affect both the forward reaction and the reverse reaction in the same way and will not have an effect on the equilibrium constant. The catalyst will speed up both reactions thereby increasing the speed at which equilibrium is reached.

Although the macroscopic equilibrium concentrations are constant in time, reactions do occur at the molecular level. For example, in the case of acetic acid dissolved in water and forming acetate and hydronium ions,

$CH_3CO_2H + H_2O$ ® $CH_3CO_2^- + H_3O^+$

a proton may hop from one molecule of acetic acid on to a water molecule and then on to an acetate anion to form another molecule of acetic acid and leaving the number of acetic acid molecules unchanged. This is an example of dynamic equilibrium. Equilibria, like the rest of thermodynamics, are statistical phenomena, averages of microscopic behavior.

Le Chatelier's principle (1884) gives an idea of the behavior of an equilibrium system when changes to its reaction conditions occur. *If a dynamic equilibrium is disturbed by changing the conditions, the position of equilibrium moves to partially reverse the change*. For example, adding more S from the outside will cause an excess of products, and the system will try to counteract this by increasing the reverse reaction and pushing the equilibrium point backward (though the equilibrium constant will stay the same).

If mineral acid is added to the acetic acid mixture, increasing the concentration of hydronium ion, the amount of dissociation must decrease as the reaction is driven to the left in accordance with this principle.

J. W. Gibbs suggested in 1873 that equilibrium is attained when the Gibbs free energy of the system is at its minimum value (assuming the reaction is carried out at constant temperature and pressure). What this means is that the derivative of the Gibbs energy with respect to reaction coordinate (a measure of the extent of reaction that has occurred, ranging from zero for all reactants to a maximum for all products) vanishes, signalling a stationary point. This derivative is called the reaction Gibbs energy (or energy change) and corresponds to the difference between the chemical potentials of reactants and products at the composition of the reaction mixture. This criterion is both necessary and sufficient. If a mixture is not at equilibrium, the liberation of the excess Gibbs energy (or Helmholtz energy at constant volume reactions) is the "driving force" for the composition of the mixture to change until equilibrium is reached.

LIQUID-VAPOUR EQUILIBRIUM

The concept of vapour pressure by means of a thought experiment. Our observation following injection of water into the box was that the pressure rose gradually from zero to 23.8 torr at a temperature of 25°C, where it levelled off and remained constant indefinitely.

The pressure resulted from formation of water vapour by evaporation of some of the liquid water. We address two interesting questions: 1) Why does evaporation occur? 2) Why does the pressure rise to 23.8 torr, then stop changing? We take first a macroscopic, then a molecular, view. Consider the process in equation:

$$H_2O(l) \rightarrow H_2O(g)$$

$$\Delta PE > 0 \text{ favors liquid}$$

$$\Delta S > 0 \text{ favors gas}$$

The drive to minimum energy favors the liquid phase. However, the drive to increased disorder favors the gas phase. Two natural tendencies try to drive the process in equation in opposite directions. The result is a compromise in which some water is present as liquid and some as vapour. This is our macroscopic interpretation of the vapour pressure phenomenon. We now seek an understanding at the molecular level.

An important result from our models of the gas, liquid, and solid phases can be stated succinctly as follows: at a given temperature, all molecules have the same average kinetic energy, whether they are present in the solid, liquid, or gas phase. Further, the distribution of kinetic energies follows the Maxwell-Boltzmann distribution, regardless of phase. The general form of the Maxwell-Boltzmann distribution is reproduced. In the ensuing discussion, we will apply this plot to the liquid phase of a pure substance.

As the curve indicates, at any moment there are some molecules moving very slowly, a large number moving with intermediate (near-average) kinetic energies, and a few molecules with very high kinetic energy. We focus now on the molecules near the surface of the liquid, because it is these that have a chance to escape from the liquid into the space above. Molecules near the surface possess a range of kinetic energies, like those in the bulk.

A molecule near the surface and moving toward the surface will escape the liquid if its kinetic energy is sufficient to overcome the attractive forces of nearby molecules in the liquid. In other words, the kinetic energy must be at least equal in magnitude to the depth of the liquid potential well. We will call this minimum required kinetic energy the escape kinetic energy. The number of liquid molecules having at least this kinetic energy is proportional to the area under the curve to the right of a vertical line passing through the escape *KE*.

When liquid water is injected into an evacuated box, it spreads out on the bottom and molecules begin to evaporate at a rate depending on two quantities. First, the number of molecules that evaporate per unit time is proportional to the number having at least the escape kinetic energy. Second, the evaporation rate is proportional to the number of molecules at the surface — i.e., to the exposed liquid surface area. In equation form,

$R_E = k_E(T)^*A$

R_E = evaporation rate, with units of amount per time

A = liquid surface area

$k_E(T)$ = rate constant for evaporation, with units of amount per unit area per unit time.

PURE SUBSTANCES

When pure substances (liquids or solids) are involved in equilibria their activities do not appear in the equilibrium constant because their numerical values are considered one. Applying the general formula for an equilibrium constant to the specific case of acetic acid one obtains

$$CH_3CO_2H + H_2O \rightleftharpoons CH_3CO_2^- + H_3O^+$$

$$K_c = \frac{[CH_3CO_2^-][H_3O^+]}{[CH_3CO_2H][H_2O]}$$

It may be assumed that the concentration of water is constant.

This assumption will be valid for all but very concentrated solutions. The equilibrium constant expression is therefore usually written as

$$K = \frac{[CH_3CO_2^-][H_3O^+]}{[CH_3CO_2H]}$$

where now

$$K = K_c \cdot [H_2O]$$

a constant factor is incorporated into the equilibrium constant.

A particular case is the self-ionization of water itself

$$H_2O + H_2O \rightleftharpoons H_3O^+ + OH^-$$

The self-ionization constant of water is defined as

$$K_w = [H^+][OH^-]$$

It is perfectly legitimate to write $[H^+]$ for the hydronium ion concentration, since the state of solvation of the proton is constant (in dilute solutions) and so does not affect the equilibrium concentrations. K_w varies with variation in ionic strength and/or temperature.

The concentrations of H^+ and OH^- are not independent quantities. Most commonly $[OH^-]$ is replaced by $K_w[H^+]^{-1}$ in equilibrium constant expressions which would otherwise include hydroxide ion.

Solids also do not appear in the equilibrium constant expression, if they are considered to be pure and thus their activities taken to be one. An example is the Boudouard reaction:

$$2CO \rightleftharpoons CO_2 + C$$

for which the equation (without solid carbon) is written as:

$$K_c = \frac{[CO_2]}{[CO]^2}$$

Multiple equilibria

Consider the case of a dibasic acid H_2A. When dissolved in water, the mixture will contain H_2A, HA^- and A^{2-}. This equilibrium can be split into two steps in each of which one proton is liberated.

$$H_2A \rightleftharpoons HA^- + H^+ : K_1 = \frac{[HA^-][H^+]}{[H_2A]}$$

$$HA^- \rightleftharpoons A^{2-} + H^+ : K_2 = \frac{[A^{2-}][H^+]}{[HA^-]}$$

K_1 and K_2 are examples of *stepwise* equilibrium constants. The *overall* equilibrium constant, β_D, is product of the stepwise constants.

$$H_2A \rightleftharpoons A^{2-} + 2H^+ : \beta_D = \frac{[A^{2-}][H^+]^2}{[H_2A]} = K_1K_2$$

Note that these constants are dissociation constants because the products on the right hand side of the equilibrium expression are dissociation products. In many systems, it is preferable to use association constants.

$$A^{2-} + H^+ \rightleftharpoons HA^- : \beta_1 = \frac{[HA^-]}{[A^{2-}][H^+]}$$

$$A^{2-} + 2H^+ \rightleftharpoons H_2A : \beta_2 = \frac{[H_2A]}{[A^{2-}][H^+]^2}$$

β_1 and β_2 are examples of association constants. Clearly $\beta_1 = 1/K_2$ and $\beta_2 = 1/\beta_D$; lg β_1 = pK_2 and lg β_2 = pK_2 + pK_1 For multiple equilibrium systems, also see: theory of Response reactions.

Effect of Temperature

The effect of changing temperature on an equilibrium constant is given by the van 't Hoff equation

$$\frac{d \ln K}{dT} = \frac{\Delta H_m^{\ominus}}{RT^2}$$

Thus, for exothermic reactions, (ΔH is negative) *K* decreases with an increase in temperature, but, for endothermic reactions, (ΔH is positive) *K* increases with an increase temperature. An alternative formulation is

$$\frac{d \ln K}{d(1/T)} = -\frac{\Delta H_m^{\ominus}}{R}$$

At first sight this appears to offer a means of obtaining the standard molar enthalpy of the reaction by studying the variation of *K* with temperature. In practice, however, the method is unreliable because error propagation almost always gives very large errors on the values calculated in this way.

CHEMICAL EQUILIBRIUM REACTION

We introduce chemical equilibrium with a simple reaction, the dimerization of nitrogen dioxide to dinitrogen tetroxide, in equation :

$$2NO_2 \rightarrow N_2O_4$$

As we have done several times before, we will study the reaction by carrying out several thought experiments designed to reveal the behaviour of the reaction under various conditions. Throughout the following discussion, bear in mind that the experiments could be (and in fact have been) carried out in the laboratory (although in a somewhat different manner than described). An initially evacuated container of volume 1.0 L, with an attached manometer.

The manometer allows the total gas pressure in the container to be measured. The temperature of the container is 298 K. The container is fitted with a piston that can be freely moved or locked in place. The following experiments are sequentially performed.

Expt. With the piston locked in place, 0.0460 g (0.0100 moles) of NO_2 gas (red-brown in colour, and toxic!) is injected into the container through a septum cap. The manometer quickly registers a pressure of 0.248 atm (188 mm of Hg).

Then, over several minutes, the red-brown colour fades and the pressure of the system falls, at first rapidly, then more and more slowly, until it levels off at a value of 0.175 atm. This is the sum of the partial pressures of NO_2, 0.102 atm (measured from the intensity of the red-brown colour) and N_2O_4, 0.073 atm (calculated by difference). The manner in which the total pressure and the partial pressures of NO_2 and N_2O_4 vary with time after injection of NO_2.

Expt. The piston is kept locked in place and the container is pumped out. Then 0.0460 g (0.0050 moles) of N_2O_4 (colorless) is injected.

The manometer quickly registers a pressure of 0.124 atm. Over several minutes, a red-brown colour develops and the pressure of the system increases, at first rapidly, then more slowly, until it levels off at a value of 0.175 atm.

The partial pressures of NO_2 and N_2O_4 are again 0.102 and 0.073 atm, respectively, once the situation of constant pressure is reached. The pressures vary with time after injection of N_2O_4. Note that the final pressures are the same as in Experiment.

Expt. With the piston still in place, the container is pumped out. Simultaneously, 0.0230 g (0.0050 moles) NO_2 and 0.0230 g (0.0025 moles) N_2O_4 are injected to the container. The manometer quickly registers a pressure of 0.186 atm, but over several minutes, the red-brown colour slightly fades and the total pressure drops to and levels off at 0.175 atm. The partial pressures of the two gases are the same at the end as in the first 2 experiments.

Expt. After evacuating the container, 0.0460 g of NO_2 and 0.0460 g of N_2O_4 are injected simultaneously. The manometer quickly registers 0.372 atm. Over several minutes, the red-brown colour fades and the pressure of the system decreases, at first rapidly, then more and more slowly, until it levels off at 0.325 atm. The final partial pressures of NO_2 and N_2O_4 are 0.155 and 0.170 atm. The pressures vary with time after injection of the gases.

Expt. The piston is now quickly pushed in until the volume of the container is cut in half. Immediately after this is done, the manometer registers 0.650 atm (twice the final pressure in the previous experiment).

However, over an interval of time the pressure and the red-brown colour decrease until they eventually level off again. The final total pressure is 0.611 atm. The pressures of NO_2 and N_2O_4 are 0.232 and 0.379 atm, respectively.

We now draw what conclusions we can from the experimental results. First, whether we start with NO_2, N_2O_4, or some arbitrary mixture, a dynamic process occurs, the result of which is a situation in which both gases are present. Second, the dynamic process leads to a situation in which there is no further change in macroscopic variables (i.e., the amounts of the 2 gases).

Third, experiments show us that the final amounts of NO_2 and N_2O_4 are the same as long as we start with the same total moles of nitrogen and oxygen atoms (in all 3 experiments, we begin with 0.0100 moles of nitrogen atoms and 0.0200 moles of oxygen atoms).

It appears that there is some regularity in the result of the dynamic process. Fourth, experiment 5 shows that we affect the reaction system by putting a stress on it, but that it adjusts to the stress and returns to equilibrium. We conclude that the system exhibits the characteristics of dynamic equilibrium.

For liquid-vapour phase equilibrium, we saw that the equilibrium state at a fixed T is characterized by a constant pressure (concentration) of vapour. No matter what we did to the system, other than change T, the pressure returned to this value. Is there a similar quantity for the reaction, a quantity that characterizes the equilibrium state as long as *T* is constant, and which in some way depends on the pressures (amounts) of the gases? We cannot use the sum or the product of the gas pressures, because these are obviously different at equilibrium in experiments 1 and 4.

The values in experiment 4 are both larger than those in experiment 1, which suggests that some ratio of pressures might be constant. Table shows the initial and final pressures, and the ratios P_{N2O4}/P_{NO2} and $P_{N2O4}/(P_{NO2})^2$ for Experiments:

Experiments 4 and 5 demonstrate that a simple ratio does not work. However, the modified ratio, in which the pressure of NO_2 is squared, does remain constant for all experiments. This ratio is interesting, because the powers to which the pressures are raised are the stoichiometric coefficients of the gases in equation. The number, 7.0 atm^{-1}, is called the equilibrium constant for reaction at 298 K, and is given the symbol K_{eq}. The ratio, $P_{N2O4}/(P_{NO2})^2$, is called the equilibrium constant expression for the reaction:

$K_{eq} = P_{N2O4}/(P_{NO2})^2 = 7.0 \text{ atm}^{-1}$ for reaction at 298 K

Concept of Chemical Equilibrium

The results of experiments on many different reactions over many years allow us to generalize as follows. For the generic reaction, in which the participating species are gases, the partial pressures at equilibrium obey the simple expression, independent of the initial pressures of the gases.

$$aA + bB \rightarrow dD + fF$$

$$K_{eq} = P_D{}^d P_F{}^f / P_A{}^a P_B{}^b$$

In words, the equation says that if we divide the product of the pressures of the products, each raised to the power of its stoichiometric coefficient in the equation for the reaction, by a similar product of reactant pressures, the result is a constant, K_{eq}, that depends only on temperature.

Every chemical reaction, simple or complex, obeys an equilibrium constant expression of the form of equation above. This is a very simple result that makes possible calculations involving the direction and extent of reaction.

If the value of K_{eq} for a reaction is large, the pressures of products will be large relative to those of reactants at equilibrium — the equilibrium lies to the right. If K_{eq} is small, pressures of products will be small relative to those of reactants at equilibrium — the equilibrium lies to the left.Our conclusions are not restricted to gas phase reactions.

An expression analogous to equation applies to reactions in solution, except that molarities must be used in place of pressures. In fact, when we recognize that gas pressure is proportional to n/V (molarity) through the ideal gas law, we realise the equivalence of expressions in terms of pressure and molar concentration. Equation therefore applies to all reactions, in the gas phase, in solution, or in some combination:

$$K_{eq} = [\Delta]^{\Delta}[F]^{f}/[A]^{a}[B]^{b}$$

The brackets signify molarity. One caution is in order for gas phase reactions. The numerical value and the units of the equilibrium constant depend on whether pressures or molarities are used. If K_{eq} is specified in units of bar, pressures are used in calculations; if in moles/L, concentrations are used. If K_{eq} has no units, either pressure or molarity may be used.

PRINCIPLE AND CHEMICAL EQUILIBRIUM

This principle applies as well to chemical equilibrium as to phase equilibrium. In fact, the principle is a qualitative manifestation of the quantitative characteristics of the equilibrium constant. Three stresses are particularly relevant to chemical equilibrium.

- Change in concentration (pressure) of a participant. For example, consider the reaction

  $$N_2 + 3H_2 \ \Delta\ 2NH_3$$

  Assume the reaction to be initially at equilibrium. Suppose that we add some NH_3 to the system. This imposes a stress on the system that will be relieved, according to Le Chatelier, by a shift that relieves the stress — i.e., uses up NH_3. The reaction shifts left until enough NH_3 is used and N_2 and H_2 produced to again make $Q = K_{eq}$. When the new equilibrium is reached, the pressures of all three gases will be larger than they were before the stress. Note that addition of NH_3 to the system does not change the value of K_{eq}. The same value applies before and after the stress.

  Please note in the figure that the changes in pressure of the three gases following the perturbation are in accord with the reaction stoichiometry: ΔP for NH_3 is negative and is twice as large in magnitude as ΔP for N_2; and ΔP for H_2 is three times the value for N_2.
- Change in system volume. This stress is important only for reactions involving gases. Consider again the ammonia formation reaction, initially at equilibrium:

  $$N_2 + 3H_2 \Leftrightarrow 2NH_3$$

  Now instantly cut the system volume in half. This instantly doubles the total pressure of the system. Le Chatelier predicts that, if possible, reaction will shift to offset the effect of the stress; to decrease the total system pressure. This may be accomplished by a shift toward the right, which will decrease the total number of gas molecules in the container (4 molecules of reactant are converted to only 2 of product). Moles of gas decreases, and so does total pressure.

In general, decreasing the volume (increasing pressure) of a reaction system involving one or more gases results in a shift toward the side with the least moles of gas. Apply this idea to a decrease in system pressure for the reaction

$$H_2(g) + Br_2(g) \rightarrow 2HBr(g)$$

A change in system volume (pressure) has no effect on the magnitude of K_{eq} for the system, as long as temperature is kept constant.

- Change in T. The reasoning here is the same as for phase equilibrium. An increase in T results in a shift in the endothermic direction, to use heat. A decrease in T results in an exothermic shift. In contrast to changes in concentration or system volume, a change in T causes a change in the value of K_{eq}.

View of Chemical Equilibrium

Consider now the general reaction in equation.

$$A + B \rightarrow 2C$$

$$K_{eq} = P_C^2 / P_A P_B$$

Why do the stoichiometric coefficients appear as exponents in the expression for K_{eq}? Chemical equilibrium is like phase equilibrium; it results from a balance of opposing rates. In this case, the rates involved are those of the reaction in the forward and reverse directions: At equilibrium, $R_f = R_r$.

Molecules must collide in order to react. This is certainly sensible, because it is not possible for atom rearrangements to occur unless the reacting atom aggregates are in close proximity. The rate of a chemical reaction is thus expected to be proportional to the number of collisions between molecules per unit time:

rate of rxn proportional to #collisions/time

For the forward and reverse processes in equation, we write

$R_f = k_f$ (#collisions of A and B)

$R_r = k_r'$(#collisions of C and C)

The rate constants, k_f and k_r', are proportionality constants in the same way that k_E and k_C are. If there are N_A molecules of A and N_B of B in a container, a particular A molecule may collide with any of the N_B molecules of B. The total number of ways in which A and B may collide is thus $N_A \times N_B$. Then

$R_f = k_f N_A N_B$

N_C molecules of C can collide in a total of $N_C(N_C - 1)/2$ ways. This arises because each molecule can collide with $N_C - 1$ others. However, the simple product of N_C and $N_C - 1$ double counts the collisions (i.e., it includes collisions of molecule x with y and of y with x; however, there can be only one collision between two particular molecules). We divide by 2 to eliminate double counting. Finally, because N_C is very large, $N_C - 1 = N_C$. It follows that

$$R_r = k_r' N_C^2/2 = k_r N_C^2$$

At chemical equilibrium, then

$$k_f N_A N_B = k_r N_C^2$$

Rearranging gives

$$k_f / k_r = N_C^2 / N_A N_B = K_{eq}$$

Since pressure is proportional to number of molecules, this equation is readily translated to pressure terms, giving the equilibrium constant expression in equation. Notice that, as was true for phase equilibrium, the equilibrium constant is a ratio of rate constants for forward and reverse processes. Chemical equilibrium, like phase equilibrium, is dynamic rather than static. Although it appears at the macroscopic level that nothing is happening since concentrations remain constant, both forward and reverse reactions continue at equal rates at the molecular level.

Free Energy and Equilibrium

To this point we have encountered two quantities that indicate the extent to which a chemical reaction will proceed: its spontaneity. These are K_{eq} and the standard free energy change of reaction, $\Delta G_R°$. We now explore the relationship between these quantities.

The sign of $\Delta G_R°$ indicates the spontaneity or non-spontaneity of a process in which reactants in their standard states are converted to products in their standard states. The magnitude of $\Delta G_R°$ tells us how far the standard state is from the equilibrium state. A process for which $\Delta G_R°$ is negative is spontaneous under standard conditions, and will proceed left to right to reach equilibrium. At equilibrium, the reactants will be present at less than the standard state pressure (1 atm) or concentration (1 M), because they have been used up to some extent in achieving equilibrium. The products will be present at greater than the standard state pressure or concentration, because they have been formed in achieving equilibrium. In the equilibrium state, products will be present in relatively large amounts, reactants will be present in relatively small amounts, consistent with $K_{eq} > 1$. Thus $\Delta G_R° < 0$ corresponds to $K_{eq} > 1$. Further, for a process with $\Delta G_R° = -50$ kJ, the standard state is much farther away from equilibrium than is the standard state for a process with $\Delta G_R° = -$

5 kJ. The first reaction will have to proceed further to reach the equilibrium state than will the second reaction, and will thus have a larger K_{eq}. We can make very similar statements about processes for which $\Delta G_R{}^\circ > 0$, except in reverse.

The larger the magnitude of $\Delta G_R{}^\circ$, the further the standard state is from the equilibrium position, and the further reaction will have to proceed to reach equilibrium from the standard state. For $DG_R{}^o > 0$, reaction must proceed from right to left toward equilibrium, decreasing the pressures or concentrations of products and increasing those of reactants. Thus $K_{eq} < 1$. The larger the magnitude of $\Delta G_R{}^\circ$, the smaller K_{eq}. Finally, when $\Delta G_R{}^\circ = 0$, the process is equally spontaneous in both forward and reverse directions; the standard state is the equilibrium state.

Example: Given are several reactions and their standard free energies of reaction. Which reaction is furthest from equilibrium in the standard state? In which direction will each reaction have to proceed to reach the equilibrium state?. Which reaction has the largest value of K_{eq}?

Process	$\Delta G_R{}^\circ$
$N_2\,(g) + 3H_2\,(g)\; 2NH_3\,(g)$	–33 kJ
$6CO_2(g) + 6H_2O(l)\; C_6H_{12}O_6(s) + 6O_2(g)$	2880 kJ
$CO_2(g) + 2H_2O(l)\; CH_3OH(l) + 3/2\; O_2(g)$	702.4 kJ

Solution: The magnitude of $\Delta G_R{}^\circ$ is largest for the second reaction; it is furthest from equilibrium under standard conditions. The first reaction will proceed left to right toward equilibrium, because it is spontaneous under standard conditions; the other two will proceed right to left. The most spontaneous reaction has the largest K_{eq}. This is the first reaction.

It would be useful to have available a way to estimate ΔG for a reaction under arbitrary (not necessarily standard) conditions of pressure or concentration. This would allow us to predict the direction of equilibrium from any desired starting concentrations or pressures. In fact, an expression relating the free energy change for a reaction under arbitrary conditions to the standard free energy change is developed. Interested readers are referred there for the full details. Here, we present only the results.

$$\Delta G_R = \Delta G_R{}^\circ + RT \ln Q$$

Here Q is the reaction quotient introduced earlier. Equation says that the free energy change under arbitrary concentration conditions can be obtained by correcting the standard free energy change, $\Delta G_R{}^\circ$, by a term (Q) whose value depends upon what the non-standard conditions are. This seems quite reasonable.

When $Q = 1$ (i.e., all concentrations are standard at 1 M), the equation tells us that $\Delta G_R = \Delta G_R{}^\circ$, as it should. When $Q < 1$ (reactants are present in greater relative amounts than products), the equation tells us that $\Delta G_R < \Delta G_R^\circ$; in other words, that reaction is more spontaneous than under standard conditions. This too is reasonable; reaction should have a greater tendency to proceed left to right if reactant concentrations are increased.

When $Q > 1$ (reactants are present in lesser relative amounts than products), $\Delta G_R > \Delta G_R^\circ$; reaction is less spontaneous than under standard conditions. Reaction has a lesser tendency to proceed left to right if product concentrations are increased.

Suppose now that we choose some arbitrary initial concentrations of reactants (they could be, but need not be, 1 atm or 1 M) and products, and allow reaction to proceed from there to equilibrium. At equilibrium, ΔG_R must be zero because the forward and reverse spontaneities are the same. Further, once equilibrium is attained, the pressures (or concentrations) of all reactants and products must be equilibrium values, so $Q = K_{eq}$. Equation becomes

$$\Delta G_R^\circ = -RT \ln K_{eq}$$

This is one of the most important results in all of thermodynamics. It gives a direct relationship between our two criteria of spontaneity. Substitution of $\Delta H^\circ - T\Delta S^\circ$ for ΔG° gives the temperature dependence of the equilibrium constant: $\ln K_{eq} = -\Delta H^\circ/RT + \Delta S^\circ/R$.

Equation is called the van't Hoff relationship. Note that it is identical in form to the Clausius-Clapeyron equation for the temperature dependence of the vapour pressure. This reinforces our earlier recognition that P_{vap} is simply an equilibrium constant, and gives substance to the statement that all physical and chemical processes exhibit temperature dependence of the same form.

Spreadsheets in Equilibrium Calculations

A systematic approach to the calculation of equilibrium pressures in gas phase reactions. However, we have been careful to choose examples that generate no higher than a second-order polynomial — a quadratic equation — which is readily solved. There are many chemical reactions that generate polynomials of order 3 and higher when our general method is applied. Such polynomials cannot be solved analytically. That is, there is no analog of the quadratic formula that gives the roots of a polynomial of order > 3. Consider the very important reaction

$$N_2(g) + 3H_2(g) \rightarrow 2NH_3(g)$$

for which the equilibrium constant expression is :

$$K_{eq} = P_{NH_3}{}^2 / P_{N_2} P_{H_2}{}^3$$

Application of our approach to this reaction generates an equation in x^4 (from the denominator of K_{eq}) which cannot be solved analytically.

However, the availability of personal computers and modern Spreadsheet programs enables such problems to be easily solved. We consider a specific example:

	$N_2(g)$ +	$3H_2(g) \rightarrow$	$2NH_3(g)$	$K_{eq} = 15.0\ atm^{-1}$
initial	10.5	0.38	0.24	

For the initial conditions, $Q = 0.10$, so reaction will proceed right to equilibrium. The change and equilibrium lines then follow:

Change	$-x$	$-3x$	$2x$
equal	$10.5 - x$	$0.38 - 3x$	$0.24 + 2x$

Now, instead of substituting into the K_{eq} expression as we normally do (which would generate a polynomial of order 4), we set limits on the value of x; i.e., we figure out the minimum and maximum values that x can have. The minimum is clearly zero, which would correspond to no reaction.

The maximum value is calculated by assuming that reaction proceeds to the right until the limiting reagent is used up. The limiting reagent is clearly H_2, so the maximum possible x value is $0.38/3 = 0.127$ atm. The numerical range in which x must lie is thus $0 < x < 0.127$. We now explore this range with a trial-and-error procedure that goes as follows:

- Vary x systematically between 0 and 0.127
- Calculate Q for each x
- Compare Q with K_{eq}
- When $Q = K$ ($Q - K = 0$, or $Q/K = 1$),

we have found x.

Calculations of Equilibrium

Extent of Reaction. We used Q and K_{eq} to predict the direction in which a reaction will proceed from specified starting conditions. We now wish to calculate the extent to which it will proceed.

Example: K_{eq} for the dimerization of nitrogen dioxide is 7.0 atm^{-1} at 298 K. Suppose that sufficient NO_2 is placed in a flask to give an initial pressure of 1.5 atm. What will be the NO_2 and N_2O_4 pressures in the flask when the reaction has reached equilibrium?

Solution: In solving this problem we develop a general approach that is applicable to any chemical equilibrium situation. Since we will study chemical equilibrium for a variety of reaction types, it is important for you to learn now how to apply the approach.

- *Step:* Write the chemical reaction, leaving space under it for further information. Write the equilibrium constant expression to the right of the reaction.

- *Step:* Immediately under the reaction, write the initial concentration (pressure) conditions. The initial concentration (pressure) of each participant in the reaction is written under its formula. If the initial concentration of a participant is zero, write this explicitly. Steps 1 and 2 are combined below:

	$2NO_2 \rightarrow$	N_2O_4	$K_{eq} = P_{N2O4}/P_{NO2}{}^2 = 7.0\ atm^{-1}$
initial:	1.5	0	

- The word "initial" is written to the left of the initial pressures as a reminder of the significance of the numbers that follow. Since there is initially no N_2O_4 present, we write 0 under its formula. It is important to note that there is no stoichiometric restriction on the initial pressures. The initial pressures need not and usually do not bear any relationship to the stoichiometric coefficients for the reaction.
- *Step:* Directly beneath the initial conditions, write the changes in concentration (pressure) that occur for each participant as reaction proceeds toward equilibrium. The amount by which the reaction must proceed to achieve equilibrium is what we want to find out, so is treated as an algebraic unknown. The usual symbol for such an unknown is "*x*". We let *x* represent the pressure of NO_2 that is used up as reaction proceeds from the initial conditions to equilibrium. If "*x*" bar of NO_2 is used, what pressure of N_2O_4 is produced? It is in answering this question that the stoichiometry of the reaction is used. The chemical equation states that for each 2 molecules (moles) of NO_2 used, 1 molecule (mole) of N_2O_4 forms. Since pressure is directly related to moles through the ideal gas law at constant V and T, the same stoichiometry applies to pressure changes. Thus for each 2 atm of NO_2 used, 1 atm of N_2O_4 forms. Thus for *x* atm of NO_2 used, $x/2$ atm N_2O_4 are formed. We write this information under the initial conditions in a line headed ΔP.

$2NO_2 \rightarrow$	N_2O_4	$K_{eq} = P_{N2O4}/P_{NO2}{}^2 = 7.0\ atm^{-1}$
initial:	1.5	0
ΔP:	$-x$	$x/2$

- ΔP means the change in pressure that occurs for each participant. The change for NO_2 is negative because its pressure decreases as reaction proceeds. The change for N_2O_4 is positive because its pressure increases as reaction proceeds. The values in the ΔP line have relative values that correspond to the coefficients of the equation. This is always the case.
- *Step:* Finally, in a third line we write the equilibrium pressures of all participants. These are obtained for each participant by adding its initial pressure to the change in its pressure that occurs as a result of reaction.

$2NO_2 \rightarrow$	N_2O_4	$K_{eq} = P_{N2O4}/P_{NO2}^2 = 7.0\ atm^{-1}$
initial:	1.5	0
ΔP:	$-x$	$x/2$
equilibrium:	$1.5 - x$	$x/2$

- At equilibrium we have less NO_2 and more N_2O_4 than we started with, consistent with expectations based on the reaction quotient, Q.
- *Step:* Substitute the equilibrium pressure expressions into the K_{eq} expression and solve for the unknown.

$7.0 = (x/2)/(1.5 - x)^2$

Expansion and rearrangement gives a quadratic equation in x:

$$14x^2 - 43x + 31.5 = 0$$

This is solved with the quadratic formula to give

$$x = 1.87,\ 1.21$$

There can be only one correct answer to our problem because physically there can be only one position of equilibrium resulting from the given initial state. Examination of the two roots shows that 1.87 cannot be correct; if it is subsituted for x in the expression for the equilibrium pressure of NO_2, $1.5 - x$, a negative value, -0.37 atm, is obtained. This is physically meaningless. It is impossible to use up more NO_2 than is initially present. Thus $x = 1.21$ atm, and the equilibrium pressures of the two participants are

$$P_{NO2} = 0.29\ \text{atm}$$

$$P_{N2O4} = 0.60\ \text{atm.}$$

These results are readily checked by substituting them into the K_{eq} expression:

$$K_{eq} = 0.60/(0.29)^2 = 7.1$$

Within the limits of round-off error, this is the same as the given value of K_{eq}. We conclude that the answer is correct. A graphical interpretation of this problem, showing the manner in which the initial pressures evolve to the equilibrium values.

***Example:*.** Suppose that the volume of the reaction container for Example is instantly decreased by a factor of 2. In which direction will reaction shift? What will the equilibrium pressures of NO_2 and N_2O_4 be?

Solution: To answer the first question we must compare Q with K_{eq}. To answer the second requires a calculation similar to that in the previous example. The strategy is

- Determine the pressures of NO_2 and N_2O_4 immediately after the volume decrease but prior to reaction. These will be the initial pressures.
- Use these initial pressures to calculate Q. Compare with K_{eq}.

- Set up the initial, change, and equilibrium information and solve the equilibrium constant expression for the unknown extent of reaction. Immediately after the volume change, but before reaction takes place, the NO_2 and N_2O_4 pressures will be twice the equilibrium values from the previous example because volume has been halved. Thus

$$P_{NO2} = 0.58 \text{ atm}$$
$$P_{N2O4} = 1.2 \text{ atm}$$

These are the initial pressures for the problem at hand. We calculate Q:

$$Q = 1.2/(0.58)^2 = 3.3 < K_{eq}.$$

The reaction must therefore shift right to reattain equilibrium. Now we set up a table similar to that in the previous example:

	$2NO_2 \rightarrow$	N_2O_4	$K_{eq} = P_{N2O4}/P_{NO2}^{\ 2} = 7.0 \text{ atm}^{-1}$
initial:	0.58	1.2	
Δ P:	$-2x$	x	
equilibrium:	$0.58 - 2x$	$1.2 + x$	

In this case we have defined x differently than in Example. Previously we defined x as the pressure of NO_2 that disappears during reaction. Here it is the pressure of N_2O_4 formed during reaction. In both examples, the pressure of NO_2 that disappears is twice the pressure of N_2O_4 formed, as stoichiometry demands. It doesn't matter how we define x, as long as the change line obeys the reaction stoichiometry. You should proceed as in the previous example to set up the quadratic equation and solve it to obtain $x = 0.55$, 0.076 atm. The root, 0.55, is physically unreasonable (why?) so x = 0.086 atm. Substituting into the expressions for the equilibrium pressures gives

$$PNO_2 = 0.43 \text{ atm}$$
$$PN_2O_4 = 1.28 \text{ atm}$$

You should check that these values satisfy the K_{eq} expression. The effect of the volume decrease and the subsequent return of the system to equilibrium.

Example:. Consider the reaction $N_2 + 3H_2 \rightarrow 2NH_3$. Suppose that the initial pressures of N_2, H_2, and NH_3 are 1.0, 1.5, and 3.2 atm, respectively, and that P_{NH3} at equil is 0.12 atm. What are P_{N2} and P_{H2} at equil? What is K_{eq} for the reaction?

Solution: This problem can be approached using the system introduced earlier: write the initial pressures first; then enter the one final (equilibrium) pressure known; calculate the change in pressure of NH_3; use the reaction stoichiometry to calculate pressure changes for N_2 and H_2; and finally, calculate the equilibrium pressures of N_2 and H_2. Once all equilibrium pressures are known, the equilibrium constant may be calculated.

	N_2	$+3H_2 \rightarrow$	N_2O_4	$K_{eq} = = 7.0 \text{ atm}^{-1}$
initial:	1.0	1.5	3.2	

Change:	
equilibrium:	0.12

The change in pressure of ammonia during reaction is easily calculated to be 3.2 □ 0.12 = 3.08 atm. Because the pressure of NH_3 decreases, this change is negative. The changes in and must be 1.5 and 0.5 times this value, respectively, and are positive. Thus = 0.5 × 3.08 = 1.54 atm; and = 1.5 × 3.08 = 4.62 atm. The changes are now inserted into the change line and the equilibrium pressures calculated:

	N_2	+3 H_2 →	N_2O_4 K_{eq} = = 7.0 atm^{-1}
initial:	1.0	1.5	3.2
Change:	1.54	4.62	-3.08
equilibrium:	2.54	6.12	0.12

Finally, K_{eq} is calculated:

$K_{eq} = P_{NH_3}{}^2 \,/\, (P_{N_2})(P_{H_2})^3 = (0.12)^2/(2.54)(6.12)^3$

$= 2.47 \times 10^{-5}\ atm^{-2}$

We make one final and very important point about the entries in the table under the reaction in the example just completed: only the entries in the ΔP line of the table are governed by the reaction stoichiometry. Neither the initial pressures (which are in general completely arbitrary) nor the equilibrium pressures are related to the coefficients of the chemical equation. This will in general be true. Although the stoichiometry governs the relative changes in concentration (pressure) that occur as the system passes from one state to another, it is not necessarily related to the relative amounts of participants present in a particular state (e.g., initial and equilibrium states in the above examples).

10

Solid Chemistry

SOLIDS IN LIQUIDS

Objectives

The first object was to find the density of various solid objects, both regular and irregular solids. The density of two liquids was to be determined. The second objective was to complete a full lab writeup as a model for the rest of the year.

- *Equipment*: Lab scales, graduated cylinder, vernier calipe
- *Safety rules*: Do Not Put the Sphere in the Graduated Cylinder!
- *Procedure*: See notecard
- *Data*: See datasheet from lab
- *Calculations*:
  - *Sphere* 1:

    $V = 4/3\pi\ r^3$ $\quad$ $(4/3)\ (\pi)\ (1.23\ \text{cm})^3 = 7.79\ \text{cm}^3$

    $\rho = m/V$ $\quad$ $2.8\ \text{g}/7.79\ \text{cm}^3 = 0.36\ \text{g/cm}^3$
  - *Sphere* 2:

    $V = 4/3\ \pi\ r^3$ $\quad$ $(4/3)\ (\pi)\ (1.79\ \text{cm})^3 = 24.0\ \text{cm}^3$

    $\rho = m/V$ $\quad$ $2.8\ \text{g}/24.0\ \text{cm}^3 = 0.12\ \text{g/cm}^3$
  - *Cylinder (metal)*:

    $V = \pi\ r^2\ L$ $\quad$ $(\pi)\ (1.35\ \text{cm})^2\ (5.10\ \text{cm}) = 29.2\ \text{cm}^3$

    $\rho = m/V$ $\quad$ $57.6\ \text{g}/29.2\ \text{cm}^3 = 1.96\ \text{g/cm}^3$
  - *Cylinder (metal using water displacement)*:

    $\rho = m/V$ $\quad$ $57.6\ \text{g}/28.1\ \text{mL} = 2.0\ \text{g/mL}$
  - *Rock*:

    $\rho = m/v$ $\quad$ $4.5\ \text{g}/2.3\ \text{mL} = 1.9\ \text{g/mL}$

– *Styrofoam block*:

$V = L \times W \times H$ (7.85 cm) (3.45 cm) (1.23 cm) $= 33.3\ cm^3$

$\rho = m/V$ $1.3\ g/33.3\ cm^3 = 0.039\ g/cm^3$

– *Small cylinder*:

$V = \pi r^2 L$ $(\pi)\ (1.23\ cm)^2\ (3.46\ cm) = 16.4\ cm^3$

$\rho = m/V$ $3.4\ g/16.4\ cm^3 = 0.21\ g/cm^3$

– *% Difference (metal cylinder)*:

% difference = | difference in 2 densities | /larger of 2 × 100

$|\ 2.0\ g/mL - 1.96\ g/cm^3\ |/2.0\ g/mL \times 100$
$= 2.0\%$

– *% error (metal cylinder)*:

% error = | actual value – experimental value /actual value × 100

$|\ 1.96\ g/cm^3 - 1.8\ g/cm^3\ |/1.8\ g/cm^3 \times 100$
$= 8.8\%$

Volume of water	*Mass of water*	*Volume of TDL*	*Mass of TDL*
10.1 mL	10.0 g	10.8 mL	14.7 g
21.3 mL	21.0 g	22.0 mL	30.0 g
30.7 mL	31.0 g	31.0 mL	42.2 g
42.0 mL	42.3 g	43.2 mL	58.7 g
50.5 mL	50.1 g	51.2 mL	70.8 g
14.456 mL	15.9 g	14.456 mL	19.7 g
76.00 mL	76.8 g	76.00 mL	103.4 g

- Density of water (from slope) = 1.01 g/mL
- Density of TDL (from slope) = 1.37 g/mL

Results:

- Density of sphere 1 = 0.36 g/cm^3
- Density of sphere 2 = 0.12 g/cm^3
- Density of metal cylinder (geometric) = 1.96 g/cm^3
- Density of metal cylinder (water displ) = 2.0 g/mL
- Density of rock = 1.9 g/mL
- Density of Styrofoam block = 0.039 g/cm^3
- Density of small cylinder = 0.21 g/cm^3
- % difference (metal cylinder) = 2.0%
- % error (metal cylinder) = 8.8%

- *Density of water*: 1.01 g/mL
- *Density of TDL*: 1.37 g/mL

The item with the greatest density (in this experiment) was the metal cylinder with a density of 1.96 g/cm^3. The item with the least density was the Styrofoam block with a density of 0.039 g/cm^3.

The TDL liquid was more dense than the water, as seen by a density of 1.3 g/mL compared to 1.01 g/mL for the water. Both spheres ended up with densities less than that of water, thus both would float in water.

The rock was more dense than water but slightly less dense than the metal cylinder. The% difference in densities between the metal cylinder (volume found by using a geometric formula) versus the density (volume found by water displacement) was low at 2.0%.

However, the 8.8% difference between the actual density of the metal cylinder and the correct value was too high (perhaps due to measurement error). Generalizations reached from this lab would include that metals tend to have higher densities than plastics, the shape of an object does not affect its density, and that Styrofoam is a material of exceedingly low density.

The lab techniques used in this lab would allow a person to identify unknown materials. The material's density would be obtained using the procedures used here and then checked with listings of known materials to help identify the material. The relationship between the dependent and independent variables would be stated as: as the volume increased (independent variable) the mass increased (dependent variable).

Discussion

Knowledge gained in doing this lab includes proper usage of the vernier calipers, graduated cylinders, lab scales, and lab notecards. No differences between prediction and result were noted.

Observations include bubbles forming in the TDL if it is added too rapidly, the difficulty of removing the TDL from the inside of the graduated cylinder, and the lack of uniformity (uniform shape) of the Styrofoam block.

Error could have been reduced in this lab by using the 0.01 gram lab scales instead of the 0.1 scales, confirming the readings on the vernier calipers with the teacher, and using more trials in the density of liquids lab (resulting in better line of best fit).

No questions regarding this lab were noted:

- Using the overflow method – fill a large container to the brim with water, add the object, capture and measure volume of overflow water (that volume = volume of object).

- The apparent volume would be greater than it should be and the density less than it should be.
- Use kitchen oil instead of water (in doing water displacement)
- To dive, large tanks are filled with water increasing density, to rise the water is pumped out.
- 5. V = m/ρ 2.00 E 3 g/0.92 g/cm^3 = 2.2 E 3 cm^3
- Use a liquid (in place of water in water displacement) that have a density greater than that of the object (so the object sinks and displaces the liquid).
- Combine the massiveness of the particles with their compactness to find density.

Method

A body is weighed in air and then immersed in a liquid. The apparent loss in weight of the body when immersed in the liquid is, by Archimedes' principle, equal to the weight of liquid displaced by the body. From these measurements the density and specific gravity of either the solid body or the liquid may be determined.

Theory

The density of a substance is defined as its mass per unit volume and in the metric system of units is measured in grams per cubic centimetre. The specific gravity of a substance is defined as the ratio of the mass or weight of the substance to the mass or weight of an equal volume of water and is a pure number having zero dimensions. A convenient method for determining densities or specific gravities is one which uses the principle of Archimedes, namely, that when a body is immersed in a fluid there is exerted on the body a vertical upward force equal to the weight of fluid displaced.

Proof of Archimedes' Principle

Suppose aright circular cylinder of height h is immersed in a liquid of density d gm per cm^3. The bottom of the cylinder is at a depth of h_2 cm and the top at a depth h cm below the surface of the liquid where $h = (h_2 - h_1)$. The pressure on the liquid at depth h_1 is $p_1 = B + h_1gd$ dynes per cm^2, where B is atmospheric pressure.

The total downward force on the upper surface of the cylinder is $F_1 = p_1A$ dynes where A is the area of cross section of the cylinder. Similarly the total upward force on the bottom of the cylinder is $F_2 = p_2A$ dynes.

Since the pressure in a fluid acts at right angles to any surface in contact with it, the pressure on the sides of the cylinder is everywhere horizontal and has no vertical component. Hence the total upward force in dynes on the cylinder is,

$$F_2–F_1 = p_2A = (h_2–h_1)Agd = hAgd$$

But hA = V, the volume of the cylinder, so that,

$$F_2–F_1 = Vgd$$

or the resultant upward force in dynes is equal to the weight of fluid displaced.While this proof of Archimedes' principle is for a particularly simple geometrical object, the principle is true for an object of any shape which is immersed in a fluid.

Application of Archimedes' Principle

- Suppose a body has a density of D grams per cm^3 and amass of M grams. The volume of the body is V = M/D and its weight in air is Mg dynes. The weight (MLg) of the body when immersed in a liquid of density d is, by Archimedes' principle, MLg = Mg – Vdg dynes. Thus ML = M – Vd or ML = M – Md/D. Since ML and M may be measured by means of a balance, it follows that if the density d of the liquid-say water-is known, the density D of the body may be calculated from,

$$D = Md/(M - M_L)$$

- If the body whose density is to be measured is less dense than the liquid, it is necessary to fasten the body to a sinker so that the two together sink in the liquid. Let M_1g be the weight in air of the body, say a block of wood, whose density D_1 is less than that of the liquid of density d. Suppose the body of mass M and density D, referred to above, is such that when fastened to the block of wood the two together sink in the liquid. Let the weight of the two together when completely immersed in the liquid be MLg. Then from Figure. it is readily seen that,

$$M'_Lg = Mg + M_1g - (Mgd/D) - (M_1gd/D_1)$$

or

$$M'_L = M_L + M_1 - ((M_1d)/D_1)$$

Hence,

$$D_1 = (M_1d)/(M_L + M_1 - M'_L)$$

- The relative densities of liquids may be obtained by finding the weight of a sinker in the various liquids. Suppose that when the sinker is immersed in a liquid of density dl its apparent loss in weight is M_1g and when immersed in liquid of density d_2 the apparent loss in weight is M_2g. By Archimedes' principle $M_1g = Vd_1g$ and $M_2g = Vd_2g$ where V is the volume of the sinker.

Hence,

$$V = M_1/d_1 = M_2/d_2$$

or,

$$M_1/M_2 = d_1/d_2$$

M_1 and M_2 may be measured directly by a balance and if one of the liquids is water at a known temperature, its density may be found accurately in tables so that d_2 may be calculated.

Part I Apparatus

A balance of the type shown in Fig. is convenient for determining the mass of a body in air or in a liquid.

The two bodies whose densities are to be determined are, for example, a block of brass and a block of wood.

A suitable set of weights, a beaker, and a thin piece of cord for tying the two bodies together are necessary.

Procedure

By means of the balance determine the mass M of the block of brass in air.

Place a beaker containing water on the adjustable platform and suspend the brass block by means of a fine cord or wire from the hook from which the pan is suspended.

Completely immerse the brass block in the water. See that no bubbles adhere to the surface of the block. Determine the mass ML of the brass block in water.

Determine the mass of the block of wood in air. Fasten the wooden and brass blocks together by the cord or fine wire and determine the masses of the two together M'_L when completely immersed in water.

The density of water at the particular temperature may be obtained from Table. If time permits, determine the density d of alcohol or an oil by weighing the brass block in air and in the liquid. Calculate the density of the brass and wood.

Fig. Blocks of Brass and Wood Suitable for Density Measurements.

Part II Apparatus

A Westphal balance which consists of a specially designed balance for measuring the specific gravity of liquids, is needed. A glass plummet, which is immersed in the liquid whose density or specific gravity is required, is suspended from the end of the calibrated arm of the balance. The apparent loss of weight of the plummet when immersed in the liquid is measured by placing known weights on the arm until a balance is obtained. Four different weights having relative values of 1.0, 0.1, 0.01 and 0.001 are supplied. The glass plummet is constructed so that when immersed in water at 15.5°C the largest or unit weight placed on the hook with the glass plummet produces a balance.

Procedure

Place the leveling screw on the base of the instrument so that it is in the position under the arm of the balance. Clean and dry the glass plummet and hang it by the fine wire from the hook at the end of the arm of the balance. By means of the leveling screw adjust the arm of the balance so that it is horizontal- that is, so that the two pointers are in line. Clean the glass hydrometre jar and partially fill it with distilled water. Immerse the glass plummet in the water and adjust the height of the instrument so that a single strand of the fine wire cuts the surface of the water. See that no bubbles adhere to the glass plummet. If the water is at 15.5°C, the unit weight hung at the end of the arm restores the balance. If the glass plummet is placed in other liquids at 15.5°C, the weights required to restore the balance directly measure the specific gravity of the liquids. For high accuracy in measuring the specific gravity or relative densities of liquids it is necessary to have the liquids at the same temperature. This is true not only because the density of liquids changes with temperature but also because the glass plummet changes in volume. If the temperatures are within a few degrees, the error introduced is not large.

Suppose that a balance is obtained when the glass plummet is immersed in water at 20°C with weights of 1.0 and 0.1 at notch 9, the 0.01 weight at notch 8 and the 0.001 weight at notch 5, and when immersed in another liquid at the same temperature a balance is obtained with weight 1.0 at notch 8, weights 0.1 and 0.01 at notch 6, and weight 0.001 at notch 4.

The relative densities of the two liquids are, by Eq.

$$d/d\omega = 0.8664/0.9985$$

The density of pure water at 20°C is given in Table I. Find the density of the various liquids provided, being careful to see that the glass plummet and the hydrometre jar are carefully cleaned each time before anew liquid is used. Read and record the temperature of the thermometre in the glass plummet each time.

Part III Apparatus

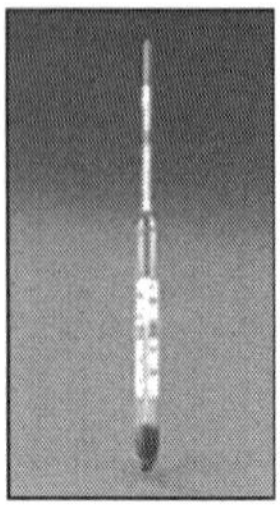

Fig. Hydrometre for Measuring Specific Gravities of Light Liquids.

A hydrometre of the type shown in Figure and a large hydrometre jar are required.

Procedure

Partially fill the hydrometre jar with the liquid whose specific gravity is to be measured and place the hydrometre in it. Clean the hydrometre and jar each time a new liquid is used. In this case the specific gravity of the liquid is read directly from the scale reading on the hydrometre. This method is not capable of giving as high an accuracy as that obtained with the Westphal balance, but the readings may be taken much more rapidly. Determine the specific gravities of the liquids used in the previous experiment.

UNIT CELL LAWS OF CRYSTALLOGRAPHY

It is perhaps not generally appreciated to what an extent modern work on crystal structure is based upon the fundamental principles enunciated by Haüy over 125 years ago. The terminology may be different, but the ideas remain the same. He spoke of"integral molecules," we say"crystal molecules,""unit cells of the space lattices," etc. He adopted as the shapes of these units the parallelopiped, octahedron, tetrahedron, hexagonal prism, rhombic dodecahedron, and hexagonal bipyramid. We still use some of these, altho certain changes in the list have been required as a result of subsequent investigations. His law of rational indices has held firm, and has furnished a starting point for many subsequent generalizations.

The point-system or space-lattice theory of crystal structure is a direct extension of it. Professor Goldschmidt's recognition of harmony and complication in the symbols of zones of forms is another. And now that the use of X-rays has furnished, especially in the hands of the Braggs, a means of demonstrating the reality of space lattices and the occupation of their nodes by atoms, rather than by chemical molecules, it is possible to go still further. The Russian crystallographer, E. S. Fedorov, has been during the past few, years carrying on extensive researches on what he terms"crystallo-chemistry," and, aided by the Braggs's working out of the structures of a number of simple salts, has recently formulated certain laws and principles extending Haüy's original law into this field.[1] Being written in Russian,[2]his papers are comparatively inaccessible to English-speaking scientists, but it has fortunately been possible to have very full and accurate abstracts of them published in Chemical Abstracts.

The principal points made by Professor Fedorov are: The space arrangement of atoms in three crystallographic directions, and the units to be used in the corresponding axes, may be expressed rationally, altho, because of our inability to determine the positions of the atoms with absolute exactness, only approximately rational relations are as a rule obtained. Planes determined by any three atoms are possible crystal faces, but the greater the density of a face the more important it is, crystallographically speaking, and the more likely to appear on the actual crystal.

The importance of planes is increased by the presence in them of dissimilar atoms, capable of attracting one another, and due to similar chemical attractions the bond between parallel planes is made stronger. The nearest distance between unlike atoms in any space-lattice is in general inversely proportional to their chemical affinity, altho exceptions may occur when an atom of one kind holds two or more of another. Thruout these theorems the influence of Haüy's law of rational indices can be clearly traced.

An extension of the idea of arrangement of atoms in layers into the field of optical properties has recently been attempted by the writer. Thus far only tetragonal crystals have been studied, but in a number of substances which crystallize in this system there has been found to be a correlation between crystallographic axial ratio and refractive indices.

Deriving from the indices, by the use of the Lorentz-Lorenz formula, the"refractions," the following inverse relationship has been found to hold in certain simple compounds,

$$\frac{W2 - 1}{W2 + 2} : \frac{E^2 - 1}{E^2 + 2} = c : a.$$

It is of course necessary that the true axial ratio, based on all the layers of atoms present, be used; and in many cases this is not the same as the standard axial ratio, which is obtained by taking the most prominent pyramid form to be (111). There are, furthermore, many disturbing factors, such as irregularity of the layers, asymmetric arrangements of atoms, which produce rotation of the plane of polarized light, and the presence of absorption bands and other colour phenomena, such as pleochroism. Because of the presence of one or more of these features, the effects of which cannot as yet be evaluated, this rule fails to hold with complex compounds, but it does hold for enough simple ones to indicate that it is a fundamental relationship.

In a preliminary paper on this subject, recently published,4 a few organic compounds were considered. Similar relations prove to hold with the minerals of the zircon group, the crystallographic features of which were first established by Haüy.

In cassiterite the refraction ratio is 0.945, the alternate axial ratio 0.951; in rutile the values are 0.926 and 0.911 respectively. The practical identity of the two ratios shows that in these minerals the space-lattice must have the same number of layers of atoms in the horizontal as in the vertical direction. In zircon and xenotime the refraction ratios are not equal to either axial ratio, but to 3/2 the standard one.

This is interpreted to show that in the unit cells of these minerals there are three layers of atoms horizontally for every two vertically. It is accordingly possible to tell in this way something about the space-lattices of crystals, and when the refraction data are combined with the observed symmetry relations, to work out in detail probable arrangements of atoms for the substances. A few minerals in addition to those of the zircon group have also been studied in this way, but in most cases the presence of disturbing factors prevents the complete recognition of their structure. Further work is planned, however, to evaluate as far as possible the influence of these factors, as well as to apply this method of study to substances crystallizing in other systems than the tetragonal.

Crystallography

"The branch of science that deals with the study of structure, geometry and properties of crystals is called crystallography".

Symmetry in Crystal

A crystal possess following three types of symmetry,

Plane of Symmetry

It is an imaginary plane which passes through the centre of a crystal can divides it into two equal portions which are exactly the mirror images of each other.

Axis of Symmetry

An axis of symmetry or axis of rotation is an imaginary line, passing through the crystal such that when the crystal is rotated about this line, it presents the same appearance more than once in one complete revolution *i.e.*, in a rotation through 360°.

Suppose, the same appearance of crystal is repeated, on rotating it through an angle of 360°/n, around an imaginary axis, is called an n-fold axis where,n is known as the order of axis. By order is meant the value of n in $2\pi/n$ so that rotation through $2\pi/n$, gives an equivalent configuration.

Centre of Symmetry

It is an imaginary point in the crystal that any line drawn through it intersects the surface of the crystal at equal distance on either side.

Only simple cubic system have one centre of symmetry. Other system do not have centre of symmetry.

The total number of planes, axes and centre of symmetries possessed by a crystal is termed as elements of symmetry.

A cubic crystal possesses total 23 elements of symmetry:

- *Plane of symmetry*: (3 + 6) = 9
- *Axes of symmetry*: (3 + 4 + 6) = 13
- *Centre of symmetry*: (1) = 1
- (Total symmetry = 232) Laws of crystallography: Crystallography is based on three fundamental laws.

Law of Constancy of Interfacial Angles

This law states that angle between adjacent corresponding faces is inter facial angles of the crystal of a particular substance is always constant inspite of different shapes and sizes and mode of growth of crystal. The size and shape of crystal depend upon the conditions of crystallisation. This law is also known as Steno's Law.

Law of Rational Indices

This law states that the ratio of intercepts of different faces of a crystal with the three axes are constant and can be expressed by rational numbers that the intercepts of any face of a crystal along the crystallographic axes are either equal to unit intercepts (*i.e.*, intercepts made by unit cell) a,b, c or some simple whole number multiples of them *e.g.*, na, n' b, n'c, where n, n' and n' are simple whole numbers. The whole numbers n, n' and n' are called Weiss indices. This law was given by Hauy.

LAW OF THE CONSTANCY OF INTERFACIAL ANGLES

Since the internal structure of any mineral is always constant, and since the possible crystal faces of that mineral have a definite relationship to that structure, it follows that mineral have a definite relationship to that structure, it follows that the faces must have also a definite relationship to each other.

This fact may be stated as follows: The angles between two similar faces on the same substance are always the same. Figure will also illustrate this point.

The face which cuts the network along the line A-C must make an angle of 45 degrees with the face which cuts along the line A-B, etc. This law is the most fundamental and important in the science of crystallography. It frequently enables one to identify a mineral by the measurement of the interfacial angles on its crystals. A mineral may be found in crystals of widely varying shapes and sizes, but the angle between two similar faces will always be the same.

And important part of the study of crystallography consists in the measuring and classifying of the interfacial angles on the crystals of all minerals. These measurements are accomplished by means of instruments know as goniometry.

For accurate work, particularly in the case of small crystals, a type of instrument known as a reflection goniometre is used. This is an instrument upon which the crystal to be measured is mounted so as to reflect beams of light from its faces through a telescope to the eye.

The size of the angle through which a crystal has to be turned in order to throw successive beams of light from two adjacent faces into tie telescope determines the angle existing between the faces. A simpler instrument used for approximate work and with larger crystals is known as a contact goniometre.

The regular internal structure of crystals requires that the ultimate individual mineral units must be at least physically alike. A physical likeness between these units necessitates that they should also be the same chemically, or at least closely similar.

Consequently we can state that in general a crystal must be made up of a regular assemblage of units which are chemically the same, and therefore that a crystallized mineral must have a definite and uniform chemical composition.

This statement is a general one and will suffice for the present; certain modifications will be found stated on under isomorphism. A crystal is a guaranty of the chemical homogeneity of a mineral. From this it follows that only definite chemical compounds are capable of crystallization.

To sum up the conclusions of the preceding paragraphs: A crystal is a solid with definite chemical composition which possesses a definite internal arrangement of its mineral units.

These internal characteristic are expressed outwardly in a definite external form. And since the internal structure of the same substance is always constant, the angles between the similar bounding planes of the crystals of that substance are also constant.

SYMMETRY OPERATIONS AND ELEMENTS

A Symmetry operation is an operation that can be performed either physically or imaginatively that results in no change in the appearance of an object. Again it is emphasized that in crystals, the symmetry is internal, that is it is an ordered geometrical arrangement of atoms and molecules on the crystal lattice.

But, since the internal symmetry is reflected in the external form of perfect crystals, we are going to concentrate on external symmetry, because this is what we can observe.

There are 3 types of symmetry operations: rotation, reflection, and inversion. We will look at each of these in turn.

Rotational Symmetry

As illustrated above, if an object can be rotated about an axis and repeats itself every 90° of rotation then it is said to have an axis of 4-fold rotational symmetry.

The axis along which the rotation is performed is an element of symmetry referred to as a rotation axis. The following types of rotational symmetry axes are possible in crystals.

Fold Rotation Axis

An object that requires rotation of a full 360° in order to restore it to its original appearance has no rotational symmetry. Since it repeats itself 1 time every 360° it is said to have a 1-fold axis of rotational symmetry.

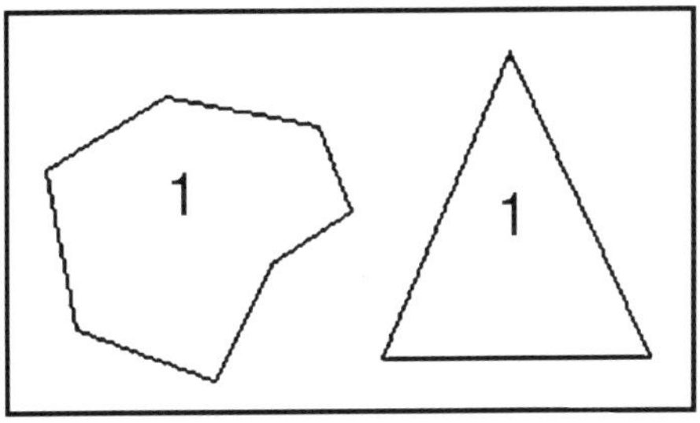

If an object appears identical after a rotation of 180°, that is twice in a 360° rotation, then it is said to have a 2-fold rotation axis (360/180 = 2). Note that in these examples the axes we are referring to are imaginary lines that extend towards you perpendicular to the page or blackboard. A filled oval shape represents the point where the 2-fold rotation axis intersects the page.

Objects that repeat themselves upon rotation of 120° are said to have a 3-fold axis of rotational symmetry (360/120 =3), and they will repeat 3 times in a 360° rotation. A filled triangle is used to symbolize the location of 3-fold rotation axis.

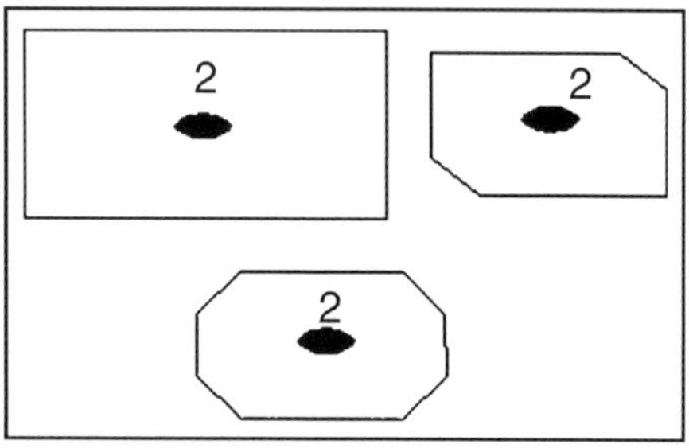

This symbolism will be used for a 2-fold rotation axis throughout the lectures and in your text. If an object repeats itself after 90° of rotation, it will repeat 4 times in a 360°rotation, as illustrated previously.

A filled square is used to symbolize the location of 4-fold axis of rotational symmetry.

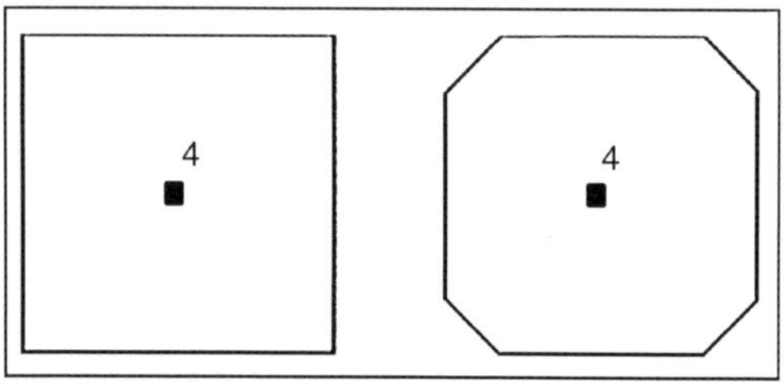

If rotation of 60° about an axis causes the object to repeat itself, then it has 6-fold axis of rotational symmetry (360/60=6). A filled hexagon is used as the symbol for a 6-fold rotation axis.

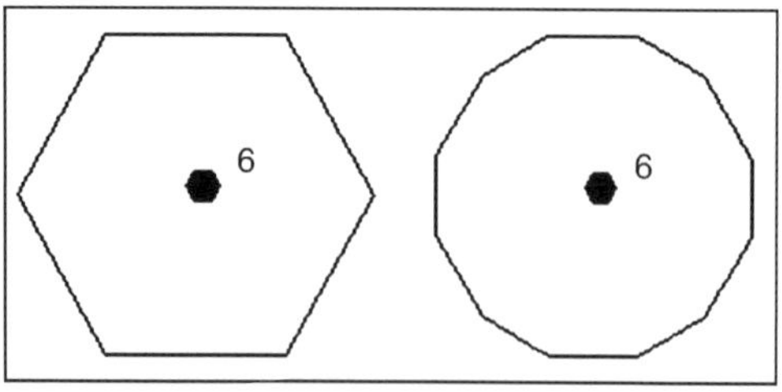

Although objects themselves may appear to have 5-fold, 7-fold, 8-fold, or higher-fold rotation axes, these are not possible in crystals.

Bibliography

Aaron Ihde: *The Development of Modern Chemistry*, New York: Dover, 1984.

Ansari, A.A. : *A Textbook of Differential Equations*, Dominant, Delhi, 2012.

Arun Sarkar: *Advanced Organic Chemistry : Reactions and Mechanisms*, Swastik Publications, Delhi, 2011.

Boyle, Robert: *The Sceptical Chymist*. New York: Dover Publications, 2005.

Chambers, K. L.: *Biochemical Coevolution: Eugene*, Oregon State University Press, Biology Colloquium, 1970.

Constantine A. Balanis: *Advanced Engineering Electromagnetics*, BSP Books, Delhi, 2008.

Cullity, B.D.: *Elements of X-Ray Diffraction*, Reading, Massachusetts: Addison-Wesley Publishing Company, 1978.

David Knight: *Ideas in Chemistry: A History of the Science*, New Brunswick, N. J., Rutgers University Press, 1992.

David M.: *Basic Principles and Calculations in Chemical Engineering*, Prentice-Hall, 1996.

Earnshaw, A.; Greenwood, N.: *Chemistry of the Elements*, Butterworth-Heinemann, 1997.

Geis, I.: *Chemistry, Matter, and the Universe*, Menlo Park, Ca., W.A. Benjamin, 1976.

Griffiths, D.J. : *Introduction to Electrodynamics*, Prentice-Hall, Englewood Cliffs, New Jersey, 1989.

Harry R.; *Contemporary Polymer Chemistry*, Pearson Education, 2003.

Herbert Morawetz: *Polymers: The Origins and Growth of a Science*, New York, John Wiley & Sons, 1985.

Ihde, Aaron John: *The Development of Modern Chemistry*. Courier Dover Publications, 1984.

Khuntia, Smruti R. : *Fundamentals of Electromagnetic Theory*, PHI Learning, Delhi, 2011.

Laud, B.B. : *Electromagnetic*, New Age International, Delhi, 2011.

Lehninger, A. L.: *Biochemistry*, New York, Worth and Co., 1970.

Linden, David: *Handbook of Batteries and Fuel Cells*. New York: McGraw-Hill, about 1984.

Mahinder Singh: *A Textbook of Stereochemistry*, Dominant Pub, Delhi, 2004.

Matthew N.O. : *Principles of Electromagnetics*, Oxford University Press, Delhi, 2012.

Meyers, R.: *The Basics of Chemistry*. Greenwood Press. 2003.

Motekaitis, R.J. : *The Determination and Use of Stability Constants*, Wiley-VCH, 1992.

Nicholas P.: *Handbook of Chemical Engineering Calculations*, McGraw-Hill. 2004.

Pandey, R.K. : *Complex Analysis with Differential Equations*, Anmol, Delhi, 2008.

Perrot, Pierre: *A to Z of Thermodynamics*. Oxford University Press. 1998.

Peter J. : *Differential and Integral Equations*, Oxford University Press, Delhi, 2008.

Phillips, M. : *Classical Electricity and Magnetism* , Addison- Wesley, Reading, Massachusetts, 1962.

Prentice, Geoffrey A. : *Electrochemical Engineering Principles*, Prentice Hall 1997

Ranpal Singh: *Advanced Inorganic Chemistry*, RBSA Pub, Delhi, 2006.

Rawat, K. S. : *Integral Calculus with Differential Equation*, Adhyayan, Delhi, 2006.

Rossotti, F.J.C. and H. Rossotti: *The Determination of Stability Constants*, McGraw-Hill, 1961

Roy Porter: *The Biographical Dictionary of Scientists*, New York, Oxford University Press, 1994.

Singh, Shalender : *Electromagnetics*, Discovery Publishing House, Delhi, 2009.

Srivastava, N.K. : *Electromagnetic Theory and Optics*, ABD Pub, Delhi, 2007.

Van Antwerpen, F.J. : *The Origins of Chemical Engineering, History of Chemical Engineering*, Washington D.C.: ACS, 1980.

Walsh, F.C. : *A First Course in Electrochemical Engineering*, Electrochemical Consultancy, Romsey, England 1993

Warren, S.: "*Organic Chemistry*" Oxford University Press, 2000.

William F. Furter: *A Century of Chemical Engineering*, New York, Plenum Press, 1982.

Yahya Rahmat-Samii: *Electromagnetic Band Gap Structures in Antenna Engineering*, Cambridge Univ Press, Delhi, 1980.

Zeggeren, F.J.C. and S.H. Storey: *The Computation of Chemical Equilibria*, Cambridge University Press, 1970.

Index

❑❑❑